DO NOT PASS GO

Tim Moore's writing has appeared in the *Daily Telegraph*, the *Observer*, the *Sunday Times*, and *Esquire*. He lives in west London with his wife and their three children.

DO NOT PASS GO

From the Old Kent Road to Mayfair

Tim Moore

Yellow Jersey Press
London

Published by Yellow Jersey Press 2002

2 4 6 8 10 9 7 5 3 1

Copyright © Tim Moore

Tim Moore has asserted his right under the Copyright, Designs and Patents Act 1988
to be identified as the author of this work

First published in Great Britain in 2002 by
Yellow Jersey Press

Yellow Jersey Press
Random House, 20 Vauxhall Bridge Road,
London SW1V 2SA

Random House Australia (Pty) Limited
20 Alfred Street, Milsons Points, Sydney,
New South Wales 2061, Australia

Random House New Zealand Limited
18 Poland Road, Glenfield
Auckland 10, New Zealand

Random House (Pty) Limited
Endulini, 5A Jubilee Road, Parktown 2193
South Africa

The Random House Group Limited Reg. No. 954009
www.randomhouse.co.uk

A CIP catalogue record for this book is available from the British Library

ISBN 0-224-06263-8

Papers used by Random House are natural, recyclable products made
from wood grown in sustainable forests. The manufacturing processes
conform to the environmental regulations of the country of origin

Printed and bound in Great Britain by Mackays of Chatham PLC

To Lilian and Felix

Acknowledgements

Thanks to Rachel Cugnoni, Suzanne Dean, Lara Soley Johannsdottir, John Bacon, Ian Hunter, Gudrun Agnarsdottir, Roger and Christina Bowdler, Simon and Catherine Moore, the Energy Saving Trust, Councillor Pat Haynes, the Audit Unit at Pentonville Prison, the staff at Lots Road power station, the Crossness Beam Engine Trust, Pall Matthiasson, Ron Beard, Susan Sandon, Mike Grabsky, and Birna, Kristjan, Lilja and Valdis.

And finally, a fitful round of derisive applause for Hasbro, who have ensured you won't be seeing a dog, boot, title deed or Monopoly board graphically represented within these pages. I am consequently delighted to confirm that this book is in no way endorsed by or associated with Hasbro, and indeed that the royalties they might otherwise have accrued are in every way endorsed by and associated with my wallet.

Contents

Foreword

Tim Moock rushed back in from the loo and swiftly counted the pink ones in the bank tray. One of us, he announced, had just stolen £500, adding that it wasn't him. I was winning 5-4 in an increasingly ill-tempered series that had seen us holed up in the attic for most of a two-week holiday with his parents in South Wales, squatting on cold lino in a dark silence broken only occasionally by vicious barks of 'RENT!' He'd been my best friend since our first day at school, the two of us bound together by a haunting alphabetical proximity, but in three years I'd never seen him like this; even as I protested my possibly genuine innocence, he flushed furiously, ran a clawed hand messily through his ginger pudding bowl, then with a terrible, strangled shriek abruptly pushed me over backwards on to the board and jumped knees first on my stomach. It was twenty-six years ago but I can still feel that battleship digging into my spine.

Everyone went through a Monopoly phase, and though my scars may be more literal than most, it has left a mark on us all. In the days when long hours of television broadcasting were devoted to the static image of a girl playing noughts and crosses with a toy clown, and when you didn't have a PlayStation to plug in your aerial socket when she came on, board games were the baby-boomers' time-sink, and Monopoly was the undisputed king. In Cluedo you plodded glumly about the billiard room for twenty minutes before a series of mumbled, half-hearted accusations heralded the real business of the afternoon: lashing Colonel Mustard and Professor Plum together with the rope and setting about their uncomplaining embodiments with spanner and lead piping. In Mastermind, which wasn't a board game but somehow felt like one, you idly constructed lewd scenarios involving that peculiar Bond baddie/Bond bird couple on the box while an elder sibling detailed with waning patience and waxing volume the limited role played by favourite colours in the laws of logic and probability.

But Monopoly you could play from the end of the *Thunderbirds* until the start of *Dr Who*, and wake up in the morning and play again, assembling and consuming hasty and inappropriate meals around the board and postponing visits to the lavatory until it was slightly too late. Because Monopoly made you feel important and grown up: managing money, doing deals, getting arrested. It was a fight to the death, a game that was all about forcing your family and friends ever so slowly down on to their knees before mercilessly punting them into the gutter. And, best of all, those were real gutters, on real streets, a real city.

I put in most of my Monopoly hours with my elder siblings. I was always the neatly streamlined racing car; my brother went for the dreadnought. My sister, clearly lacking self-esteem, was the dog or the old boot. At home we played on a sixties board almost torn in half along the fold; at my grandparents' house we played on a wartime set with a cardboard spinner instead of dice (pity the

SS officer who peered out of his Panzer hatch and copped six sides of Empire Bakelite in the teeth). When my father came back from a business trip with an American set, we used to overlap the GO squares and play two-board, figure-of-eight transatlantic marathons. In the school holidays, entire weeks were swallowed whole.

We learned to teleport our tokens without tock-tock-tocking them along for each dot on the dice: if you were on Trafalgar Square and rolled a ten, you cut right across to Bond Street. We learned to pass the little plastic cubes on to the next player with such practised nonchalance that they wouldn't notice you'd parked your motor on their Mayfair until they'd rolled and it was too late. And we learned each other's tactical quirks. My sister swore by the stations and the orange set. I always paid the £10 fine instead of taking a Chance. My brother inevitably assumed control of the onerous dice-related calculations that were the lot of the utilities landlord.

Some of the small-print clauses in the deals we brokered reached management/union levels of arcaneness: I'll give you Oxford Street for Strand and £350, but if she swaps Regent Street and you get the whole green set then I'm exempted from paying any rent on it for ten laps. At one stage there was an experiment with insurance policies: a fixed per-lap premium paid to a landlord in exchange for free lodging in any of his hotels you might land on.

After honing our poker-faced virtuosity it was a terrible thing to play with outsiders, amateurs, people who counted out their numbers, who twittered 'Just visiting!' through smugly pursed lips whenever they passed through Jail, who sat there for an hour scanning the rules for any evidence to back up their insistence that you weren't allowed to buy property on the first round of the board. In my pre-teenage prime I could look round a board of cousins and family friends and with a hustler's practised eye pick out their aggravating foibles before we'd even started: he'll try to put houses on GO; she'll find that second-prize-in-a-beauty-contest card sofa-soilingly comical; and, dear God no, every time you hand over the rent to that one he'll say, 'It's a pleasure doing business with you!'

It didn't take much to start a fight in Monopoly, particularly after the hotels started going up – if you've played it more than twice, you'll have seen title deeds fly. Where theft wasn't involved, these incidents could usually be traced to ugly triumphalism; in our family this was neatly defused by the smile-wiping 'winner-puts-the-game-away' rule which required the victor to sort out all the money into denominations and the title deeds into their sets. Get really mouthy, Mister Mayfair, and you might even find yourself putting the Chance cards into alphabetical order.

Monopoly taught us the politics and diplomacy of brokering deals, the basic laws of probability, the art of bending outmoded rules. In Moore Monopoly you couldn't collect rent when you were in prison, there were no auctions, and if anyone tried to sell their Get Out of Jail Free card they got a flick on the ear. I still remember my brother going down under a hail of hotels for invoking the right to buy houses when it wasn't his turn, as enshrined in the terms and conditions of play. You simply couldn't imagine any rival pastime developing such a life of its own, evolving to suit its players. 'Scrabble *with* the Ns? Well; it's your house.' 'Sorry, Miss Scarlet always starts in the Naughty Corner.' That my siblings and I enjoyed a special relationship with Monopoly was obvious – unavoidably so for the apple-cheeked uncles who jovially proposed a quick game of something before Morecambe and Wise and hobbled out to their Rovers at midnight, pale and broken men – and this relationship was soon blessed with progeny. We began adopting unwanted sets: a fifties one with flat tin tokens, a much earlier board with the stations marked LNER instead of BRITISH RAILWAYS and a dull, mid-eighties set with Mayfair purple and Pall Mall pink. I developed a draughtsman's obsession with those Chance question marks, and painted one very badly on to a badge which I can only hope never got worn. But by the time *The Monopoly Omnibus* came into my possession, it was too late: the dog had bolted, the boot was on another foot, the battleship had long since steamed out of port. I was twenty and hadn't played the game for years, not in fact since my siblings hit their mid-teens and became more preoccupied with the sort of activities familiar to me from the cheekier Chance cards. And in any case, it was written by Gyles Brandreth.

The man famous not so much for appearing regularly on TV wearing ludicrously novelty pullovers as for doing so without even once being punched hard in the throat by a public-spirited member of the audience, Brandreth was until recently a Tory MP whose Commons speeches were instantly drowned out by endearingly unimaginative bellows of 'WOOLLY JUMPER!'. I hardly need to catalogue the many good reasons for never opening this book – though it would be unprofessionally remiss not to mention his funny bug eyes and Teddy Bear Museum – and yet I couldn't quite bear to dispose of anything decorated with those majestically evocative black capitals. Too large a percentage of my pre-pubescent life had been eaten up by Monopoly; the cord was too thick to cut. The book stayed and so did the boards. There was a brief Monopolistic resurgence during further education, and for my father's sixtieth birthday my siblings and I created a bespoke Monopoly board tailored to his status as cruel and grasping overlord of many student tenants in Bath. That same year I fathered a son of my own, and I will leave you to imagine the lurid pagan rituals enacted when, at the appointed time, the boy was inducted into the Monopoly brotherhood. But though even as a six-year-old Kristjan proved so promisingly competitive that I had to read him the winner-puts-the-game-away riot act after less than fifteen minutes, a year later he still seemed reluctant to acknowledge its unique appeal. When he emerged from an obscure cupboard in my parents' house with a look of feverish anticipation on his face and a dusty Cluedo box in his arms I knew I'd need to have words. But I'd yet to decide what these words might be when one morning soon after he came upstairs with the newspaper, his brow too deeply furrowed for one of such tender years.

'Bad loser at Monopoly may go to jail' read the headline he solemnly indicated, a headline which introduced a harrowing insight into the terrible hold the game could still exert on those of a certain age. The bad loser in question was a former Army sergeant who would regularly 'cajole' his reluctant son into lining up two tokens on GO; when the thirteen-year-old made the mistake of winning, there were 'flare-ups'. Eventually the mother threw the game in the bin, but it was mysteriously retrieved and after a final ill-advised victory the boy found himself being kneed in the groin and slapped. Charged with assault, the man said the attack was incited when the child became 'smarmy'.

'Will you slap me if *I* win?'

'Only if you're smarmy,' I could have said, but instead I placed a hand on my son's shoulder and smiled sadly. Kristjan needed to know that Monopoly didn't have to be like that, but at the same time he needed to know why it *was* sometimes like that. Actually, he didn't at all – the boy was still only seven – but there we were anyway, settling down with Uncle Gyles for a glorious tutorial on the days when Monopoly ruled the world.

Introducing *The Monopoly Omnibus* with the eye-catching claim that he owed his life to the game – his parents having met during a session that evidently got out of hand in a fashion I'd certainly never experienced – Brandreth's essential theme was, and I quote, that 'People seem to like playing Monopoly!'. Not a revelation in itself but the following pages offered Kristjan ample evidence of the game's dominance of the post-war cultural scene. Taught the rules by their parents – as I suppose we must have been, though I don't ever recall playing them – the children of the fifties and sixties clocked up so many laps of the board that for more than a few, a simple game was soon insufficient. When my siblings and I succumbed to Monopoly ennui we doubled the GO money for landing exactly on that square with the big red arrow; for others, this wasn't quite enough.

Once the non-stop straight-game record got up to fifty-nine days, people – or anyway students – quickly diversified. They played Monopoly in baths, in lifts, in tree houses; they played it underground or upside-down, suspended from helium balloons with the board stuck on the ceiling. They played on boards one-inch square, or painted them out on car parks and threw huge foam dice off a third-floor fire escape. Most especially, they played it underwater. The game's American manufacturer went so far as to hire out a special sub-aquatic set, with a steel-backed board weighing 7 stone and houses stuffed with wire wool. In the seventies, it never had time to dry out.

The mania soon went official, with Britain's Monopoly manu-facturer John Waddington organising championships in locations felt to be appropriate. It wasn't so bad at first: the inaugural British finals took place on platforms 3 and 4 of Fenchurch Street station, and subsequent finals were played in Park Lane hotels. In 1977, however, a determination to work up a stunt appropriate to Electric Company ended with four unhappy contestants being zipped into anti-radiation suits and frogmarched up to the roof of the main reactor at Oldbury-on-Severn nuclear power station.

Over 160 million Monopoly sets, I learned, have been sold worldwide, and most estimates suggest the game has been played by at least five hundred million people. Extrapolating from these figures, revealing as they do that each set is played by an average of three and a bit people, the twenty million sets sold to Britain's fifty-eight million inhabitants since the game's launch in 1936 have been played by 62½ million people. Even allowing for the sad but enduring truth that people sometimes die, this essentially implied that *absolutely everybody in the whole country has played Monopoly*. And there was more.

I quickly acquired a repository of fancy-that Monopoly facts. In the war, silk maps were hidden inside Monopoly boards and sent out to Allied prisoners, inspiring hundreds of escapes and even more Get Out of Jail Free jokes. The game is sold in eighty countries and has been translated into twenty-six languages. The Great Train Robbers played Monopoly with real, stolen notes while holed up in that Buckinghamshire farmhouse. During the 2000 May Day protests, an anti-globalisation demonstrator hovered precariously around the relevant streets in a mobile hotel outfit.

Soon, these facts filled my brain and began to overflow out through the mouth below. 'In Finnish Junior Monopoly,' I'd announce to a pub full of acquaintances, no doubt in a dispiriting nasal drone, 'jail is a lavatory.' Unusually, though, only a few heads would drop and begin to nod cravenly into their drinks; most eyes sparkled with animated glee and soon the room would fill with reminiscences of cheating and chicanery; inevitably, too, of boards overturned and tokens raised in anger. People helplessly blurted out the catchphrases, most often the nay, nay and thrice nay declamation on the Chance and Community Chest cards that sent you off to jail. Ours, I was reminded, was a generation brought up in a happier society where strangers threw about birthday cash, where banks made errors in your favour. Someone said their father had made a set, and then so did someone else, and the next week I'd find myself admiring individually crafted hotels and boards lovingly hand-painted in Humbrol enamels. Monopoly made people do things that other games didn't.

And everyone seemed to have questions of their own: why was there an American car with whitewall tyres on Free Parking and a New York cop on Go To Jail? Who else noticed that the site-only rent on Piccadilly was the same as the other yellows when it should have been £2 more? Did anyone *ever* bother with mortgage interest?

Fielding these queries, I began to realise that despite the game's straight-batted premise – the financial annihilation of your loved ones – the weirdnesses lurking behind Monopoly were reflected in its details. Take the head-melting arithmetic heralded by the landlord of several dozen red and green plastic edifices turning over the Chance card headed You Are Assessed for Street Repairs: £115 per hotel, £40 per house – it is as mindlessly convoluted now as it was then. And what of Community Chest, which has bothered me in a background way for years, ranked in my third division of incomprehensible enigmas between magnetism and the horridness of Somerfield supermarkets? It hardly helped when I learned it to be some sort of semi-official welfare system prevalent during the American Depression. Surely only the most cruelly capricious benefactor pays out £100 for matured annuities with one hand while snatching it all back as doctor's fees with the other. There are sixteen Community Chest cards: would you apply for housing benefit if to do so incorporated a one in eight risk of either being carted instantly off to the nick or entered in an impromptu beauty contest?

The tokens were another popular topic, largely because whereas in most games players pushed a nondescript nub of coloured plastic around the board, some loose cannon in the Monopoly design department had somehow managed to win over the directors with a diecast selection of pathological randomness. 'Well, we've got a racing car, obviously, and this rather nicely detailed dreadnought. Oops! Yes, sorry, the funnels are a bit sharp. This? Well, it's a hat. A slightly squashed top hat, you know, like a tramp might wear. Ah! I knew you'd love the little dog. A Scottie. Isn't he sweet? Oh, and then there's this sort of old jester's boot thing. And an iron.'

To a chorus of slightly deflated sighs I'd relate how these days Monopoly is under the global aegis of the toy giant Hasbro, whose desire for corporate uniformity has swept away most eccentricities. There are cowcatchers now on the trains at Fenchurch Street, Piccadilly's site-only rent is £24, and the 'Uncle Pennybags' character leaps out of Monopoly's middle O on boards the world over. But it's not their fault, I'd say, it's ours: when the firm held an international vote a couple of years back to decide on a new token, the public's choice was unforgivingly dull. When precedent demanded an owl, a lighthouse, a fir cone, a bib, the world's Monopoly players opted instead for a bag of money.

But though tweaks could be tolerated – a new typeface here, a differently coloured banknote there – I encountered a fierce loyalty to the 1936 board's eclectic but apparently sacrosanct property portfolio, usually when discussing the 'special editions'. In recent years Hasbro has produced or licensed a burgeoning range of themed sets – Manchester United Monopoly, Newcastle and Gateshead Monopoly, World Cup Monopoly, Star Wars Monopoly, Scooby-Doo Monopoly, Coca-flaming-Cola Monopoly – but to mention these was to elicit reactions of an intensity to shame even the most maverick Europhobe. 'My son tells me you can get Pokémon Monopoly now!', I'd trill fatuously to my neighbouring dinner guests, and for long, silent seconds there'd be a lot of jaw-muscle and neck-artery work around the table, perhaps even a still-quivering knife buried point first in the beech veneer. 'It's only a *game*,' someone might eventually pipe up, realising as they did so that the only time you hear those words is when they are plainly untrue. It especially wasn't true because the Monopoly streets weren't silly fabrications – they were real. Tell someone that the Rovers Return occupied Mayfair's berth in Coronation Street Monopoly and you'd get a tersely dismissive reply. 'But the Rovers Return isn't Mayfair. *Mayfair* is Mayfair.'

And it wasn't just the British. An Australian who came round to paint our exterior woodwork said he'd arrived in the mother of the Empire's capital anticipating a city of angels and vines and fairs in May. After a little more research I discovered that millions of disparate former colonials had been brought up with the London board: Kiwis, Canadians, Indians, Singaporeans, even Saudi Arabians. Before the war even Frenchmen and Belgians were obliged to set off down the Old Kent Road, and Monopoly was the closest Hitler ever got to parading up Piccadilly.

All those hours and days and weeks of tocking tokens round that board branded its addresses into the nation's – the Empire's – subconscious. Doctor Oliver Sacks, who set formidable new challenges for his fellow neurologists in events portrayed in the film *Awakenings*, and presumably did the same for opticians with his book *The Man Who Mistook His Wife For a Hat*, finds space to discuss family Monopoly marathons in an early chapter of his autobiography. 'Extreme passions developed over Monopoly,' he recalls, speaking for all who have played the game around the world. But its legacy affected the young Oliver more profoundly and directly, literally colouring his mind's-eye view of streets he had yet to walk down. 'To this day I see the Old Kent Road and Whitechapel as cheap, mauve properties, the pale blue Angel and Euston Road next to them as scarcely any better. By contrast, the West End is clothed for me in rich, costly colours: Fleet Street scarlet, Piccadilly yellow, the green of Bond Street, and the dark, Bentley-coloured blue of Park Lane and Mayfair.' (Even more direct associations were possible on our sixties board, in which the Old Kent Road and Whitechapel were, as they remain today, a basely unequivocal poo brown.)

How different it was on the original game's Atlantic City streets, known to me so well from those board-on-board school-holiday epics. Even though I'd lived all my life in London – albeit a suburban London way out west of the West End – I was still infinitely more intrigued by the lingering mysteries hinted at on our own board than the tedious roll call tolled out during a lap of Atlantic City. Indiana Avenue, Illinois Avenue, Kentucky Avenue, Tennessee Avenue, Pennsylvania Avenue . . . if you closed your eyes you could almost see a grid of identical streets knocked up by the mayor's construction cronies in a week and named by his alcoholic wife in an afternoon. And Mayfair was Boardwalk, which as far as I'm aware is a type of plank-paved shoreline promenade that people drop chips on and tramps sleep under.

But how many centuries of deranged linguistic alchemy were distilled into Pall Mall and Piccadilly? Who was the angel of Islington? What white hall and which white chapel? 'Ah – your famous Pentonville Road,' exclaims the Singaporean tourist; and if his cabbie stifles a derisive snigger then, he'll be laughing on the other side of his face an hour later while desperately scanning the *A–Z* for any trace of Vine Street. Because, as I was beginning to realise and as many of my associates had suggested, however stoutly we might defend it as an untouchable icon, that board made some very unlikely legends. We've all packed up penniless in Park Lane, bailed out bankrupt in Bow Street and, most memorably, met our makers in Mayfair. And when we did so, who didn't slowly emerge from the clamorous aftermath of defeat and take a moment to ponder the mysteries of those malls and squares and fairs, to reflect on the rags-to-riches progress around a board which found a home for all human life; and having done so, looked anew at the triumphant landlord and thought: this top hat is still going in your ear, mate.

Chapter 1

'Maybe it's because I'm a Londoner'

Maybe it's because I'm a Londoner, that I love London so,
Maybe it's because I'm a Londoner, that I think of her, wherever I go,
I get a funny feeling inside of me, just walking up and down,
Maybe it's because I'm a Londoner, that I love London town.

I'm sorry, but what the parted buttocks is that all about? Hubert Gregg penned the capital's best-known anthem less than ten years after the launch of the London Monopoly board, but its lyrics hardly offer much in the way of insight. As an aid to establishing what it is about London we're supposed to like, Hubert's maddeningly circular argument proves stubbornly unhelpful. I'm reminded of the scene in *Oliver!* where Bill Sikes roars his response to Nancy's whimpered inquiry as to the extent of his affections: 'I *lives* with you, don't I?' Then twenty minutes later he beats her to death. And what about this funny feeling? Contemporary cynics might mutter about atmospheric pollution; at Hubert's time of writing it could just as easily have been shrapnel.

Where were the majestic landmarks? Whither the Beach Boyish paeans to the irresistibility of London's womanhood? Couldn't Hube have fleshed things out with a chorus extolling its parks or pigeons or river? The most famous song about what at the time was certainly the world's most renowned city, and there's no so good they named it twice, the scandal and the vice, no Rio by the sea-oh, no I like Paris in the springtime. Men of Harlech is a better song, and precisely twelve people live in Harlech.

In fairness, Hubert's failure to pin down London's elusive charms is preferable at least to the dire lamentations of urban decay that have dominated the capital's musical anthology since someone with an ear for a tune noticed the bridge kept falling down. The 'Streets of London' described by Ralph McTell are unsteadily trodden by shambling, filthy loons, and the Clash's 'London's Burning' cruelly raised false hopes for the fate of my school's physics blocks with its confident assertion that even quite considerable structures might literally burst into flames by simple virtue of their capacity to generate tedium. Of course, you'd hardly imagine Bucks Fizz to have majored on dead cats and tramp's vomit in their 1983 hit 'London Town' – although for all I know they did exactly that: I couldn't bring myself to listen to it then and I'm certainly not about to now.

It's not easy to find a Londoner ready to stand up for their home town: when the most recent Lonely Planet guide lambasted a city of filth, traffic and 'yobbos', the newspaper reporters despatched into the capital's streets to procure some outraged vox-pop ripostes came back with their tapes full of mumbled assent. Demand an explanation as to what a Londoner likes about his home town and the floundering consequences are hilarious to behold. Minor celebrities witter unconvincingly to the *Evening Standard* about restaurants and architecture. A City gent stopped in the street by Newsroom SouthEast talks it up stalwartly as a global transport hub. Mayor Ken Livingstone's departmental website proudly asserts that 'London is special because three people a week try to kill themselves by jumping under a Tube train'. Overall, I think I'm happiest to align myself with an eight-year-old's paean exhibited on a corridor wall at my children's school: 'It hardly ever gets flooded and it's never too hot.'

I'm not sure how this reluctance to praise London came about. Perhaps it's to do with embarrassment at the sheer dominance of the metropolis over its provincial brethren: London was once eleven times larger than its nearest rival, Liverpool, and today there are more Londoners aged over seventy-five than residents of Manchester. So what did *I* like about London? Though always aware of a slight swelling in the chest area when informing Continental acquaintances of my lifelong residence in what after all remains one of the world's most famous cities, I still couldn't understand why so many of their footballers came here in apparent preference to Rome or Barcelona.

Only when you break the city down into manageable postcode-sized pieces does London begin to come into focus. The principal sporting teams of almost every other important capital proudly incorporate the city's name in their own – the New York Mets, Paris St Germain, Real Madrid – but London's footballing giants flaunt their parochial origins. Tell a north Londoner that west is best – as I've often done – and they'll suddenly remember they've got a tongue in their head, as well as a sock full of snooker balls in their hand. The reluctance of cab drivers to venture south of the river is a London cliché. And it's certainly not difficult to think of warm lyrical tributes to constituent parts of the unwieldy whole – 'A Nightingale Sang In Berkeley Square', 'Waterloo Sunset', and of course Marvin Gaye's 'Sexual Ealing'.

This at least raised some hope for my hatching scheme: London *did* begin to make sense if you cut its big picture up into small snapshots, and although I might have no idea how to do this, I knew a man who had. An old man with a top hat and a moustache, bursting through a capital O near you today. From the Old Kent Road to Mayfair, the Monopoly board distilled London into twenty-two cameo performances; if I went and watched them all perhaps I'd make sense of an otherwise overwhelming production. What did those twenty-two snapshots reveal about London? And as you stuck them all together would you watch a profound truth about this enigmatic city gradually take shape before your eyes, or just end up with a really shit collage?

If I'd known then what I subsequently discovered – that no fewer than seven Monopoly streets, starting in clockwise order from Pall Mall and spanning every set on the way to Park Lane, had been described as either London's finest thoroughfare, or Europe's, or the world's – I'd have realised that even culling Greater London's 45,687 streets into twenty-two hardly unmuddied the waters. But at the time it seemed a reasonably straightforward method of answering questions that were beginning to acquire a strange urgency: who was actually responsible for choosing these twenty-two streets back in the thirties, and what did their choices reveal about London then and now?

I began telling people that I was going round the Monopoly board, though because even when I got my children to whisper 'but, like, in *real life*' afterwards this didn't sound particularly epic – sponsored Boy Scouts do it in an afternoon – I soon adopted a rather more grandiose mission statement. I was going to tell the story of London, or at least its last few chapters, through the Monopoly board's twenty-two streets. That did the job for me, but if there was one thing I should have learned it's that when it comes to Monopoly everyone feels entitled to the last word.

'Not bothering with the stations, then?' snided a neighbour, and I tutted and said, yes, all right, and the stations.

'What about Jail?' asked Birna, my wife, and with my blood up I fired back a reckless retort – fine, and I'll do the utilities and Free Parking and all.

That should have been that, but it wasn't quite. 'But Daddy,' began Kristjan, in a voice painstakingly purged of smarm, 'who are you going to play against?'

It wasn't quite so snappy now. 'I'm going to tell the story of London by visiting the twenty-six streets and stations on the Monopoly board, along with appropriate but as yet undecided activities on every other square except the Chances and Community Chests, and in order to . . .'

'Well, and Super Tax and Income Tax.'

'. . . and in order to . . .'

'And GO, obviously.'

'. . . and in order to achieve this I will be playing myself in a cashless, one-player facsimile of a game, equipping myself with a board and concomitant accessories and throwing the dice to dictate my progress between the colour groups, which for the sake of simplicity I shall treat as a single entities rather than three . . .'

'Or two.'

'. . . or two individual properties.'

And when they realised I'd finished everyone would dutifully raise their eyebrows and nod slowly, and then someone would say, 'So you're counting Go To Jail as part of Jail, then.'

CHAPTER 2

Advance to Go

Filth-faced stevedores, bowler hats streaming out of Tube subways, milkmen pushing handcarts, dicky-bowed Bertie Woosters and plump old women waddling uncertainly through gaps between trams: as revealed by my trawl through the capital's photographic libraries, few cities have ever more richly earned the flogged horse-corpse appellation 'City of Contrasts' as London in Monopoly's year zero.

In 1936 London stood on the threshold of the consumerist age, yet had somehow got its pelvis wedged in the Victorian porch out front. So although there were Maltesers and the speaking clock, there were also chimney sweeps and lamplighters cycling through the streets. Britain's millionth telephone was cast in gold and presented to the City of London's elders at Mansion House, and in October the world's first proper televisions went on sale in the West End; but then again sheep grazed in Green Park and St Paul's – as it would be until the sixties – was still the city's tallest building.

Most of these contrasts suggest a city split between the very rich and the very poor, but in 1936 Britain was beginning to squeeze its population in from the extremes: a transition, in effect, from a Cluedo nation split between Colonel Mustard and his servants to a populist Monopoly, where with a bit of luck and judgement an Austin Seven and a Metroland semi was within everyone's grasp. A bit more of both and you could bag a place in Mayfair. The game was emblematic of a new economic and social mobility.

Exuding the grateful humility of a lottery-winning pensioner, I've always thought Uncle Pennybags made an inappropriate ambassador for such a cut-throat game. Far better that slicked-back, winking conman phased out by Waddington in the early sixties: the original Loadsamoney, waving his wardrobe-sized wad with a horribly cocky leer that told you it had not been acquired through honest toil. If he represented London, it was a very different London from the E.M. Forster depictions. Greed was good; if you've got it, flaunt it. In London, you could out-Yank the Yanks.

This was what drove people to the capital. London was the planet's financial centre, and handled almost 40 per cent of Britain's trade with its vast and sprawling Empire. Almost 1,700,000 Londoners commuted to jobs in offices, shops or hotels in the City and West End, and almost as many worked on the shopfloor: 35,000 alone at Ford's new Dagenham plant out at the East End, and more still along the light industrial parades lining the dual carriageways as they wound out towards the new suburbs. Of the 644 factories opened in Britain in the five years after 1932, 532 were in Greater London.

A 1937 eulogy of the capital, subtitled *Heart of the Empire and Wonder of the World*, concluded, 'It can truthfully be said that nowhere else in the world today is there so large a community enjoying so high an average level of comfort as London, nor has there been at any time in history.' Well, if you put it like that, said the miner's daughter in Jarrow, and ran down to the station for a single to King's Cross.

This, in truth, had been going on for rather a long time. In the sixteenth century, the city had been a European backwater and a global irrelevance. By 1800 it had grown into the continent's largest city, and by 1900, when only six European cities needed seven figures to total their populations, London was more than a million ahead of its nearest rival, Paris. In the last decade of the nineteenth century, four hundred newcomers were settling in London *every day*. By the twenties it was the largest city the world had ever known, and driven by an astonishing expansion into the countryside around still it grew: the number of commuters using Rayners Lane station, out near the Piccadilly line's western extremity, rose from 20,000 in 1931 to a monstrous four million just six years later. In 1938 the city's population would break through nine million, a total that has since been falling consistently and is likely to remain as the high-water mark.

It was all terribly exciting. Most of the information I was acquiring shouldn't be soberly acquired in clock-ticking libraries, I felt, but blared out of Tannoys by an over-animated newsreel commentator. I couldn't wait to get going. But there was only one place to start my tour of London, and that, of course, was Leeds.

I once went out with a girl from just outside Leeds, so I know there are some very nice places in Leeds, or anyway just outside Leeds. It was difficult to imagine a locale entitled Sheepscar being one of these, particularly given its challenging proximity to the unpeopled post-industrial wastelands of Chapeltown. Marooned in a bleak urban prairie of under-trafficked roundabouts and Victorian rubble, the West Yorkshire Archive Service had the air of a decommissioned signal box. Housed in a squat red-brick building, it was identified by rusting capitals spelling out SHEEPSCAR.

Digits over the door dated the archive warehouse – once a local public library in the days when there had been a local public – to 1936, of appropriate, and I hoped auspicious antiquity. It smelt of Plasticine; a boss-eyed alderman glared down from his frame on the stairwell. The elderly archivist I'd spoken to had my material ready on a big oak table: three dusty cardboard boxes tied with cotton tape, very like those my grandfather used to have his laundered shirts returned in. 'The Waddington files,' he said, withdrawing immediately to a distant office.

'Manufactured in Great Britain by John Waddington Ltd, Leeds' was a phrase burned into my cerebral cortex. It was on the front of the box, and on the back of the rules, and I'd always known that if I wanted to get any closer to finding out why the London board was as it was I'd end up in West Yorkshire. I lifted the top one's lid, sneezed twice, withdrew a 1946 Parker Brothers catalogue and in opening it felt corroded staples perish in my palms.

'The Monopoly Story' detailed within was very much the official one, describing how unemployed boiler salesman Charles Darrow had invented the game at his kitchen table in Germantown, Pennsylvania, during the spring of 1930. Darrow, a typical victim of the Depression, fancied himself as an inventor but had enjoyed little success with previous efforts that failed to find that elusive middle way between the dull (an improved bridge scoring pad) and the daft (anyone for a 'combined bat and ball'?). 'Why he chose to devise a game based on real estate nobody knows,' a Monopoly website had claimed. 'In later years he couldn't remember.'

Darrow died in 1967, still stubbornly failing to recall any contact with The Landlord Game, patented in 1904 by Elizabeth Magie of Philadelphia (Germantown's nearest city) and widely played across Pennsylvania in the years after. Intriguingly intended to ridicule an unjust tax system and condemn rather than glorify ruthless property speculators, her game was played on a board with nine squares between corners, two of these being Go and Go To Jail. Proceeding around this board, players bought properties (as well as railways, water works and an electric company) and charged rent for them. The game became known as Auction Monopoly, and then – yes – Monopoly.

In fact, Darrow's sole contribution – not on the face of it one that merited a life of improbably moneyed leisure as the first millionaire game inventor, particularly when set against the $500 Magie later accepted to shut her up – was to place the emphasis on acquiring sets to build houses. A small but hugely significant step. Monopoly wouldn't be much fun without the thrill of acquiring what the rules kept telling us to describe as 'all the sites of a complete colour group'. Getting a set in Monopoly is a little like becoming a parent: you devote all your financial and emotional resources trying to nurture and develop your little ones, and when they let you down, you flog them to the bank.

Monopoly would be no sort of game without the joy of sets. Elizabeth Magie might have invented the wheel, but Darrow came up with the axle that made it roll. And roll and roll: having first played his friends on an old piece of tarpaulin hand-painted with the names of Atlantic City streets, Darrow was soon taking orders from local department stores at four bucks a throw. When the orders went wholesale, Darrow's cottage-industry production line couldn't cope and in 1934 he contacted toy giants Parker Brothers.

Knowing a thing or two about board games, but clearly no more than that, Parkers rejected Monopoly out of hand. The most heinous of the game's 'fifty-two fundamental errors' was its lack of a specific end: a Parker Bros title was expected to last no more that forty-five minutes, but here was one which didn't know when to stop. What Parkers failed to grasp was that in 1934 there were many millions of people with a lot more than forty-five minutes on their hands, but no money for extra-domestic entertainment. Here was a game that filled all those unemployed hours, and did it by pressing a satisfying wedge of fantasy dollars into your hand with the opportunity to develop this into a barely manageable mountain of cash through ruthlessness and wily investment. It was like the Crash never happened.

It should have been one of those portentously spurned opportunities, like Decca turning down the Beatles or Margaret Thatcher's chauffeur staying awake in the fast lane, but Parker Bros were given a second bite at Darrow's plump and ripening cherry. Parkers' chairman, Robert Barton, heard a friend of his wife's raving about a board game she'd just been playing, and having borrowed her Monopoly set he didn't get to bed until 2 a.m. Three days later Darrow was in Barton's New York office signing on the dotted line.

'Taking the precepts of Monopoly to heart,' said Darrow, recalling his decision to flog the rights rather than build up a one-man business, 'I did not care to speculate.' *What?* Reading this I questioned not just whether Darrow had invented Monopoly, but if he'd ever even played the game. The first law of Monopoly is *always* to speculate, to buy everything you land on (except possibly the crap-arse utilities), to invest in houses as soon as you get that first set. Play against someone who spurns even a single property-purchasing opportunity on that first lap of the board and you know you're playing a loser.

That was in January 1935. By mid-February, normally a dead time for the firm, Parkers were shifting 20,000 sets a week. In the company's fifty-year history they had never seen anything like it: by Christmas, the backlog of orders was stuffed into laundry baskets stacked up along the head office corridors. For every dollar bill produced by the US Treasury, Parkers were knocking out ten Monopoly bucks – it really was a licence to print money.

Founded in 1898, fifteen years after Parker Brothers, the John Waddington revealed in the archival documentation was a very different sort of company. Leeds, as everyone except the purveyors of youth fashion will be aware, is not New York.

Waddingtons were printers, specialising originally in theatre programmes, who in 1922 had diversified into playing cards. In 1924 the firm was accused of plagiarising rival De La Rue's ace of spades, which should by rights have spawned an entertaining slanging match in the press – 'PACK OF LIES!'; – 'YOUR ACE OR MINE?' – but these were gentler times, and after a court case ended in Waddingtons' favour the two firms buried the hatchet so deeply that they were soon playing each other in an annual cricket match.

Nothing else happened until the mid-thirties when Parkers shipped a Monopoly set over to Leeds. One Friday night in the spring of 1935, the managing director of Waddingtons, Victor Watson, handed the set to his son Norman (at that time in charge of the playing card division) saying, 'Look this over, then tell me what you think of it.' Years later, Norman recalled this event in appropriately momentous terms. 'I played an imaginary game against myself continuing through Friday night, Saturday night and Sunday night. I was enthralled and captivated. I had never found a game so absorbing and thus the Monopoly game was first played in England at my home.' Red-eyed, unshaven and consumed with evangelical zeal, Norman rushed into the office on Monday morning and persuaded his father to get on the phone. The transatlantic call that connected Victor Watson and Robert Barton that day was the first ever made by Waddingtons and the first received by Parkers. By the end of it, Victor had snapped up the Empire and European rights.

Despite his son's enthusiasm, when casually volunteering to head down to London to scout out appropriate equivalents for the Atlantic City addresses Victor can have had no idea how much he was biting off, even though he'd take his secretary Marjorie Phillips along to help him chew it.

The whole business was clearly rather half-cocked: the Waddington art boys knocked up some nice British locomotives to replace the cowcatchered Atlantic City jobs, but didn't get around to sticking a Metropolitan wooden-top on that New York cop's head or switching the Free Parking Chevrolet for an MG. The Electric Company light bulb remained a standard US-issue Edison screw; Charles Darrow's crass error on the yellow set's site-only rents sneaked across the Atlantic undetected. The prisoner looks British enough, a gaunt and shifty old lag you can almost hear blagging snout in a cracked hiss; but beneath his bars is a word few would have encountered in thirties Britain. In news stories and detective novels, 'jail' was always 'gaol' before Monopoly came along.

Lifting the dusty lids off those Waddington boxes had been an act charged with portent. These forgotten documents would unravel all the enigmas of Victor Watson's more obscure decisions: why he chose the streets he chose, and how he felt they encapsulated London as it then was. I'd imagined finding Victor's handwritten notes from that weekend down in The Smoke with Marjorie, explaining that Tottenham Court Road was excluded after a bellboy in Heal's laughed at his spats, and how Vine Street made it in when the wily Marge calculated that substituting it for Upper Burlington Gardens would save £59 4s. 3d. a year on ink.

But rifling through to the bottom of the third and final box with ratcheting desperation, I'd uncovered nothing whatever from the relevant period. Waddingtons' in-house magazine, *The Team*, had a complete run of back issues from the turn of the century until 1981 – complete, that is, except for a mysterious void from 1931 to 1940. Victor had died, aged just sixty, in 1943; Marjorie Phillips retired in 1952 after thirty years as the MD's PA, still addressing her boss as 'Mr Norman'. They had taken their secrets with them.

Somehow putting out of my mind the implication that I had completely wasted my time, I leafed back through the files in search of anecdotal succour, and soon found myself becoming engrossed in the correspondence between Norman Watson and Parker boss Robert Barton, watching it develop from 'Dear Sir' in the first box to 'My good friend Norman' in the third. The initial talk was purely of business: 'Regarding the games Oscar and XYZ – we must at all costs stamp very hard on any people who infringe our Monopoly copyrights.' But these were men shackled together by a steely bond – each had played epoch-making late-night games of solo Monopoly. Theirs could never be a cold-hearted commercial relationship. The tone seemed to change after Norm sold Bob the US rights to Cluedo, a game Waddingtons had recently bought from a Birmingham solicitor's clerk, Anthony Pratt. Released in 1948, Cluedo tapped so deeply into a global fascination with country house whodunits that it was able to overcome the daunting twin handicaps of a silly name and being completely crap: marketed as Clue it shifted a hundred million copies in the US and was licensed in twenty-three countries.

With their business association on a more equal footing, Norm and Bob's friendship blossomed. Their letters began to touch on politics, or at least a shared and strident distaste for 'socialism', and there were exchanges on the birth of Prince Charles, the Korean War and the voyage of the US submarine *Nautilus* beneath the North Pole.

But through it all ran a constant theme: Norm and Bob were living out their respective roles in parochial Blighty and the cosmopolitan US of A as the balance of economic power tilted dramatically across the Atlantic. Bob on his summer: 'I returned last night from ten beautiful days in Bermuda.' Norm on his: 'I have been somewhat miserable with an attack of the shingles.' Bob's visit to England in 1953: 'I have reserved us tickets for the Coronation parade: third-floor window in St James's, fifty guineas each.' Norm's reciprocal trip to the States: 'It was the waste that was most noticeable – almost whole cigarettes thrown away before entering an elevator.' That thirties smile had certainly been wiped off Leeds's face, and by association it didn't look good for London. In lifestyle terms, Bob was advancing to

GO while Norm went back three spaces. The humiliations of rationing stretched the gap ever wider. In 1947 Bob had sent Norm a Christmas box comprising '5 lb of rice, bacon, butter and tea'. 'Will you also be kind enough to give me Mrs Watson's exact stocking measurements?' he blurted the following November. Another note accompanying Bob's 1949 food parcel read: 'Sally has just reminded me of our terrible mistake last year regarding the size of Ruby's legs.'

Possibly through coincidence, the correspondence thinned out thereafter. After the winning revelation that Switzerland's Cluedo players accuse not Colonel Mustard but Madam Curry I came to the final run of in-house magazines. It was all rather poignant. Even as Joyce Grenfell presented the board with the four hundred millionth Waddington-printed theatre pro-gramme, the hands on the games division tiller in the early seventies were steering the firm directly towards the rapids.

It staggered me that a human composed of standard-issue parts could ever imagine that Beat The Elf or The Great Downhill Ski Game were worthy of development and promotion. While the printing side of the firm branched lucratively into fag packets and frozen-food cartons, the board-game boys were issuing press statements attempting to justify the release of an ordnance-defusing entertainment entitled Bombshell! in the midst of an IRA blitz on the capital (following complaints from the recently bereaved family of an Army disposal expert, the game was quietly withdrawn). Tesco threw a spanner in the Waddington works in the mid-seventies by stacking its shelves with imported Yugoslavian Monopoly sets, and disastrous investments in a hopeless home video-game system almost brought the company down in the early eighties.

Stacking the letters and magazines back into their boxes with a sigh, I noticed a sheet of paper that had slipped out on to the floor. On it was a single pencilled paragraph: 'The average gathering of friends in these days seems to revolve around cocktails and dirty stories sprinkled with spicy bits of scandal. These prevailing conditions trouble the conscientious parent who wishes to keep their children at home. They encourage their young people to bring friends home. It is the alternative to cinemas, the foxtrot. The cure is games in the home.'

Perhaps because of that youthful exposure to the Atlantic City original, I'd always thought of Monopoly not as a stout home-grown bulwark against inappropriate American imports – cocktails, cinemas – but rather the thin end of the transatlantic wedge. You could change the streets and stick on trains like Henry out of Thomas the Tank Engine, but as with Cliff Richard's youthful hip rotations or the vestigial fins on a Vauxhall Victor, the country of origin was obvious. But now I saw the game had been marketed in Britain not just as a simple family pastime, but as a governess, an hour-devouring parental con-spiracy to keep us indoors when we could have been out sprinkling spicy bits of scandal into our vodka martinis. That strident manifesto painted a vivid picture of a nation as it stood at the cultural crossroads, and now it was time to go back to that crossroads and put the signs straight again. It was time to advance to GO.

CHAPTER THREE

King's Cross

KING'S CROSS STATION

GO, I suppose, was the perfect motto of an age and a nation transfixed by speed. In the thirties Britons were the first to drive at 300mph and fly at 400mph; the water speed record set by Malcolm Campbell on Coniston Water in 1939 stood until the fifties. And the train Victor and Marjorie alighted from at King's Cross on that unrecorded date in 1935 was a London and North Eastern Railway A4 class, the fastest steam locomotives the world had ever seen.

If I'd known where GO had gone, I'd naturally have started there. Impatience and economy had lured me into my car for the Sheepscar run, and despite involuntarily recreating certain environmental aspects of Victor's portentous journey when smoke started billowing out of the dashboard coming back down the M1, having eschewed the more authentic rail option I still felt slightly fraudulent. Grappling with the GO issue, it occurred to me that if not quite killed, two birds could at least be badly hurt with one stone by beginning my game at King's Cross. It was Vic and Marge's gateway to the capital; their GO would be mine.

Wedging my pre-war board into a backpack I set off into a veil of September drizzle. Despite the weather I felt warmly happy, partly because I was going to play Monopoly, but mainly because of the peculiar thrill of being a tourist in my own city, undeniably commuting and yet somehow on a giddily novel voyage of discovery. Between SE28 and NW11 there were 119 postcodes in London, and my lifelong residence had been almost wholly lived out in two adjacent ones well away from Monopoly's main focus, the West End. Of the twenty-two streets on my board I could claim easy familiarity with fewer than half, hadn't set foot in five and had no idea where one was. I'd never taken a train from three of the four stations, visited a water works or been in prison, just visiting or otherwise. I loved London, but like Hubert Gregg I couldn't really tell you why. Perhaps when I'd advanced to Mayfair, taken a trip to Marylebone station and gone back to Old Kent Road I'd have found out. But if I tracked down some Free Parking, I'd be keeping it to myself.

Hyde Park gave us a lane and the Battle of Trafalgar a square, but it was a further indication of the sprawling majesty of my ignorance of London that, these two and that old road to Kent aside, I'd had no idea how any of the Monopoly addresses got their names. King's Cross hadn't struck me as especially outlandish, so I was reasonably astounded to learn that the landmark which gave the area its name had survived for less than a decade. In the 1820s Battle Bridge was a benighted shantytown, stalked by highwaymen and dominated by a smallpox hospital and a towering slagheap of waste rubble piled up outside a brickworks. In the first round of what has proven to be a two-hundred-year struggle to make the area even slightly nice, the slagheap was imaginatively sold to the Russians to rebuild post-Napoleon Moscow and in 1836 a rather attractive 60-foot monument erected in its place. Not in any way cruciform, this octagonal structure was topped by a statue of the recently deceased King George IV, a monarch popular only amongst those of his subjects with an unusual tolerance for preening, fat-faced indolence.

This surely explains why the statue was pulled down after only six years, and why few thought it disrespectful thenceforth to employ the structure beneath, which had been a police station, as a pub. It hadn't been a cross, and now it didn't have a king. Three years later the whole thing was demolished along with the smallpox hospital, and on its site arose what was at that time the nation's largest railway station.

A transport hub with a dozen axles, as well as the mainline station King's Cross was serviced by London's first bypass, the west–east New Road, the Grand Union Canal, and, from 1863, the world's first underground railway. In all the bustle and noise it wasn't surprising that no one stopped long enough to notice how rundown the area was becoming.

In 1935 King's Cross still rang with whistles and clanks and the shouts of trunk-trundling porters – that year there were 400,000 unionised railway employees – but in the contemporary photographs I'd seen the neglect was already obvious. Scenes more typically associated with British Rail's well-chronicled seventies nadir tolled out in black and white: sullen operatives scraping trolleys along ravaged plaster and brickwork; a de-wheeled old goods van in farmyard condition pressed into service as the platform 1 staff room.

I'd never before stopped to pay much attention to the station or its environs, and I doubt that Victor Watson would have either: Waddingtons' London office was in St James's, a few stops west down the Piccadilly line which he'd have hopped straight on to. For Vic and Marge, though, that day would be different. To appraise London's real estate in terms of its economic and aesthetic value they'd need to keep their eyes open. Standing outside the plain brick arches of the station and peering through four lanes of Euston Road traffic, they'd have been faced by the ornately tiled Reggioni's restaurant, Stewart and Wight's Cocoa Rooms and Temperance Hotel and the splendid twin turrets of the Regent Theatre. It was still a place for nice people to hang about in, respectably idling away the hours before their train left.

At least that was the theory. Because with all those new bus and Tube connections there *were* no hours to idle away: you just turned up and got on your train. And so the nice people stopped hanging about King's Cross, to be replaced by others for whom the huge throughput of humanity represented both an enviable customer base and perfect cover. In the early thirties, a huge banner slung across the Regent Theatre's façade read: 'Visitors to London: Enjoy a Good Play and Catch Your Train'. The Regent isn't around now, but if they'd kept the banner that Good Play would have devolved into a Grubby Shag, and Your Train into Hepatitis C.

King's Cross these days is nationally synonymous with kerb-crawling, football violence and brazenly conducted class A drug deals. Feeling like, and in my bedrizzled old anorak uncomfortably resembling, a character in that 'touch of flu' heroin-screws-you-up campaign, as I emerged from beneath the mid-seventies car-port canopy I felt the CCTV cameras that now infest King's Cross turn on me like the paparazzi on Posh, panning and zooming restlessly.

Out front the downbeat, neglected transience that characterises many European railway terminuses still lingers: an amusement arcade, two McDonald's, kebab shops and the sort of convenience stores that sell stupidly strong lager, crisps illegally split from multipacks, and pornography. But a lot of money is being spent in the area – £4 billion over the next fifteen years on both the Channel Tunnel rail link and an improbably ambitious commercial and residential development – and no one wants the pitch queered by undesirables. A local TV news report I'd seen the week before revealed that the hoardings lining all the pavements around the station weren't erected solely to conceal construction work, or even to ease pedestrians into the bus lanes, but to deny cover to tarts and dealers. That and the nosy cameras had apparently eased much antisocial behaviour a few streets back from the station, but by the same token the overbearing surveillance seemed a provocation, inspiring a desire to rebel against the police state, to play up to the cameras, to do the bad stuff they were so keen to stop you doing. King's Cross was a naughty place, and if you wanted to find out why, perhaps you ought to deal with some of the naughty people on their own terms.

I tried to disabuse myself of this preposterous theory while despatching a rather toothsome £5.95 lunchtime special at a curry house opposite the station, a three-course delight blemished only by the management's decision to describe the main dish's principal ingredient as 'bird'. It shouldn't have been too difficult. Through the furious mess of traffic I noted two lank women effecting some dead-eyed sleight-of-hand exchange on a stepping-stone traffic island; outside McDonald's a blistered wino was heroically engaging an imagined foe. If you were going to sail that close to the wind, you might at least hope it blew you off on some voyage of discovery. What would I learn while hastily selecting a foil-wrapped rock of adulterated crack from a dealer's mouth or splitting eight cans of Diamond White with an incoherent gentleman of the road?

Aware that my focus was tightening in on the only remaining element of King's Cross's unholy trinity, I absent-mindedly paid up and set off towards the mean-street hinterland. Tarts were by tradition blessed with hearts of gold, I assured myself, in a way that crack-heads and piss-artists were not. I had merely to locate a suitably approachable example and engage her in streetwise banter; the inside story of King's Cross would be laid out before me by someone who'd seen it all, who'd been there, done that and wet the T-shirt.

But if there's one thing Monopoly should have taught me, it's that you've got to pay to play. No fees, no favours. I'd taken barely a step before acknowledging the dominant flaw of a scheme which effectively required one to chat up a prostitute. Bob Hoskins had a go in *Mona Lisa*, and even he hadn't been able to handle it. However traumatic it would be, money was going to have to change hands.

With bits of bird and knots of anxiety binding my innards I wondered if this could really be happening: that after thirty-seven years of generally stout moral conduct I was going off to pay a street courtesan for her services. It made it only slightly less awful, but substantially more ridiculous, to decide that these services would comprise a game of Monopoly.

Though as with everything I am about to say this fact is coloured by an unfamiliarity with the protocol, I imagined three in the afternoon as an off-peak time in the sex industry. Certainly there were no obvious candidates standing by lampposts with hands on pencil-skirted hips. And though my board-game plan had initially seemed a brilliant face-saving, and indeed marriage-saving compromise – one could convincingly argue Monopoly to be the definitive opposite of sex – even vaguely formulating a relevant business-touting approach conjured scenes which invariably ended with me being assessed for face repairs by a huge man wearing half a branch of Ratners about his person.

'Excuse me, I've got a rather unusual request . . .'

If the apologetic Hugh Grant gambit warranted the most serious physical retribution, any cheeky upfrontness was hardly better: 'Take a Chance with me, love, or you'll end up with another £10 fine.' 'Wanna win second prize in my beauty contest?'

For half an hour I kerb-walked the district, pausing momentarily outside a couple of promisingly tawdry massage parlours but otherwise finding no evidence of the vice plague I'd heard and read so much about. I was thinking of less irksome methods of encapsulating the outlaw ambience of King's Cross when I walked past a phone box and noticed its glazed area completely obscured by a mosaic of coloured postcards.

With the coast clear I snatched a handful, crammed them into my rucksack and strode briskly away, through the inconsequential annexe that houses the most famous railway platforms in Britain: 10, under which, some say, Boadicea is buried, and 9¾, from where Harry Potter catches the Hogwart's Express. On the grounds that Harry Potter is a fictional wizard I suppose it doesn't matter that the furthest you can travel from any platform in the annexe appeared to be Stevenage, any more than it matters that the some who say the Boadicea thing are foolishly deluded (expert opinion places her bones near Colchester).

The solitude required for my awkward task wasn't hard to locate given the proximity of the old marshalling yards behind King's Cross, earmarked for that huge redevelopment but currently a brownfield wasteland so extensive that some quick-witted entrepreneur has knocked up a 250-yard golf driving range in a far-flung corner.

With the unearthly turbine roar of departing northbound expresses reduced to a spin-cycle drone I sat down on a broken pallet by the shell of a building labelled 'Coal Depot' and examined my haul. Top of the deck was a snarling Valkyrie in a rubber dress and a Catwoman mask: 'DOWN ON YOUR KNEES!' barked the motto above a phone number. Hers was the first to be cast aside with an inner yelp of distress, quickly followed by a hairy chest labelled 'I was a woman' in a discard pile that soon grew into a teetering stack. Baby cosseting, clinical fantasies, water sports – with a little lateral thought I could usually work out what type of awfulness I was avoiding, but sometimes ('A level Greek'; 'TV shoplifter') I couldn't.

I reached the last card – 'If you don't find the same nurse as in this picture, you leave straight away' – with a sense of bewilderment and dread. Such was the spectrum of perversion it had seemed at least possible that I'd turn up a card headed 'I'll make your house into a hotel' above a winking Auntie Pennybags, but after an extensive cull I was left with just four, two emblazoned with the radiant catchphrase 'I like my job', one 'fun, fat and fifty' – I figured at least she'd have been round the board a few times – and a 'melon relief'.

The ensuring mobile calls engendered levels of telephonic apprehension unknown since adolescence. By failing to pick up their phones the first two offered perhaps a more honest assessment of their levels of career satisfaction, and the owner of the voice that answered fun, fat and fifty was either only two-thirds right or they'd printed the number of the local builder's merchant by mistake. I slammed the phone down as literally as current mobile technology permits, and it was melon relief's turn at the next call when I initiated our conversation by blurting out that I just wanted to play a game of Monopoly without any funny business.

Features puckering in distaste, I picked up the discards and slowly flicked through them. Bound to please, blow your mind with my behind, thank you sir may I have another – oh no. No no no no no. However nasty Monopoly sometimes turned, it never turned *that* nasty. Rarely, anyway. In the end I decided to try everyone who didn't threaten to wee on me or inflict pain.

'Hellogabbyspeaking,' fluttered the softly Hispanic voice at the end of the line.

'Good afternoon,' I said, in a brisk and strident tone intended as the antithesis of the textbook salivatory perv-o-mumble. 'I came across your . . . I found your card in a telephone box and was just wondering about your schedule for the afternoon.'

'Yes . . . is OK today. Wish service you require? You know my rate?'

'No, no I don't,' I said, still as if arranging a quote for weatherproofing external woodwork.

'Is forty pounds for thirty minute sensual massage.'

'Right . . . um, what it is, I mean, what I'm interested in isn't so much that as playing Monopoly.'

'Playing in Napoli?'

'No, no. It's, um, a game. A board game? Very popular all over the world. I'm sure you'll know it when you see it. Yes. And obviously your company, maybe having a chat while we played. The game. Of Monopoly.'

There was a pause, and for a moment I thought I'd lost another one. When at length the voice spoke again it was both tentative and reluctant.

'The game . . . is, ah, *dangerous* in some way?'

And so there I was half an hour later, walking away from a cashpoint with £40 out of the spousal joint account, £40 I was about to hand over to Gabby, who perhaps at this point I should explain described himself as a pre-operation Brazilian transsexual new to the UK. Shielding face with backpack I pressed the relevant intercom in an only slightly rundown street round the back of Camden town hall, as confident as I could be that the looming experience would simply involve an expensive game of Monopoly with a bloke in a dress rather than the joyous throwing open of some previously treble-locked door in the darker corridors of my sexual psyche.

The Gabby who opened the door of the first-floor flat bore little resemblance to the Gabby who appeared on the postcard – less of the willowy lady-boy and more of the wobbly lady-man. Brushing a strand of his waist-length wavy black hair from a broad face thickly caked in powder and dominated by bulbously collagen-crammed lips, Gabby smiled slightly and gestured me in; I nodded gruffly and wondered if shaking hands would send out the right signals.

Gabby's flat was in fact rather fun in an eighties art student way: tall walls decorated with zebra-skin tapestries and an enormous chrome-Sputnik light fitting swinging gently from the ceiling. On the other hand – and at this point I'd like to welcome you aboard the Euphemism Express – its air was overbearingly impregnated with an unwelcome aroma, the aroma in fact of an adolescent male's bed linen after a month of prodigiously consummated nocturnal imaginings.

Trying to ignore the signals my nose was bellowing to my brain I whisked out the board with a manly cough. 'Right. We might need a table for this.' I'd gone for my fifties set, comfortably the most presentable – in such pristine condition that it had quite clearly never before been played (though regrettably, as with all but the very earliest Darrow-era sets, of diminutive *Antiques Roadshow* potential given the enormous number produced each year). It even retained the little slip you were advised to include with any complaints about missing contents; scanning the room for a flat surface I wondered how the cited John Waddington employee who had approved the set for despatch, Checker 22, would have felt on learning that the next pair of hands on the banknotes he'd counted up fifty years earlier were tipped with maroon varnish and belonged to a pre-operation Brazilian transsexual.

'We play here,' said Gabby, indicating a long blue sofa which wasn't nearly as spartan or businesslike as I might have wished.

I slapped the board down on the upholstery and set out the title deeds and Chance and Community Chest cards, holding out the tokens for his perusal. 'I take . . . this,' he said, plucking the dog from my hand.

'My sister always chose that,' I replied automatically, and Gabby looked at me, his immaculately decorated brown eyes soft with a kind of matter-of-fact empathy.

'I understand. So you are . . . *addict* to this game?'

That was a bad moment, one that became worse as I endeavoured to disabuse him of this interpretation. Hoping to palm Gabby off (oh, *please*) with a story about researching an alternative guide to Monopoly-board London, I succeeded only in convincing him that my mission was to play the game with as many transsexuals as possible. Once happy that the newspapers were not involved in any way, he couldn't have cared less, nodding distantly through my increasingly garbled bletherings before politely requesting payment up front. Handing over those crisp twenties I realised that by Gabby's standards there was nothing unusual about a client initially reluctant to confess an obscure and shaming fetish. Reluctant, anyway, until the arousal became too intense to bear, until the trigger point when Gabby turned over the adulterated Community Chest card that would begin his brutal manual harvest: 'IT IS YOUR BIRTHDAY: COLLECT 10 PINTS FROM EACH PLAYER.'

While narrowing my choices I'd instantly dismissed the two post-operational transsexuals, along with the grotesquely butchered shambles implied by the card labelled '½ opt'. But now I found myself contemplating the stark reality that in a purely physiological sense, we are all pre-operation transsexuals. And forty quid was forty quid – I might want to get my money's worth.

'Yes, yes – we have like this in Brazil. Some long time ago I play . . . but in Brazil game is called Bank, Banco . . .' As I'd predicted, Gabby's ignorance of the game diminished once he'd taken stock of the board's layout.

'Banco Imobiliario,' I said, and was again treated to that limpid, understanding gaze as Gabby pulled the hem of his PVC microskirt down over wide stocking tops and sat by the other side of the board. From a coffee table cluttered with unopened Tia Maria miniatures and – oh dear – boxes of Kleenex, he retrieved three identical mobile phones and lined them up neatly on the board beside the Chance cards.

The meter was running and I ran swiftly through the rules, sticking the dog next to the racing car on GO before handing Gabby the dice. With admirable nonchalance he rolled, and eschewing the highest-score-goes-first rule, I let him go with his double three. 'The Angel,' he said with a wry smile. 'I buy this.'

Almost immediately everything somehow seemed more normal; Monopoly was a homely international language and we were both speaking it. Handing over the title deeds of properties

Gabby purchased allowed me to discuss the game and the streets without sounding too mad. He seemed more familiar with the board's extremes – a good friend lived in Whitechapel, and with a shy half-laugh he confessed to many professional assignments in Mayfair.

I hoped someone would land on King's Cross, and when he did I falteringly managed to coax out a few biographical details. After leaving Brazil for a protracted tour of Europe's capitals, Gabby had settled in London two years ago, and though King's Cross was 'maybe ugly' – snapping up Piccadilly he stated a wistful desire for a West End flat – he felt at home here because of its tolerance. 'All London is like this,' he breathed in that child-like monotone. 'The people are not always so . . . happy, but so many different people and culture and everybody get on, make no trouble.'

In 1935 the King's Cross immigrants were Italian: Reggioni's was one of half a dozen such catering establishments around the station. Today, you'd be wasting your time attempting to define the cultural make-up – almost half the UK's ethnic-minority population lives in London, and King's Cross has an almost randomly picked-and-mixed cross section. The impression I'd had around the station was of an aimless, rootless absence of community, an inhuman vacuum embodied in the revelation that fourteen years after the escalator fire in the Underground there, one of the thirty-one victims, a man in his forties, has yet to be identified. But the King's Cross Gabby spoke of was different, a lively and all-welcoming community. Everyone comes and anything goes: as Gabby could no doubt assess from rich personal experience elsewhere, in London even the most colourful individualist was accepted on streets that had already seen it all. As a native I can say I felt a surge of civic pride. At least I hope that's what it was.

Gabby, I could sense, was beginning to enjoy the game, largely because of an incredible run of fortune that within two laps of the board had bagged him a pair each of light blues, purples and yellows and no fewer than three stations. For my part I'd landed on two of his properties, been sent to jail, copped a speeding fine and a hospital bill and been stung twice for income tax – down to three hundred odd quid and with only Marlborough Street, Water Works and Regent Street to show for it. Funded by a bank error in his favour, my rent and an advance to GO, Gabby hadn't even broken into his five hundreds.

Almost every turn was interrupted by a call on his mobile switchboard: one he answered with a strangely baritone 'bom dia', one with a rather suspicious 'mmm?' and the third – the work line, the one I'd rung – with that breathy 'hello-gabbyspeaking'. I'd hoped that in the apparent absence of further appointments I might be allowed a bonus hour or two, get a few houses up and make things more interesting than they already were, but it soon became obvious by the incoming calls on that last line that my time was running out.

'We have maybe ten minutes,' said Gabby as I handed him the Park Lane title deeds, his way of telling me to cut the crap and whip it out.

'Just time for another couple of rounds,' I said, too loudly and too heartily, and for the first time Gabby looked mildly surprised – this really *was* the easiest £40 he'd ever earned. And his luck didn't change on the board, either. When I called a sudden halt, abruptly imagining Gabby's next client leering out a salty, collaborative wink as we passed on the stairs, I'd already had to turn down Mayfair and even Bow Street on economic grounds.

'So I win?' said Gabby. Quickly I divvied up: eleven properties and £766 in cash for him, five and £174 for me. Not for anticipated reasons, it was the most dreadful Monopoly performance of my life.

'You are busy today?' he inquired mildly as I crammed and slammed bits into box and board into backpack.

'No, not really,' I said quickly, making for the door.

'Oh,' nodded Gabby, 'I ask because you have many, many ah . . .'

And following his gaze to the floor I saw the wodge of buckled cards displaced from my backpack during the over-eager preparations for departure. 'Mistress Nina's School of Correction: PUNISHMENT AT ITS BEST' read the legend across the visible half of the one on top.

I half-stooped to pick them up, then righted myself. 'No need for her now,' I jabbered, fingers already twisting the Yale. 'You've just beaten me.'

In my haste I'd forgotten to ask Gabby to do something for me, and jogging back past the station in light drizzle I set off to do it myself. Not at this stage confident enough to risk exposing my Water Works in public, I retraced my steps to the old coal depot and whipped the board out of the backpack.

Despite that outlandish baptism, it was still a lovely thing to behold. Even in a light rain I could see what Oliver Sacks meant: the colours were indeed rich and costly, strident Technicolor blurts in a time of monochrome austerity, a beige age. Befitting its manufacturer's heritage, the Waddington board is a triumph of the printer's art.

Surveying the bushes growing out of the coal depot's upper walls, between windows missing like empty eye sockets, I accepted how little of London is a triumph of anything any more. The Channel Tunnel rail link scheme is already teenaged but at this end of the line was still years from taking recognisable shape. Why did it take us so long to get anything useful done these days? The enormous Piccadilly line extension to Cockfosters – opened in 1933 and incorporating eight new stations – was knocked up in less than two years. In that same year, the ribbon was cut on three new bridges across the Thames. Below I watched as an incoming express was swallowed up by the huge mouth of St Pancras station, in its time the largest enclosed space in the world; these days, we're reduced to heralding that express line to Folkestone as the 'first major railway to be built in Great Britain for one hundred years'. Intended as a proud boast, this comes out sounding more like a shaming indictment. Where once we excelled at building large things, these days it's all we can do to knock them down: English Heritage had insisted that the mighty cylindrical skeletons of three gasholders lying in the rail link's path must be dismantled and reassembled nearby, and even 100 yards off I could hear the ineffectively strangled obscenities of yellow-hats battling to loosen screws tightened in 1880.

It should have all been rather melancholy, but in the light of my encounter with Gabby I instead found the surrounding shambles cheerfully inspiring. The tolerant individualism that drew Gabby to London was symbolised by its jerry-built anarchy: there has never been the civic will, let alone the way, to reshape the capital to some centralised and inhuman grand design. Most European capitals are dominated by great boulevards and sweeping vistas, created by wiping the map clean and starting again. But even after the Great Fire, even after the Blitz, there was no wholehearted attempt to grasp the opportunity for wholesale urban overhaul: there were discussions, and blueprints for a new future, and then in the end they just stuck up taller buildings along the original medieval street lines. Writing in 1938, a *Sporting Times* journalist reported how, while enmeshed in horrendous traffic up the Strand, his cabbie had turned round and muttered, 'Damn fine city, London – or it will be when it's finished.'

And that's it: London will never be finished. We make do, we mend. Of the eighteen Monopoly streets which are actually roads (as opposed to squares, districts or pubs), no fewer than six were originally built by the Romans. Although, in a feeble attempt at maintaining suspense, I'm not at this stage going to tell you which ones.

Squatting down, balancing the board precariously on my lap and cursing King's Cross for straddling the fold hinge, I placed my racing car in position. As I wiped away the worst of the drizzle, it occurred to me that I was taking this a lot more seriously than Vic and Marge. Blithely, blissfully unaware of the historic enormity of their looming task, that what they were about to do would impact upon millions of British lives, and millions more in the globe's far-flung pink bits, their approach was, to be charitable, cavalier.

'What's this big road out front here, Marjorie?'

'Euston Road, Mr Victor.'

'Never heard of it. How about that one running up the hill to the left?'

'I believe that's Pentonville, Mr Victor.'

'Never heard of that neither.'

'Well, I don't think they're especially notable, Mr Victor. Now, if we were to walk just along there we'd get to Tottenham Court Road and Great Portland Street, some of the best kno . . .'

'Don't be daft, woman. It's only a flaming game. Grand – that's two streets and a station done already. I think tea is in order, Marjorie.'

'Of course, Mr Victor. There's a rather nice Lyons Corner House just up there in Islington. The Angel, if I recall.'

I rolled. Both dice skidded smartly beyond Free Parking and into what I discovered, unwisely employing touch in favour of sight, to be a patch of nettles. Having treated at least four postcodes to an ignoble and protracted oath, with as much precision as my poisoned digits would permit I rolled again. A five and a three: Whitehall.

CHAPTER 4

The Purples

PALL MALL
CITY OF WESTMINSTER

WHITEHALL
CITY OF WESTMINSTER

NORTHUMBERLAND AVE
CITY OF WESTMINSTER

Sombre, stately and regal, no street on the board is more aptly coloured than purple Whitehall. If you're *Country Life* you call it 'our noblest thoroughfare'; if you're Michael Caine you call it 'the most overrated place in London – just extraordinarily dull'. Once a 2,000-room behemoth, the palace that gave the street its name was the official residence of every monarch from Henry VIII to William III; originally York House, there is (as is often the case in a city that's not even sure how it got its own name) some doubt as to how it became known as Whitehall Palace. Expert opinion links it to 'the custom of naming any festival hall a "White-hall"', but I prefer to side with the stubborn minority who entertainingly insist that the name is derived from some of the newer walls, these being, let me see, beige.

Henry died at Whitehall, as did Oliver Cromwell. Many of Shakespeare's plays were premiered there. Charles II once lost 4½ lb during a palace tennis match, slightly less than his dad did shortly after being escorted through a first-floor window on to a lofty scaffold. Then, in 1695, the 2,000 rooms were reduced to one after a Dutch laundry maid inadvertently started the fire that razed all but the Banqueting House.

The royals had already moved out, and now their ever-expanding governments moved in. Emerging from Westminster Tube with Big Ben donging out midday, the yawning breadth of Whitehall tapered distantly to Trafalgar Square before me, both its flanks staidly overlooked by the museums of bureaucracy. Though I might easily be sharing its pavements with a disproportionate number of fellow Gabby clients, it was no little relief to welcome Whitehall as the clean, crisp chalk to the sleazy cheese of King's Cross. Here was the vice versa of Oscar Wilde's comment about old women having faces like public buildings – aside from Richmond House, a sort of Brutalist Hampton Court knocked up for the Department of Health in the eighties, every edifice looked stolid and humourless; Victoria's we-are-not-amused catchphrase in bricks and mortar. The Treasury: Buckingham Palace with net curtains and strip lighting. The old War Office: a Stalinist department store with two and a half miles of corridors. Dourly decorated with dusty 'VR's, the towering mahogany doors of the Foreign and Commonwealth Office seemed more like the long-sealed entrance to a mausoleum, and surveying what is now the Scottish Office it wasn't easy to imagine the phrase 'mad, bad and dangerous to know' being coined behind its doors by Lady Caroline Lamb in the throes of her affair with Lord Byron.

The Victorians and Edwardians deliberately fashioned Whitehall on an impersonal, imperial scale – befitting, after all, officials who held ultimate administrative power over a fifth of the world's population. People could argue about where in London you might find the Empire's heart and soul, but there was no doubt that here was its brain. A lot of Vic and Marge's choices might generously be described as out of left field, but you

46

couldn't leave Whitehall out. It'd be one of the first names on any London street team sheet: if Whitechapel and Old Kent Road were the tough and sometimes dirty centrebacks, Leicester Square the temperamental playmaker and Mayfair the big-money signing up front, Whitehall would be the solid and dependable midfield general. When the Treasury took a direct hit from a huge Luftwaffe bomb in 1940, so effectively did its massive walls absorb the blast that surveying an unscathed exterior nonplussed emergency crews thought they'd been called out on a false alarm.

The most serendipitous reward for endless weekends sneezing my way through the shelves of second-hand booksellers was a 1933 Post Office London Street Directory, which helpfully supplied an exhaustive list of the residents and proprietors of every address in the immediate pre-Monopoly era. The Whitehall entry told its own story of a colonial bureaucracy run riot. Strolling up its broad pavements Vic and Marge might have rubbed shoulders with an official of the Aliens Branch or the Inebriates Act Department, an inspector of the Schools of Anatomy or Explosives or – autograph books and Kodak Brownies at the ready – the actual chairman of the Bengal Military Orphan Society.

Near the Cenotaph, a WPC rode past, her mount giving a fulsome reminder of this area's continuing reign as London's horse-poo capital; a chatter of remarkably enthusiastic German students strode by in a blur of backpacks and camcorders. We were into the statues now. A curiously stunted Sir Walter Raleigh sandwiched between two meaty field marshals I'd never heard of, then one I had: Haig, a controversial choice in the thirties because the artist made him almost as big as his horse, and today because we've found out that the Somme was all his fault. Monty's come out worst – a graduate of the fight-with-a-lawnmower school of sculpture – but he's got the best view, staring straight down Downing Street with the slowly revolving iris of the London Eye behind him should he fancy a quick peek over his melting, lacerated shoulder.

At 12.30 the traffic at either end of the thoroughfare was embroiled in its usual pinball frenzy, but Whitehall itself retained an appropriately respectful calm: there aren't many major roads in central London you can cross at a saunter, particularly one so extravagantly broad. Ambling over to the tourist gaggle at the Downing Street gates I understood that, as well as emphasising Whitehall's role as Empire High Street, the sheer width was also a crowd-control measure.

Back in Charles I's time there were mob riots in Whitehall, and as executive power began to concentrate here so political malcontents periodically gathered to express their grievances. On this basis, it's astonishing to think that until 1990 you could walk right up to the front door of No. 10. Not that you'd necessarily have wanted to in the mid-thirties, when according to contemporary tastes the modest Queen Anne terrace (constructed, incidentally, by Sir George Downing, the second person to graduate from Harvard) was considered so poky and rundown that there was a campaign to demolish it. Historian Harold Clunn, a strident advocate of such schemes, complained that 'provided a place is old and rich in historical interest, the uglier it is the greater the reluctance to pull it down'.

It's certainly filthy. The exteriors of most of Whitehall's buildings have been or are being buffed and blasted and steam cleaned, but peering through the tourists and the steel and the flak-jacketed police, the façades of Nos 10–12 presented a stubbornly stained and smutted reminder of the steam age.

Despite recent claims that the capital's air is now cleaner than at any time since 1585, no one would promote lungfuls of modern London as a cheek-reddening tonic: Mayor Ken Livingstone admitted recently that the air quality is inferior to any city in the UK and ranks among the worst in Europe. But how much worse it was in the thirties. Coal production didn't peak until 1900, and even twelve years later 76,000 tons of soot were falling on London annually. Not for nothing was it called The Smoke.

Monopoly was very much a coal-fired product: as well as the steam train at each station, until the sixties the centre of the board was decorated with a mural depicting two speeding expresses shuffling smokily past a brace of Metroland homes, themselves belching smuts through four chimneys. At the start of the fifties, 98 per cent of British homes still had an open fire, and the notorious pea-soupers of 1952 contributed to the deaths of 12,000 Londoners. And I still cannot quite believe that London Transport did not decommission its last steam engine until 1971: an absurd, nonsensical fact that, like asparagus making your pee smell funny, should not be true but somehow just stubbornly is.

A souvenir stall selling Mind The Gap knickers heralded the start of Whitehall's slightly more vibrant northern half. Following a guided tour group of Antipodeans through its gates I realised I'd never been into the Horse Guards before, and certainly not known that it remains the official entrance to Buckingham Palace. And only by virtue of further brazen eavesdropping did I discover that they still increase the number of guards when the Queen is in residence – a bold move if one considers the modern terrorist's proven resistance to men in conical Rapunzel hats wearing even the very shiniest stirrups.

Horses buffed to suede and boots to PVC, a troop of guardsmen rode into the courtyard through a battery of camera flashes. Beneath an arch, another two with lofted swords grimly resisted four bell-bottomed Italian girls approaching the tunic-tickling phase of the time-honoured tourist pastime of give-us-a-giggle, and I recalled how surprised I'd been to read that such saucy disrespect was at least as widespread around here in the thirties. Waiting at the top end of Whitehall for George V's funeral cortege to pass, the crowd, adopting the catchline from a contemporary ad campaign for Lyons Corner Houses, began chanting, 'Where's George?'. And this at a time of staunch, almost feverish royalism: to mark George's silver jubilee the year before, London's schoolchildren were all given two days off school and a commemorative spoon, and tens of thousands had slept out in the rain to bag a front-row view of the regal procession ('I can't understand it,' he said to his family as they stood before a wildly cheering mob on the Buck House balcony, 'I'm really quite an ordinary sort of chap.').

Through a gateway etched with nineteenth-century I-woz-'ere's I emerged into what in 1935 had been the largest clear space in London for over two centuries. Though a distant also-ran in the era of the B&Q car park, the Parade Ground still impresses. In an earlier age royal jousts had been held here, and looking through the fountains and flowers of St James's Park towards Buckingham Palace it was impossible not to be stirred by a sense of history or pomp or something reasonably epic. And then I realised that standing here in 1935 you'd have seen swastikas flying from the German Embassy just in front of Pall Mall, and fascist bundles draped across the nearby Italian State Railway office, and I thought of the single lonely wreath I'd seen at the foot of the Cenotaph and felt my innards flutter.

To put all this in context, my visit to Whitehall came less than two weeks after the World Trade Center awfulness, which as well as casting a general pall over most personal ruminations had whipped up an atmosphere incompatible with dawdling aimlessly about in front of important government buildings holding a notebook. In every reception area stood a stark placard reading 'ALERT LEVEL – BLACK SPECIAL'; when I inquired of a chap in a blazer outside the Royal United Services Institute what this meant his response was the sort of look that greeted Oliver Twist's request for seconds. The same query at the threshold of the Parliamentary Counsel at least elicited a verbal reaction: 'It wouldn't mean much to you if I told you, which I won't.' Asked more cordially to explain myself by a plump security officer patrolling outside the old War Office, I struck up what was threatening to become a conversation until I made the mistake of referring to its tenants as the Ministry of Defence. 'I think we'll just call it a government office, *shall we?*'

Then both road and buildings narrowed, and Whitehall shrank to a mercifully more human scale. Turning around to look back down towards Westminster, I was presented with a view that uncannily replicated the photocopy of a 1936 panorama I now retrieved from my backpack. Every building, every statue was unchanged. Double-deckers with the same route numbers (77 and 12, as you don't ask); the same lampposts in the same places. All you needed to do to the old photo was dangle security passes round the necks of that little knot of lunch-hour Civil Service strollers, Tipp-Ex out the Keystone Cop taxis, homburgs and bowlers and give the plane trees a healthy slug of Miracle Gro. I was almost relieved when I turned back round and saw my view framed by Tostig Souvenirs and a J.D. Wetherspoon.

Lured into the latter by an absurd offer – a pint and a burger for £2.49 – I took up a seat by the window. In accordance with the current urban trend this had until recently been a venerable old bank, but I wasn't going to cry into my beer – certainly not at 99p a pint. How can a pub not be better than a bank? If it had stayed the latter I wouldn't be in here now, I reasoned, working back to my seat under mahogany and old portraits with a refill in my hand. In any case, peering across and along the street and cross-referencing from my 1933 directory I noted that not much else had changed here either. The Silver Cross restaurant was still trading under the same name, as was the Clarence Tavern and home of farce, the Whitehall Theatre. So too the Old Shades, established for comfortably over a century and still supplying its patrons with honest ale and hearty fayre. On the other hand, the British Union of Vivisectionists had evolved into a McDonald's.

Suffused with the rosy, ill-focused glow of a man who has enjoyed a quantity of bargain ale inappropriate to the hour, I set

51

out into the street. This end of Whitehall was distinctly more stimulating, I now found, winking at a slightly mad-eyed old man in a yellow bib emblazoned with 'COMPASSION IN WORLD FARMING' and wondering if I should tell him about McDonald's. There were anarchist stickers on the lampposts and a witness appeal for an assault that could never have happened further down the road.

I don't suppose for a minute that without that second pint inside me I'd ever have gone into Tostig Souvenirs, and not even for a second that after a lifetime of weary scorn I'd suddenly have been so richly entertained by the stalwart tourist T-shirt slogan, 'I like the Pope – the Pope smokes dope'. Laugh? I almost bought a bouncing clockwork penis.

There wouldn't have been any foreign tourists in London in the thirties, at least not as we know them today. The Depression had broken middle-class piggy banks across the world, and the *belle époque* of the old European aristocracy was finished. Blue-collar provincials couldn't afford a week in London even if they'd been allowed to: I'd been mildly horrified to discover that paid holidays were almost unheard of at the time of Monopoly's birth. When the Amalgamated Engineering Union secured two weeks' annual paid leave in 1937, it was seen as a landmark.

How different it had all been half a century earlier. In the 1860s and '70s a new breed of vast luxury hotel colonised this part of London, along wide thoroughfares that helped demarcate what became known for the first time as the West End. Piloting my way slightly unsteadily across the Italianesque free-for-all encircling Trafalgar Square – the only place in London where I'm still scared to drive – I turned into one such street, a street that didn't exist until 1876 and is therefore comfortably the newest on the Monopoly board.

Created on the site of Northumberland House, the eponymous aristocratic family's London base and a well-loved seventeenth-century mansion demolished only after much protest (and a helpful half-million for the Duke), Northumberland Avenue was expressly designed to accommodate hotels. The five-hundred-room Metropole, the Victoria, the seven-floor Grand – all were built in the Continental style for Continental travellers arriving at the new Charing Cross station. And all showcased the latest new technology: contemporary photographs emphasised not starched linen and chandeliers but en suite plumbing and telegraph facilities. The Victoria was one of London's first electrified buildings, with a prodigious generator in its basement, and two-piece telephones were soon installed in most of the Grand's three hundred rooms.

Until 1954 it was almost impossible to obtain planning permission for a new building taller than the width of the street before it – a regulation supposedly imposed as a result of Queen Victoria's fury at her view from Buckingham Palace being interrupted by a fourteen-storey mansion block – so in order to build high hotels they first had to lay a wide carriageway. A turn-of-the-century snap taken from a Northumberland Avenue rooftop showed its considerable girth crisscrossed by top-hatted promenaders and straddled by horse-drawn hansoms lined up in the middle of the road around a pitch-roofed cabbies' shelter. If Monopoly had come out then, Northumberland Avenue would have been a shoo-in.

As it was, by the time of Vic's tour all the hotels had gone. The dwindling number of fur-collared foreigners decamped to the newer establishments around Park Lane and Piccadilly, and, as the Midland Grand Hotel, St Pancras, had discovered to its cost in the thirties, the typical domestic rail user was no longer a well-heeled visitor from the shires but a breathless commuter. On the day he sold the Grand to a whisky firm for use as their London headquarters, Sir Francis Towle commented regretfully that 'a great hotel resembles a battleship, inasmuch as it becomes obsolete after twenty years'.

Today Northumberland Avenue is a tree-lined Whitehall

annexe, equally under-trafficked and so broad about the beam that the central reservation is used as a bus park. That width, those trees and the Parisian look of the old hotels rising monotonously upwards impart an atmosphere redolent of some obscure boulevard round the back of the Arc de Triomphe; and in fact the building that had in 1935 housed the London HQ of the ill-starred League of Nations was now reincarnated as a French-run 'apart hotel', offering 'aparts' at £170 a night (without breakfast, for pity's sake).

The generous conclusion is that in selecting Northumberland Avenue, particularly as the purple set's top-rent daddy, Vic and Marge had briefly let their fingers slip off the zeitgeist button. Yes, Monopoly was all about hotels and so was Northumberland Avenue, or anyway had once been – maybe Vic had stayed at the Grand in its Edwardian prime; maybe he'd spent the Great War ferrying military memos up and down the Metropole's marbled corridors. Or maybe, in accordance with the Pentonville/Euston model, he'd reached the top of Whitehall, stared bleakly about the pedestrian-hostile no-man's-land girdling Trafalgar Square, turned to Marge and after a meaningful exchange of looks muttered, 'Oh, just stick that one down.'

Succumbing to a horribly premature hangover, I shuffled unenthusiastically along. On my left, generally identified with great reluctance by tiny bell-plates outside thick and glassless doors, the offices of Enterprise Oil, Investment Manager Selection Ltd and PBR Financial Services. On my right, the grubby-windowed, pigeon-netted Northumberland House and Metropole Buildings, once respectively the Victoria and Metropole hotels and now clumsily welded into an anonymous governmental labyrinth on Black Special Alert. Security guards in sweat-circled blue shirts paced about the dulled brass and eroded woodwork of a once grandly bustling reception; just beyond, pausing outside a net-curtained window, I beheld the silhouettes of half a dozen motionless heads arranged around an overhead projector screen on which was felt-tipped 'Any Answered Questions? Action on JBJ/SC'.

Referring to my 1933 directory as I stood in the porch of a long-closed branch of Barclays strewn with last year's newspapers, I understood how much less tedious London's commercial existence had once been. Then, Northumberland Avenue had accommodated offices of the Mechanical Pulp Consortium Ltd, Velva Silent Flooring, Simon Brothers champagne merchants and the Peruvian Construction Company. That dead Barclays had once been Nevill's Turkish Baths; a Ladbrokes bookies currently stood in for the Welsh Plate & Steel Manufacturers Association. Aside from Virgin Bride and, in happy proximity, the International Sacred Literature Fund, every current concern was faceless and globalised and somehow shadily offshore. The rich foreign tourists were now rich foreign businesses.

But Northumberland Avenue isn't very long, and things picked up at the end. Inside the Nigerian High Commission, half a dozen visa applicants lounged in plush armchairs amidst an endearing disorder of deflated balloons and upside-down beds: the cheering antithesis of Whitehall's dour administrations. Two sun-yellowed sheets of A4 taped to the door detailed the price of Nigerian tourist visas by country of origin, and I scanned it in wonder – Austrians were charged £23.20; Germans £10.50; Tunisians £2.32; Libyans £33.33. No two countries shared a price in a list whose pathological inconsistency could only be explained by a refreshingly human brand of bureaucratic capriciousness. While enjoying a city break in Lagos, Björk leads away a plague of rats with her beguiling ululations: Icelanders find their visa fee slashed to £6. The Filipino ambassador beats his Nigerian counterpart to the last Ferrero Rocher at a diplomatic do: next morning the Tipp-Ex is bitterly cracked open on Northumberland Avenue and the relevant figure bumped up to a monstrous £125.

Back over the road I came up to the Playhouse Theatre, known to some as the venue of Alec Guinness's stage debut and to me as the location of no fewer than thirteen early BBC Beatles sessions. You can't beat a good theatre, though you can beat a good play. I hate plays. I've never seen the point of paying money to watch people shout a lot and pretend to die, and now that I'm the father of three young children I don't have to. But then the Playhouse doesn't seem to have concerned itself with good plays. In 1912 you could have come here to see *Bunty Pulls the Strings*, a production which it's difficult to imagine being much better than it sounds, yet which somehow endured for 620 performances. Currently on stage, though, was J.B. Priestley's *An Inspector Calls*: an apposite examination of pre-war middle-class morality which I was nonetheless obliged to shun due to the lingering shame of how during a youthful – and very brief – journalistic engagement I entered it in the *Evening Standard*'s listings as *Anne in Spectacles*. And in any case beyond, to my great delight, was the cabbies' shelter, clearly the self-same structure in my photo but now replanted 50 yards down the road.

Perhaps because I would rather crawl home on bare and bleeding knees than ever consider flagging down what are Europe's most expensive licensed taxis, London's cabs retain a certain fascination for me. In 1904 there were 11,400 horse-drawn cabs in the capital, a staggering total not surpassed by their mechanical successors until the late 1970s. (The fearful congestion thus engendered forced the authorities to establish ranks on which cabs were obliged to wait for a fare.) Vic and Marge could quite feasibly have hopped into a horse-drawn hansom – the last was still galloping around London in 1947 – but given the choice he'd probably have preferred not to. It was the hansom drivers' reputation for drunken abuse that inspired London's do-gooders to finance prefab cabmen's shelters – essentially Victorian Portakabins – where they might enjoy a cheap and hearty meal and a strictly teetotal beverage. Sixty-four went up; the Northumberland Avenue shelter is one of less than ten survivors.

The century-old green door was open and in I peered. At one end an undertoothed Joan Sims who certainly rounded off all sentences with the word 'love' was boiling carrot slices on a gas stove at least as old as her; at the other a cadaverous, cardiganed cabbie sat drinking tea beneath a *Sun* calendar. Miss September would have walked away with the Community Chest beauty competition, with the gas stove a good bet for that ten-quid second prize. I coughed.

'Yes, love?'

By way of reply, suddenly concerned at breathing second-hand lunchtime ale about a teetotal establishment, I withdrew my Victorian street scene, along with a later close-up of the shelter. 'Where d'you get them foaters?' she asked, poring over the photocopies with quiet amazement. A pleasing ten minutes ensued. After a brief revelation that the shelter was leased to her by the Transport & General Workers Union, we sat down around the Formica, and with a complimentary cuppa forced towards me I explained what I was doing. In scenes that were to be repeated at almost every stop around the board, the word 'Monopoly' unlocked a trove of eagerly recalled adolescentries, mostly centred around sibling conflict and cousin-conning gamesmanship.

'My brother used to hide a few cards under his side of the board before we started,' said the cook. 'I always saw him sliding them out later but I never said nothing. He was six foot before he was twelve.'

The cabbie leaned back against Miss September until her breasts picturesquely crowned his head like Mickey Mouse ears, and then, as a cabbie should, slowly reeled off the streets around the board in precise order. When he'd finished he looked into his tea for a while, then muttered, 'Used to be a trough for horses next to this shelter.'

I stepped out into the long autumn afternoon shadows feeling oddly inspired. A shyly grinning Japanese youth carrying an

upside-down map came up and whispered 'Tems reever?';
directing him towards the Embankment set me on my way
through the striding commuters with a maybe-it's-because-I'm-
a-Londoner spring in my step. It was a Monday, and it was late
September. But I was not having to take any action on JBJ/SC,
nor carrying a Filipino passport into the Nigerian High
Commission. Even here, on what surely had to be the least
exciting street on the board, I had met good people who had told
me good stories.

With a name handsomely more foolish than any other on the
board, I always suspected the story of Pall Mall would kick off
with a memorable opening chapter. And so it proved to be. In the
early seventeenth century, Irish travellers returned from Brittany
stopped off in London to introduce a pastime they had acquired
there, one perfectly adapted to the wide flat bits around St
James's Park. Requiring players to propel a large boxwood ball
through iron hoops by means of a big hammer, 'paille-maille' is
variously suspected to derive from the Italian for 'ball-mallet' or
the Breton phrase, 'Are you sure this isn't croquet?'.

At any rate, the game proved so popular with Charles II that he
lopped off a few vowels and built a special alley in a field round
the back of Whitehall to play it, and indeed played it with such
uncroquet-like ferocity that after additional vowel surgery it
spawned the phrase 'pell-mell'.

Even the bloke in the Rothmans of Pall Mall shop didn't know
all that, and after I'd told him he thoughtfully raised a large, red
hand to a large, red cheek and in obscure reciprocation said, 'This
is the best place in London to get a cab. An unhired one passes
every thirteen seconds.'

As we watched, half a dozen sped past in a one-way, slot-car
frenzy, joyously liberated from the gridlocked torpor of
Trafalgar Square. The Rothmans right-hander is no place for
daydreaming jaywalkers, offering enthusiastic drivers a rare

opportunity to outbrake rivals going into a sweeping corner. Clip the apex and get the power on hard and fast up towards Piccadilly: it always brings out the Michael Schumacher in me, and the Michael Tyson in my rear-seat passengers.

The pace of life without his establishment was not, however, matched by that within. We talked about restrictions on tobacco advertising and sports sponsorship. The phone rang; a wrong number. He told me that the funny thing was, he'd never smoked. The phone rang again; another wrong number. 'We get a lot of those,' he said. 'Dunno why.' Beginning to understand that the taxi survey had not been culled from a local news report but painstakingly compiled over many years from behind this very till, I felt obliged to comment that his daily routine seemed cruelly at odds with the 'Rothmans World of Excitement' emblazoned on the merchandise that surrounded him. Nodding wistfully, he said he often had only one customer a day – a cabbie, of course, who came in at lunchtime for a pack of Royale 120s.

The phone rang again and this time, mercifully, a brief conversation ensued. 'A Japanese lady wanting advice on posting books home,' he said after downing the receiver. 'We get all sorts of calls. That's the trouble with being a famous address. Post comes in from all over the world just labelled "Rothmans of Pall Mall, London".' He showed me one such recent arrival, a rumpled envelope with an exotic stamp.

'What do they write about?' I asked, suddenly recalling a conversation with an aged Mancunian taxidermist who told me how he'd rushed over to the chairman of British American Tobacco at an inter-war race meeting and blurted, 'Hey up, Sir Hugh – I really like your fags.'

'Just trying it on, mainly. They smoke nineteen and send the last one in saying the packet was duff and could you send them a replacement.' He ran his fingers across the manila wrinkles and, detecting a small, soft cylinder, nodded indulgently. 'That's this one's game, anyway.'

The Monopoly addresses beyond jail have always reflected precisely the sort of raffish, world-of-excitement urbanity that cigarette manufacturers have been traditionally so desperate to imbue their products with. Taking their lead from Sir Walter Raleigh, who at his house by The Angel, Islington, became the first European to light up, no fewer than six fag brands have borrowed from the board: Pall Malls are smoked around the world, Germans still pop down the corner shop for *zwanzig* Bond Street, and though seventies lad-fags Piccadilly and the ill-fated Strand have long since coughed it, Mayfair remains a stalwart among Britain's pennywise smokers. Most notably of all, in 1902 Philip Morris adapted the address of its London factory in Marlborough Street when launching the brand that is now the world's most famous (originally featuring a red tip to disguise lipstick marks, Marlboros were the first cigarettes aimed specifically at women). It's probably unhelpful to speak of a golden age of smoking, but in the thirties the pastime certainly reached its browny-yellow London zenith. George Orwell's *Keep the Aspidistra Flying*, a contemporary study of gas-lit boarding-house tawdriness in the capital, is dominated by Gordon Comstock's quest for fags, bought with rent money and consumed in place of food. Almost every Monopoly street accommodated a cigar dealer or small-scale fag firm: five of the former up Bond Street; no fewer than twelve of the latter down Piccadilly. In the thirties Britain had the world's highest incidence of lung cancer, and by the war seven out of ten men and a third of all women smoked.

Studying one of the cowering huddles of pavement smokers that congregate outside all London offices, I was reminded how rapidly attitudes have evolved. It's only ten years since the top deck of every London bus was permanently wreathed in a speakeasy fug, and it is astounding to recall that smoking was banned on the Tube only after investigators blamed the 1987 King's Cross fire on a discarded cigarette falling into escalator machinery. (During the inquiry they discovered the scorched remains of five smaller fires beneath other escalators that had burned themselves out undetected in earlier years.)

As I walked out beneath the Rothmans shop's stripy Dutch gables a troop of busby-topped guardsmen marched from the side of St James's Palace and stamped splendidly off into The Mall's foggy morning sunlight. Before today, all Pall Mall had been to me was a corridor of blurred street furniture entered and exited at immoderate speed; already I could see it was going to impress me a good deal more than I'd imagined.

The monarchy is still a part of Pall Mall, although because today's royals either aren't interesting or aren't allowed to be, the connections are now limited to crests over regally appointed suppliers of waterproof clothing. Under Charles II's enthusiastic patronage things were a little different, and Pall Mall rapidly acquired what was to prove an enduring reputation as a playground for the rowdier sort of toff. Sporting rough and tumble gave way to slap and tickle: Charles installed Nell Gwynne and at least one other mistress in the new houses springing up along Pall Mall. Gambling clubs began to cater for hardy pioneers bravely pushing back the boundaries of that money/sense ratio, and there were inevitably a broad range of drinking options.

Ever willing to embrace the latest human vice, Pall Mall began to attract tobacco firms, and the street's indelible association with smoking requisites was cemented in 1866 by the future Edward VII. Outraged at being banished to the smoking room at White's Club for a post-prandial puff on one of his famous cigars, the then Prince of Wales went straight out and bought his own Pall Mall club – one where a chap could set light to tobacco wherever he bally well pleased. The Marlborough, as it was called, had an ideal heritage – the building had once been a gambling den with an in-house pawnbroker, and there was a skittle alley out back for those 'paille-maille' moments – and after its acquisition the Prince visited almost every day in order to mingle with cronies while cradling a huge brandy snifter and smoking his head off. He was big mates with the head porter, Warwick, whose fifty-year reign comfortably exceeded his own; he played billiards with courtiers in full evening dress and top hat. It was almost as if the adjective 'clubbable' had been coined for him.

Almost. A friend and fellow member, the Italian-born artist Pellegrini, was once enjoying a morning (*morning?*) drink in the Marlborough when Edward joined him. Fancying a top up, Pellegrini nudged the Prince and, boldly eschewing royal protocol, drawled, 'Be a good chap and ring the bell.' Dangerous words to a man who beneath the funny beard and ribald banter was, after all, Queen Victoria's son. Without a word, Edward duly rang; the summoned servant promptly arrived. 'Please show Mr Pellegrini out,' breezed the Prince, and never spoke to the artist again.

In the 1650s British gamblers were getting through almost five million decks of cards a year and, keen to keep themselves a cut above the pack, the punters of Pall Mall began to seek more rarefied profligacies. They started making bets on how many cats would cross the street outside or whether that chap who'd fallen down on the club steps had fainted or dropped dead. In 1756, Lord Byron, your man's great uncle, endeavouring to resolve a bet with a friend on whose estate had the most deer, fatally ran the man through in a Pall Mall tavern. It was no surprise that the silly wager which challenged Phileas Fogg to circumnavigate the globe in eighty days was taken on in the smoking room of the Reform Club, Pall Mall.

In between throwing it down the drain, Pall Mall's patrons did also manage to spend large amounts of money tarting the place up: in 1807 it became the first street in London to be fully illuminated by gas. Mainly, though, members lavished fortunes on club houses with columned porticos and double staircases hung with rare artworks. An £80,000 copy of the Farnese Palace in Rome, the Reform Club was twice as expensive to erect as its near contemporary Nelson's Column, and in 1909 the RAC's members blew a quarter of a million on their new gaff.

By the turn of the century there were eighty-seven clubs in London, though, regrettably, none of the particularly silly ones set up shop in Pall Mall – the Ugly Club, the Wet Paper Club or the No Pay No Liquor Club, 'whose members were obliged to wear a hat of peculiar construction'. But maybe they should have, because as the jazz age dawned the Pall Mall clubs were already losing their appeal to the young. Up West there were cinemas, cocktails, dancing and – yes – women.

In the thirties the idle rich were a dying breed; Bertie Wooster's comic appeal depended on the anachronisms of his lifestyle. Everyone had to work, even some of the aristos, and after a hard day you didn't want to unwind in a room of old men snoring into their port. Of the twenty clubs based in Pall Mall before the war, only seven remain. The Marlborough closed in 1953: 'Costs rose, members died, and none came to take their place,' an ex-member explained succinctly.

Such a fate would seem to await the Army & Navy Club, judging from the hunched figures in brogues and felt hats I watched holding on to each other as they tottered in, but the braided doormen outside the RAC were ushering in a very different breed of member. Seeing yet another Japanese businessman and his immaculately cashmered wife being wafted inside I wondered what it was about crusty British institutions – Burberry, Aquascutum, single malt whisky, Bentleys, brutal imperialism – that so excites this distant nation.

'We're doin' all right,' mumbled the largest doorman, jowls chafing across his vast epaulettes as he scanned the reckless traffic for incoming taxis. 'Think all the clubs are doin' all right. All redecoratin' and all that. We got 15,000 members.'

'That's only 5,000 less than in the thirties,' I said, hoping to ingratiate myself and so sidle in for a quick peek at 'the most beautiful swimming bath in Britain' and whatever else £250,000 bought you in 1909. 'Um, I don't suppose I could . . .' I said, flapping an arm vaguely towards the museum-like atrium where Burgess and Maclean met for their pre-flee tea.

The doorman raised an elaborately cuffed hand, as much to silence me as to flag down the cab which now peeled off the race circuit and halted extravagantly in front of us. 'Private,' he muttered grimly into a small cloud of tyre smoke, despatching a bow-tied Oriental into the back seat.

After being accorded a similar reception at the more intimately panelled (and studiously anonymous) doorways to the Reform and the Athenaeum, it occurred to me that this was the appeal of club membership: it allowed the nineteenth century back into the twenty-first, granting new money the haughty exclusivity of old. By turning away people they don't like the look of, Pall Mall's club doormen guarantee their members feel not just richer than you, but actually better. I could go into the Ritz in my anorak and provided I had the cash no one would turn me away, but here I was scum, a subspecies to be allowed a tantalising glimpse of dark marble and balustraded mezzanine over a burly uniformed shoulder before being brusquely banished. I suppose it should have bothered me – a Londoner humiliated on home soil before an audience of ponced-up foreigners with armfuls of Harrods bags – but the theatre was so preposterous I felt more inclined to laugh. Seeing a man wearing a bowler hat fulsomely decorated with salmon flies I actually did.

Throughout the clubs' heyday membership passes would have been superfluous: if you looked like a toff, you were a toff, and if you didn't you had no recreational business being in Pall Mall at all. But by the end of the thirties, it was becoming more difficult to judge a Londoner by appearance alone: the strict 'hat code' which demarcated the classes – flat caps for the blue collars, trilbies for the middle market, bowlers and homburgs for City types and professionals – was breaking down, and developments in artificial fabrics were blurring the female fashion boundaries.

And though a part of Pall Mall is trying very hard to re-erect those barriers, watching two black-glass Rollers with scantly charactered number plates idle outside Consolidated Real Estate Management Services I understood the street's dominant theme is that rich people now have to spend more time earning money and so have less time to spend it.

Though the gentlemen's clubs still dominate the dark side of Pall Mall, the culling has been severe: turning back and gazing down the way I'd come I noted the stark sixties mid-rise office boxes that regularly jutted out and above the ornate club buildings, like house bricks dropped in a wedding cake. Sometimes the building survived, only to be stealthily invaded by new money. The gas-lit torches still stand proudly along its façade, but the United Service Club is now the Institute of Directors, full of flow-chart addicts nodding purposefully at each other while recharging their laptops where once they'd have been playing cricket with bread rolls and buttering the porter's tie. 'The IoD is a place of business,' emphasised a heart-sinking notice in the reception.

No one lives in Pall Mall now, but while snooping around trying to find out if they did I found myself rewardingly waylaid. Between the glass blocks and colonnaded clubs ran tiny, ancient alleys, home to places you might expect to find, such as milliners' shops with bow-fronted Quality Street windows, but plenty you wouldn't, like cafés with slashed foam benches and the sort of hardware shops that flog a four-pack of loo rolls for 99p. I can only assume that so perpetual is the redevelopment process that the area permanently supports a floating population of builders and tradesmen. Only later did I find a picture of one of those hardware shops dating from 1930, when it had been a second-hand dealer whose window-blind slogans stridently requested 'office waste and rags – white & coloured' and promised to pay 'the best price for dripping and kitchen stuff'. Easily visible to Vic and Marge as they strolled down Pall Mall, one imagines this may have sealed the street's fate as the purple-set runt, wedged rudely up against Jail.

On Pall Mall itself, though, the surviving retail premises are appropriately faithful to the new-money-for-old club theme, latching on to a fashion amongst City parvenus to play at country gentlemen. Culturally obligated to indulge in more acceptable upper-class pursuits, the patrons of Pall Mall have turned to huntin', shootin' and fishin' in place of smokin', gamblin' and shaggin'. (The drinkin' only survives in a corporate sense – the old wine merchants Berry Brothers have offices here, as do the Cutty Sark lot.) There were six gun and tackle shops in Pall Mall in the thirties and three remain, selling rods, rifles and publications whose titles benchvaulted joyously over the innuendo parapet: *Just Black Labs*, *A Passion for Grouse*, *Monster Rods: A Hands-on Guide*. Really – you couldn't make it up (although in the case of the last one I did).

I went into one of these places, a tackle shop whose absence of price tags eloquently identified its work-hard/play-hard (or rather earn-hard/spend-hard) customer base. After partially upsetting a small display of £120 trout-fishing sunglasses I approached the plummy and balding Prince Edward behind the counter and began asking him questions. Unaffected by their persistent crassness, the cheery confidence with which he replied to these suggested it wasn't the first time he'd been asked what his most expensive rod was or if he stocked anything in solid gold, presumably by customers who had no intention of purchasing anything less.

'We do a salmon rod for £2,500,' he said, smiling proudly. 'Top-quality graphite. Special order.' No gold, I was told with a sympathetic tilt of the head, but if titanium was my thing they had a £1,500 reel.

My gaze was wandering up to a wall-mounted display of J.R. Hartleyesque feathery hook things when the phone rang. Snatches of assured patter drifted over as I pondered that I might never again have this opportunity: to fix a man in the eye and demand, 'Right – whip those flies down and let's have a good look at your tackle.'

'Yuh . . . stunning little rod. Smashing. Put it like this – we sold one to Eric Clapton last week.'

I imagined the proud endorsement emblazoned across a Fender Stratocaster in a music-shop window: 'As played by Captain Birdseye.' Then, unwilling to distract the assistant from what was clearly a lucrative call, I wandered out and up the regal pavements. This was the sunny side of the street, and with the stupidly snooty clubs hidden in shadow I began to feel warmed by Pall Mall's aura of timeless nobility. So much so, in fact, that I made rather an arse of myself after strutting pompously up to a shop assistant as he lugged the last of his establishment's stock – curtain rings, knobs, brackets and other items of what you might call brassmongery – into a removal van.

'Ah! The end of an era,' I sighed dramatically, as if speaking on behalf of the countless generations of Moores whose fancy peg and hook requirements had been taken care of by his establishment's craftsmen.

'I guess so,' he said, stooping to shoulder a plastic bin full of door handles as I riffled importantly through my 1933 directory. 'Though that era only started in, er . . .' – and here he considered briefly – '. . . in 1998.'

Yet my spirits were still up, and surveying the gloriously ornate stucco façades around me I recrossed Pall Mall with a dandy's spring in my step, before clicking showily down a grand flight of stairs into St James's Park. There, in wincing sun, I despatched my packed lunch amidst geese, secretaries and distant Big Ben bongs in happy anticipation: this was good, but as I set off back to the Rothmans end, I knew I'd saved the best for last. Casting your gaze upon the threshold plaques identifying it as the shared headquarters of Norwich Union and the National Neighbourhood Watch Association, upon those tea ladies carrying boardroom refreshments into its lifts, you'd hardly guess that all of Pall Mall's most engagingly wayward excesses were embodied in Schomberg House. Not unless you noticed the nude Greeks propping the porch up.

A red-brick pocket palace erected by William III for the eponymous Dutch mercenary who later copped it leading the English forces at the Battle of the Boyne, Schomberg House had to wait almost a hundred years for notoriety to come knocking in the form of Dr James Graham, who in 1781 lured London's jaded thrill seekers to what he had irresistibly rechristened 'The Temple of Health and Hymen'.

If walls really did have ears, those of Schomberg House would have blushed themselves crimson many centuries ago. Part quackshow, part peepshow, the maverick Scottish physician's therapeutic regime included sessions involving obscure 'medico-electrical apparatus' and a demonstration of the benefits of mud baths featuring the future Emma Hamilton (she of naughty-Nelson fame) stripped to the waist and wearing a feather headdress. Presiding over events in a 'Celestial Throne', Graham delivered lectures on infertility, and more particularly how this malaise could be overcome by slipping him fifty quid for a night in his 'Grand Celestial State Bed'. On coloured sheets and serenaded by music (presumably, given Graham's voyeuristic background presence, fervently accompanied by the fabled sound of one hand clapping), couples were guaranteed to conceive here 'as even the barren must do when so powerfully agitated in the delights of love'.

As would the thirties, so the late eighteenth century offered favoured sanctuary to purveyors of offbeam medicine: Graham didn't get any grief from the authorities until he allowed illegal card games to be played in an adjoining room, and even then he was let off. Only when he began referring to himself as 'Servant of the Lord OWL' did clients begin to doubt his competence, doubts only partly allayed when he explained that 'owl' stood for 'Oh! Wonderful Love'.

After the fucking, the shopping. Graham was in an asylum by the time Dyde & Scribe converted Schomberg House into an upmarket haberdashery, and dead when in 1796 it evolved into what was Europe's first department store. With separate sections for fabrics, jewellery, clocks and fashion, Harding, Howell & Co. advertised itself widely in the press as stocking 'every article of foreign manufacture which there is any possibility of obtaining'.

Ever Pall Mall's bellwether, in the mid-nineteenth century Schomberg House gave itself a firm slap in the face and settled into institutional sobriety. The War Office moved in, along with a few residual royals: my 1933 directory lists two of the tenants as Helena HH Princess, GBE, CI and the similarly ennobled Marie-Louise, old-maid granddaughters of Queen Victoria. Internally overhauled for office use in the fifties, it has been hosting dull annual general meetings ever since – though having said that, I'd love to have seen Dr Graham grab the wrong end of the stick in two eager hands when he read that bell-plate and saw that peeping Toms were no longer merely tolerated, but apparently encouraged by a national association.

It was time to shake again. This time half hoping a security operative would rush out and ask me what the flaming hell I was playing at, though still mildly concerned that in the current Black Special hysteria he might first drop me with a leg shot, I angled a hand behind my head and grovelled laboriously about in the backpack like a drunk archer trying to find the last arrow in his quiver. At length I withdrew the board, squatted down and placed it squarely over a paving stone.

Along with an ability to calculate and deliver change for a five hundred in less time than it takes to shout 'RENT!', another of Monopoly's conferred mathematical legacies is a solid grounding in the laws of probability. Even as I lined my motor up between the inverted £140s on Whitehall I knew that the most commonly rolled two-dice total would take me to Free Parking, but as the four and the three showed up I also knew that I still had no idea what to do when I landed there.

CHAPTER 5

Free Parking

Disturbed no doubt by its infuriating arbitrariness, the previous owner of one of my old boards had forcefully amended the P in Free Parking into a B. And why not? Why not give the Scottie a share of the limelight? Why this utterly isolated assumption that we're all driving round the board, when in fact we're just as likely to be booting it down Bond Street or ironing up to The Angel? And why didn't anything happen when you landed on Free Parking? The only completely impotent square on the board, it was no surprise that the people should eventually force Free Parking to work for its living.

The most popular method, certainly within the Moore household, was to employ the central-board void as a temporary vault for the accumulation of income or super tax, to be scooped by whoever next landed on Free Parking. Later this lottery windfall was extended to include all fines deriving from Chance and Community Chest cards; a regular consequence was the unstoppable growth of a huge multicoloured cash mountain that dwarfed the bank's reserves and whose eventual destiny played havoc with Monopoly's finely tuned game mechanics.

For the landlord of Mayfair and Park Lane a Tory-style fat-cat rebate from Free Parking represented inevitable and crushing victory over his miserably cowed tenants; on the other side of the same coin, a sudden and dramatic socialist income-redistribution in his favour could send the humble Old Kent Roader off on a nouveau-riche spending spree more reckless than any sixties pools winner. He might blow it all pebble dashing Bond Street, or raucously offer the Chance-card birthday boy two grand to stand up and do the Lambeth Walk with his old mum, God bless her.

The answer to the Free Parking riddle is that Charles Darrow was an American, and so was Henry Ford. The motor vehicle was a potent aspirational symbol, one appropriate for any would-be property tycoon, but it was also such a presence in American life that cities were already being designed around cars. As early as 1921 one in fourteen Americans were car owners; the comparable British ratio was one in 168.

That said, Londoners didn't need the internal combustion engine to knock up a decent gridlock. That over-quoted statistic unfavourably comparing today's transcapital traffic speeds with those of mid-Victorian London takes no account of the fact that mid-Victorian London was a stinking logjam of handcarts and hansoms. Contemporary surveys showed that some of the busier junctions had to deal with a horse-drawn vehicle arriving every three seconds; travellers in the 1850s complained that it took less time to get up to London from Brighton than to cross the capital's central district once you got there. No wonder the Underground proved such a hit – the first line, though consisting of only seven uncomfortably smoke-filled stations, was soon carrying forty million passengers a year.

Initially playthings for the very wealthy (why else was the RAC based in Pall Mall?), motor cars only began to make a significant contribution to London's Traffic Hell in the late twenties, when mass production dropped the prices to Everyman level – by 1936, you could pick up a second-hand Austin Seven for a fiver. An obsession with vehicle ownership was one of the first urban American trends to cross the Atlantic; Monopoly, of course, followed soon after. Motorists started to grumble that jams 'often lasted twenty minutes, and sometimes half an hour', and though this complaint might tempt the modern London motorist to drum two fingers on his lower lip and so emit a derisive warbling hum, more sympathy is due to the 40,000 motorists enmeshed for six hours in Britain's first epic gridlock at the 1928 Derby.

London was growing outwards, and though the public transport network did its best to follow it into the countryside most new homes were nowhere near a useful station. For the hundreds of thousands who lived in ribbon developments along huge new arterial roads devoid of local shops or facilities, there was no choice but to drive everywhere. This wasn't a particular problem out in the distant suburbs, but it certainly was when they pootled into town: by 1931, 61,000 cars were inching around Hyde Park Corner every day. Just as American cities were designed expressly for cars, so the medieval alleys of London emphatically were not. Yet so effectively vocal was the motor-vehicle lobby (as early as 1920 *The Times* was boldly declaring that 'the future of British industries lies on the roads') that plans were almost immediately drawn up to completely reshape central London for their benefit.

It is in the writings of Harold Clunn, a man whose fanatical devotion to motorised transport marks him out as the Mr Toad of 1930s civic planning, that we find the most startling excesses. Clunn's 1934 book, *The Face of London*, kicks off with a complaint that 'London's life blood is compelled to run through veins and arteries that have not expanded since infancy', and thenceforth proposes drastic bypass surgery on almost every such vessel.

With the ultimate aim of transforming the entire Monopoly zone into an American-style grid of multi-lane highways, Clunn casually proposes demolishing Oxford Street and starting again, knocking a new four-laner smack through the middle of Soho and cutting off huge swathes of central London's dwindling parkland to widen every surrounding street into a dual carriageway. With a completely straight face – or, who knows, a twitching and wet-lipped pornographer's leer – he even advocates demolishing buildings at the end of every London cul-de-sac in order to accommodate mechanical turntables, thereby saving motorists 'the trouble of making the right-about turn'. And that's all by page forty, long before he really hits his stride. 'Now that HM Office of Works has sanctioned mixed bathing on the Serpentine,' he later intones in one of the last century's more vexing parallels, 'perhaps we may still hope that some day they will permit the creation of the Piccadilly boulevard.'

Combined with an unabashed anti-Semitism that has him loudly decrying 'British homes are being appropriated and their businesses snowed under by the Jews' it is easy to dismiss Clunn as a ludicrous fascist – easy and actually quite fun – but the uncomfortable truth is that in the mid-thirties he was by no means a lone voice in the wilderness on either score. 'We want a through road from the Bank to Marble Arch capable of taking four lanes of traffic for the entire distance,' declares Clunn, and whoever this sinister 'we' might have been, plans to drive what amounted to a motorway straight through London's historic heart were well in hand when war broke out. In 1934 he says, 'The horse which sets the pace for all traffic in our narrow streets is a scandal which ought not to be tolerated'; two years later, horses are banned from the central area (thousands were sent to the knacker's yard and one grief-stricken driver topped himself). And in 1935 the *Daily Mail* – Britain's most widely read paper – came out to support Oswald Mosley; the next year Mosley's Blackshirts were marching through the East End.

Both strains of totalitarian viciousness seemed to converge in 1952, when the trams that had so infuriated Clunn as he queued behind them up at the Elephant & Castle were finally banished from the streets of London after fifty years' service and many billion passenger journeys: in 1943 alone, 2,500 trams carried seven hundred million travellers. Londoners – particularly the silent carless majority – loved their trams, and hundreds of thousands turned out on 6 July to cheer E/3-1904 along her valedictory run from Westminster to Woolwich. Crowds placed pennies in the track before her to have them bent as souvenirs, chalked poignant farewells on her noble scarlet flanks and linked arms to sing 'Auld Lang Syne'. 'No King or Queen received a better reception,' recalled a wet-eyed local boy watching her clank up the Old Kent Road for the last time. Let us hope he wasn't there when, in preference to seeing E/3-1904 preserved for future generations in a transport museum, the authorities instead chose to have her pushed over and burnt outside her old tramshed in Charlton.

Anything that interfered with the private car's progress across the Monopoly zone was simply wiped off the board: after horses and trams, trolleybuses disappeared in 1961. It is impossible to overstress this fixation with the free movement of motor traffic, one that taken to monstrous extremes would, eventually and inevitably, scoop the soul out of large swathes around the cheap end of the Monopoly board.

But even this has to be seen as a let-off: if Clunn and his ilk had been given full and free rein half the Monopoly streets would have disappeared for ever and my journeys along the remainder restricted to cowering central-reservation cameos. Thanks only to the war and 'the English method of doing things by halves' bemoaned by Clunn was the full horror prevented. I'd often have cause to thank the English for this method, to the point where the consequently half-baked shambles of much of London once again shone out as its defining and most endearing quality.

I suppose it isn't surprising that the Harold Clunns of this world would never consider what to do with deliberately stationary vehicles in their obsession with speed and movement. Cars were better than trams and horses because they could, at least in theory, go faster; driving about was somehow an end in itself. No one seems to have spent too much time considering the possibility that, having arrived at B, motorists might actually want to stop for any reason before heading back to A or on to C.

In fact, London's parking problems pre-date the motor age. Just off Marylebone High Street there's a garage which had earlier been a stable, and which until thirty years ago was dominated by an enormous hydraulic lift that facilitated multi-storey horse parking. When cars arrived, the issue became rather more pressing and in 1901, only three years after a handful of vehicles lined up outside the Henley Regatta to form Britain's first car park, the City & Suburban Electric Carriage Co. built a seven-floor multi-storey just behind Piccadilly. London's age of free parking ended almost before it had begun, so inaugurating a hundred-year quest for that secret place round the back of D.H. Evans where the wardens ran out of yellow paint.

The newly widened Park Lane was laid over what in 1963 was the world's largest underground car park, but even this proved a token gesture. A single parking space near The Angel went under the hammer in 2001 for £37,000. Alan Clark, maverick MP and patrician petrolhead, mothballed a fleet of slightly knackered Bentleys and Rollers under the House of Commons: 'The cheapest parking in central London,' he said, ignoring all official demands to move them.

These days, of course, it's not so much about finding free parking as finding *any* parking. Every Londoner knows what it is to join a dispirited crocodile of motorists crawling around the back streets looking for kerbside gaps and craning their necks to read the small print on those infuriatingly evasive restriction plates. So intense is the competition and so stacked the odds that it was an uncanny ability to find a parking space in London that first led David Icke, former television presenter and Coventry City goalkeeper, to suspect he might be in some way spiritually favoured.

Westminster Council, which in Monopoly terms is nicely set up with every property on the board in its possession except the five crappiest ones and Fleet Street, has in recent years established an enviable reputation – enviable, that is, amongst truly evil men and cyclists – as the undisputed champion of parking levies. In 2000, it issued 897,467 tickets, an increase of 13 per cent on the previous year's total and almost three times more than any other London council managed. The fine is something like £9,000, though if you pay four hours before the ticket was issued you can get this reduced on appeal to £7,000. And at 20p for three minutes, Westminster's meters are more expensive than Hamburg's peepshows. You don't even get any free tissue, though at those tear-inducing rates you could probably find a use for some. If you had a counter job at a West End McDonald's and drove to work – an unlikely scenario in any number of ways, I know – at the end of an eight-hour shift with your motor on a meter you'd be left with precisely 80p in your salt-speckled, sauce-smeared palm.

Most of my previous dealings with Westminster Council's parking department have involved sending them very long letters and, after an interval of many months, receiving very short replies. As a moth-wallet whose unappealing tendency to bear grudges against officialdom stands comparison with America's militia movement, I should by rights have built up an impressive armoury of payment-avoidance tactics; the regular appearance of words such as 'forthwith' and 'proceedings' in these short replies pays eloquent testament to the opposite.

Talking to an unusually forthcoming old chap in the council's ticket-appeal office I began to understand why. Accepting that *bona fide* Free Parking was a hilarious improbability, in fact a traveller's *non sequitur* to rank alongside Great North Eastern Railways or Happy Eater, I'd phoned him to procure a next-best compromise – if you don't pay to park, you get a ticket; but if you don't have to pay the ticket then you haven't paid to park. Ergo, free parking.

'The general rules when you write an appeal,' he confided, 'are to know the terminology and not to lose your rag.' Though my cocksure mastery of the phrase 'penalty charge notice' ticked the first box, a tendency to invoke unflattering comparison with administrative procedures in the Third Reich left the pen hovering over the second. 'More particularly, most people say the meter didn't work or was somehow running fast – they're wasting their time down that road.'

While he was inevitably reluctant to give me precise directions to more productive roads, reading between the yellow lines it seemed that unless you could prove your vehicle was in the service of a visiting military force, the best option was to say it had broken down. 'Though you'd ideally need photographic evidence that you'd displayed a note to that effect, as you would to back up any allegation of missing or faded lines or a misleading or ambiguous sign.' Photographic evidence? 'Keep a disposable camera in the glovebox. I do.'

That was too mad, even for me. 'Listen,' I said, in a more expansive, confessional tone, 'I'm not going to do that. I just want to park in your borough without paying.'

'Right.' There was a pause. 'We've got some quite cheap parking up Harrow Road,' came the eventual reply, quickly followed by the caveat that 'quite cheap' in this context actually equated to the approximate hourly cost of playing pinball if you were really bad at it and had a broken wrist. Nothing actually free, then. 'Not currently, not at the moment,' he replied teasingly, somehow implying that the outcome of an imminent council debate on the abolition of all parking controls and charges was too close to call. 'At least not unless you've, er . . .'

and here he issued a little snort of private amusement, '. . . you've got an electric vehicle. Then you can park on double yellows or wherever you want.'

An agreeable young man called Anthony duly delivered my electric vehicle six evenings later. Fashioned from enough bright blue plastic to have a whole borough of schoolchildren wondering where their lunchboxes had gone, this cheeky-faced, tiny-wheeled conveyance irresistibly recalled the playground in many other ways. To send it shooting off down the road the casual observer wouldn't try to plug the car into the mains but press down the roof and roll it backwards before letting go. It was so short that Anthony was able to park it face on to the kerb in front of my house without causing obstruction, and so silent that as he did so I could hear the nine-year-old from three doors down teasing, 'Look out, here comes Noddy.' Circumnavigating it in half a dozen strides I noted the vehicle identified itself as the TH!NKcity, a name certain to dominate the index of my forth-coming treatise, *Brand-Name Typography – A Wanker's Guide*.

But all this was perfect, not just because of the free parking angle, but because in every important respect the TH!NKcity was both an idealised embodiment of twenty-first century London and the vehicular antithesis of thirties London. What Londoners were told to aspire to now was a TH!NKcity; in the thirties it had been an open-topped Bentley with the cubic capacity of a meat fridge. And it's because they had all that noisy fun racing each other to Croydon Aerodrome and back that we now have to face a future of humming slowly about in plastic toys (batteries included).

In those days it was all about speed and glamour, and getting there quickly, loudly and in a huge cloud of smoke; for the TH!NKcity to have been any more diametrically opposed to these principles, it would have had to have been made out of marzipan. The TH!NKcity was made by metal-spectacled technocrats in Oslo, not leather-aproned apprentices in Walsall.

Its top speed was 54mph. When Anthony applied the horn it made a sound like someone down the road receiving a text message.

'I can't believe you're allowed to park this on double yellows,' I said to Anthony as we squeezed in together for a demonstration drive round the block. Anthony worked for the Energy Saving Trust, a charitable foundation whose eagerness to promote alternatively fuelled zero-emission urban vehicles extends to letting idiots like me borrow one of their cars for a day in order to drive about town parking like Starsky & Hutch.

'That's because you're not,' he said, blankly, setting us off down the road with a rising milkfloat hum.

My father, with whom I share both a keen interest in motoring novelty and a lifelong determination to disprove that maxim about free lunches, had arranged to come up specially and was crestfallen at this news when he arrived the next morning. 'It's not so bad,' I said, grappling with the bonnet-mounted charger socket into which Anthony had inserted my extension lead the night before. 'We can still park free in pay and display bays and meters. For the maximum time specified on the restriction plate.'

'At least no one's pulled out the plug,' he said, helping me reel the cable back through the sitting-room window (don't even consider a TH!NKcity if you suspect any of your neighbours harbour either Luddite sympathies or a weakness for unimaginative practical jokes).

We set off circumspectly, starkly conscious both of the TH!NKcity's head-turning silliness and its limited range. Anthony told me that a friend of his had taken one to Brighton, though under questioning confessed this had involved an overnight stop in Guildford. If you didn't have the radio on, or the lights, or the wipers, if you accelerated like a tranquillised vicar and made optimum use of a 'regenerative braking' system which charged the battery under gradual and controlled deceleration, you could, possibly, make a fully juiced up TH!NKcity run for fifty miles.

Always at the back of your mind, though, was that if you left the hazards on or got drawn into a protracted – and certainly mismatched – exchange of horn sounds you'd coast to a halt on a flyover and realise your extension lead was, ooh, seven miles too short. Even if your batteries went flat outside a Magnox reactor you'd still need to sit there for eight hours getting a charge. It would be like driving into a petrol station and filling up with a turkey baster.

The charge meter was already down to 70 per cent as we droned to a Tube-train halt in an empty meter bay round the back of Oxford Street. 'What now?' said my father, who had spent most of the outward journey bellowing 'Regenerate!' whenever a distant green light changed to amber. 'Wait for a warden,' I replied, and out we got.

By the time we spotted one sauntering up to our TH!NKcity we'd saved £2.20 in parking, thereby very nearly offsetting the bill for coffee consumed while on surveillance in a Starbucks over the road. The warden circled the car, appraising it with a smirk identical to the many directed at us through neighbouring drivers' windows on the journey up. 'How will he know he's not supposed to ticket it?' asked my father in a stake-out whisper.

'It says "electric" somewhere on the tax disc,' I said, then speaking for both of us added, 'so in other words, he won't know.'

On cue, the warden looked at his watch, withdrew his little computery thing and began to enter our registration number into it. 'Go, go, go, go!' I should have screamed before rushing across and spreadeagling him over the bonnet, but it had belatedly occurred to us that as the ticket he was now beginning to issue would be invalid there was perhaps no need. I could, in fact, have done what my father was preparing to do and just sat and watched him do it. But here was the table-turning opportunity of a lifetime. Out I bolted. 'Please, please!' I yelped, breathing rather harder than my short burst across the street demanded. 'I'm really sorry, but I think the meter must be running a bit fast.' He eyed me evenly. 'Also, I've broken down.'

'Well, if that's the case,' he said, starting to sound slightly but rewardingly narked, 'you really should put a note to that effect in the windscreen.'

I covered my forehead with one hand and nodded slowly. 'It's just . . . the lines,' I said in a pained and pitiful rasp, 'they're so faded, so . . . so . . .' Abruptly I lowered the hand and after theatrically scanning the street left and right looked straight into his eyes. 'Listen,' I hissed urgently, 'I shouldn't really be telling you this, but I'm here in the service of a visiting military force.' He took a small step backwards. Cradling my chin as if in reconsideration, I addressed a prolonged and wondering hum to the pavement, then blurted, 'No. No. No, that can't be right. No. What I mean is' – and here I arrowed my index finger to the relevant ballpoint scrawl on the tax disc – 'this is an electric vehicle.' It was cruel, really, and almost totally unwarranted. Traffic wardens have a miserable job, at least when it's snowing, and I wholeheartedly endorse all efforts to discourage people driving into the middle of London. And so does my father, who confessed as we rounded Piccadilly Circus that in years of executive employment in central London he had never once commuted by public transport.

The current proposal to impose a daily charge of £5 for taking a car into the central area is promising, though one that will discriminate in favour of all those fat-cat gas-guzzlers who clog the relevant streets. A fiver? That's not even half what a BMW-driving executive ponce shoves down a lap dancer's G-string at lunch time. What they should really do is ban all private cars except the TH!NKcity and see how those City boys fancy wheezing into the company car park in what looks like the sort of machine Communism would have produced if it had worked better – a twenty-first century Trabant.

Though it might easily be a hangover from the Bentley Boys of inter-war London, or even the sorry legacy of Margaret Thatcher's helpful comment that any bus passenger over the age of thirty was by definition a failure, for most people a car stubbornly remains not just a means of transport but a statement. It shouldn't be so, given the depressing absurdity of motoring around the Monopoly zone – with parking tariffs rivalling the minimum wage and 50,000 cars an hour barging into the central area in the morning rush hour it's no wonder that 'the traffic' regularly tops those 'worst things about London' *Evening Standard* celebrity surveys – but it simply is. And if a BMW says, 'Out the way, poofhouse', a TH!NKcity says, 'Oh, OK. Sorry!'. Of course I drive a Volvo estate, which says, 'Please pass – self-vasectomy in progress.'

Attempting to accommodate my wife and children in a TH!NKcity would be to recreate what seventies students did in Volkswagen Beetles when they couldn't find their underwater Monopoly sets, but for my father and I it seemed a grand little runabout. We saw Anne Robinson waiting on a street corner and, throwing charge-conserving caution to the winds, gave her a cheeky, though sadly inaudible, parp. After cameo standoffs with two further wardens in Covent Garden ('The meter isn't broken? Right . . . oh, that's it: I was misled by an ambiguous sign. Don't go away – there's a disposable photographic laboratory in my glovebox'), we blundered across an underground car park off Harley Street that not only advertised free parking for electric vehicles – and at £13 for four hours' parking in a conventionally powered conveyance, this was the jackpot – but also free charging in two designated bays.

Slightly surprisingly, one of these was occupied by a Peugeot electric van; slightly less surprisingly, the plugs were completely incompatible with our socket. Honestly. It was clear from the wardens' ignorance that this whole electric car/free parking stuff was a token gesture – rule out the ones with the crates of gold top on the back and there can't be more than two dozen electric vehicles in the capital – but they could at least have made those tokens the right size.

With the charge meter dropping towards 50 per cent I began to focus more closely on regenerative braking. So effectively did this compromise the more traditional priorities of urban motoring that coasting around a corner near the British Museum I almost knocked over a woman on a bicycle. Oh, all right, I actually *did* knock over a woman on a bicycle. But somehow it didn't seem to count: not having heard my stealthy approach, she looked so surprised as she bounced off the plastic wing that instead of the merited wildly abusive gesturing I was treated to a raised, open palm of apology.

It was an encounter that recaptured the spirit of '35. Roundabouts arrived in London's anarchic streets in 1926 and the capital's first set of traffic lights went up at Piccadilly Circus the same year, but both innovations were inspired by a desire to increase traffic speeds rather than reduce accidents. In consequence, death rates were fearful: in the twenty years between the wars, 120,000 people died on Britain's roads – equal, as one commentator noted, to the full strength of the British Expeditionary Force despatched to France in 1914.

In an interesting road-safety initiative, the government abolished all speed limits in 1930 and waited until the annual death toll hit 7,000 – still a record and twice the total we manage today with twenty times as many cars on the road – before reinstating them five years later, reluctantly throwing in a compulsory driving test. Even then there were complaints: opposing the 1935 Bill, Lieutenant-Colonel Moore-Brabazon made the ear-catching claim that is was essentially a motorist's civic duty to mow down jaywalkers: 'No doubt Members of the House will recollect the numbers of chickens we killed in the early days. We used to come back with the radiator stuffed with feathers. It was the same with dogs. Dogs get out of the way of motorcars nowadays. It is true that 7,000 people are killed in motor accidents . . . but there is education even in the lower animals. These things will right themselves.'

No pedestrians so richly deserved such education as the lower animals walking the capital's streets. 'Nobody who drives a motor vehicle in London can fail to be astounded at the folly of which pedestrians are capable,' commented *Motor* in 1934. 'It is no exaggeration to say the man at the wheel of the motorcar is constantly saving the lives of walkers.' Victor Watson for one would have roundly endorsed such bold sentiments. Monopoly was released the year speed limits were introduced, and as detailed in its Chance card penalties the frustrations of driving are already more in evidence than its pleasures. Just months earlier, you wouldn't have been fined £15 for speeding but given an indulgent wink of encouragement by the traffic cop as he respectfully flicked bits of pedestrian off your grille with his truncheon.

And what of ' "DRUNK IN CHARGE" FINE £20'? Even as a child I thought it seemed a little distasteful to soil a wholesome family pastime with the image of some ginned-up landlord wrapping his Alvis round a West End lamppost. Bracketing a conviction for drink driving alongside mundane bills for education and healthcare, Monopoly made the practice seem not just acceptable but inevitable. In fact, by putting the phrase in inverted commas, Waddingtons were implying that it somehow shouldn't be an offence at all. But remember that drink driving wasn't really frowned upon socially until the eighties, and that speeding is only now coming to be considered unacceptable. Pondering which motoring practices indulgently termed 'cavalier' by today's Londoners will appal their descendants in sixty years' time, my father and I smugly came up with illegal parking and excess emissions.

Having carefully checked the pay-and-display signs to ensure we hadn't strayed into a less enlightened neighbouring borough, we left the TH!NKcity off Tottenham Court Road and lunched at a nearby curry house. When we leadenly emerged ninety minutes later, there was a ticket on the windscreen. And just an hour after that, having parked the TH!NKcity by Lincoln's Inn Field to wander about the surprising and genuinely splendid Soane Museum, there was another, this time accompanied on the passenger window by a fluorescent 'AUTHORISED FOR CLAMPING' sticker of the type whose removal necessitates the vigorous and constant application of wire wool and lung-melting solvents for anything up to four years. It wouldn't have been at all funny if the car actually had been clamped, of course, or if we'd felt any moral obligation to tackle that sticker, but it hadn't, and we didn't, and so it was.

My father did the maths as we whined home through the traffic. Using criteria that have no place in rational contemplation but made eminent sense to us, he calculated that after deductions for curries and coffees, our paper profit in terms of unfed meters and unpaid fines was a whopping £71.40.

We parked nose up outside my house with the charge meter down to 20 per cent; happy but oddly exhausted – please don't say I can no longer handle a vehicle even as poxily stunted as this one without power steering – my batteries felt even flatter. This may explain why, when my father came out with a plastic bag and advised me to wrap the extension lead in it in case of rain, I chose to ignore him.

I was in bed when the first, gentle drops fell, a sound picked up by my ears but which my brain elected not to pass on to my legs. The extent of the downpour and its fearsome consequences only became apparent retrospectively, when in the morning I flicked on the bedside light and nothing happened.

CHAPTER 6

The Yellows

LEICESTER SQ
CITY OF WESTMINSTER

COVENTRY ST
CITY OF WESTMINSTER

PICCADILLY
CITY OF WESTMINSTER

Birna's Icelandic grandfather – a larger-than-life trawler captain whose life was an especially large one – regularly visited London in the thirties. Shortly before he died I talked to him about these trips, who he'd stayed with, what he'd done. When I asked him where he'd gone for a good night out as a young blade at large, his wet blue gaze drifted out of the window, and with a small but indisputably saucy smile of recollection he murmured, 'Leicester Square'.

I'd been frankly astonished by this at the time, and was again after Anthony had repossessed my TH!NKcity with a good deal more grace than its minimal battery charge, garish adhesive decorations and accompanying sheath of penalty charge notices demanded. But after I'd sat down, opened the board for the first and only time under my own roof and rolled six, I rather belatedly made an obvious connection. The yellows – Leicester Square, Coventry Street and Piccadilly – were the good-time set, the night-on-the-tiles set, the party-till-you-drop set.

Relegated on the board below Coventry Street – familiar to all tourists and most Londoners as 'Where?' – Leicester Square's reputation in the thirties was clearly as brassy as it is today: the Blackpool of London. 'I would love Leicester Square to be like a Florence-style piazza, but at the moment it's more like Ayia Napa,' moaned the Metropolitan Police's deputy assistant commissioner recently, addressing a Westminster Council meeting that planned to redeem the situation by licensing buskers, installing (sigh) thirty new CCTV cameras in the streets around the square and building six Parisian-model outdoor 'pissoirs'. 'That's not the kind of entertainment we're looking for,' added council leader Simon Milton, probably referring to the happy hours rather than the pissoirs.

Simon and the deputy assistant commissioner might love the idea of a gracious promenade *à deux* about some trattoria-strewn Florence-style piazza, but in the absence of Florence-style weather I'm happy to bet they'd be staying in watching *Top Gear*. The only volunteers for a stroll about Leicester Square on a wet autumn evening are very likely to be both teenage and drunk, and hats off to them on both counts. Here at least was a part of London that knew its heritage, a place where young Londoners could draw on a many-generationed history of gathering to binge drink. When Euan Blair needed a gutter to keel over into, where else could he have gone?

Laid out as a handsome residential estate on fields owned by the Earl of Leicester in the 1670s, the square's noble intentions were compromised almost immediately. The Earl's son let in shops and stalls, and the rot set in with uncomfortable literality at the start of the eighteenth century, when someone stuck a tele-scope in the grass in the middle and aimed it at the decomposing heads of traitors impaled at Temple Bar down the hill, charging for each peek.

Artists brought in their questionable theatricalities – Joshua Reynolds had his staircase at No. 47 specially widened 'to accommodate the ample skirts of female patrons', and the engraver William Woolett was the square's neighbour from hell, firing a cannon from his roof to mark the completion of a piece of work. At No. 30, William Hogarth drew much of the inspiration for his graphically tawdry caricatures from the streets around. And Bohemia, after all, isn't a million miles from Transylvania – in 1761 a Swiss miniatures painter renting a room at No. 36 had a set-to with his landlady which culminated in his ferrying bits of her out of the door in parcels.

A defining moment in Leicester Square's history took place in 1726. Partly because it took place in a brothel (at No. 27), but mainly because in involved a woman, Mary Tofts, who claimed to have given birth to a litter of fifteen rabbits. Clearly selecting the wrong sort of doctor for the job, the local hospital despatched a surgeon, who watched in utter astonishment as Mary spawned another couple of bunnies. Heaven alone knows what medical counselling he offered her – 'No dear, we breed *like* rabbits, not *with* them' – but the case was now the talk of London and King George I sent his own surgeon to investigate. The fact that this gentleman could claim only to have delivered Mary of 'rabbit portions' should possibly have raised suspicions, but it wasn't until she was apprehended 'trying secretly to buy a rabbit' that the fraud was exposed. This incident sealed Leicester Square's reputation as a cabaret of the bizarre; the sort of place where to make a name for yourself in the rabbit game, it wasn't enough merely to pull one out of a hat.

It was all studiously lowbrow, and attempts to crowbar that brow upwards were invariably doomed. In 1851 an entrepreneur built a 'Great Globe' in the square's muddy middle, at 60 feet high the largest ever built. Essentially a stylised model of our planet, visitors climbed up platforms in its gas-lit interior to examine from beneath 'the physical features of the earth'. Or rather they didn't – it was demolished after only ten years. Even more disastrous was the grandly titled 'Royal Panopticon of

Science and Art', a series of lecture halls arrestingly decorated in the Moorish style. This ill-conceived marriage of the garish and the worthy also showcased a hydraulic 'Ascending Carriage' and the world's loudest organ, features that helped bump the cost up to £80,000; a sum which, with reference to my now-traditional idiotic price index, could have bagged you Marble Arch, with enough change left for Big Ben's clock.

If London's squares, as many have said, are its jewels, then by the middle of the nineteenth century Leicester Square was the capital's tarnished navel ring. The garden in the middle, by now a barren wilderness, was sold by a dentist to a ship's purser, who sold it to an ivory turner, who sold it to a goldsmith. A grandly gilded statue of George I on horseback that had dominated the garden for a century was already looking a bit sorry when the builders turned up and found it right where they wanted to erect their Great Globe. Confounded by a law forbidding the statue's removal from the square, they hit upon the cheeky solution of burying it 12 feet underground and sticking their big orb on top. When the globe's bubble burst the statue was disinterred and, though George and his mount had in the interim shed all their gold leaf and five limbs between them, re-erected on its plinth. Now presiding over what had degenerated into 'an open rubbish dump where kitchen refuse lay in heaps beside the rotting remains of dogs and cats', George was left to the mercy of local children, who rode pillion behind him, pulled more bits off and one night in October 1866 endowed the decaying monarch with a dunce's hat, pipe and moustache, having first painted his horse white with black polka dots. So notorious did this spectacle become that it even inspired what must surely have been a memorable show at a nearby strip joint.

In 1760 George III had been proclaimed king in Leicester Square; just over one hundred years later the now headless statue of his great-grandfather was flogged there for £16 scrap. Leicester Square's decline was complete. The only way was up, or at least across. Music halls moved in, the Alhambra occupying the Aladdinesque Panopticon building and the Empire setting up shop in the similarly shortlived Royal London Panorama. Leicester Square had found its level, and quickly proved adept at giving its public what it wanted. By 1936 both Alhambra and Empire were showcases of the new breed of super cinema, and between them the square was thoughtfully punctuated with all-night restaurants such as the Quality Inn with its clean, nautical Art Deco interiors and the self-service Honeydew, offering 'Canadian Pie in containers to take away'.

With a long-standing reputation as the starting point for many a lad's night out – a reputation name-checked in the chorus of 'It's A Long Way To Tipperary' – Leicester Square was clearly a good place to hang about in if you wanted to know what the man in the street got up to when he fancied an evening as a man about town, and one night in May 1937 there were a lot of people with notebooks wandering about it doing just that. The Mass Observation movement was a bold attempt to take a snapshot of everyday British life: social science was in its infancy in the thirties, and there was a general sense of urgency (general at least among earnest middle-class lefties) to take this snapshot before rapidly evolving patterns of work and leisure blurred it beyond recognition. On Coronation Day – 12 May 1937 – hundreds of Mass Observation volunteers insinuated themselves into crowds around the country, scribbling down incidents witnessed and conversations overheard in pubs and on buses, watching how people walked and behaved. No one is sure what the operation achieved – it must have been terrible for the organisers to see their worthy venture mutate into the clipboard-clasping horror that is market research – but if you're trying to get an impression of London life in the thirties, there is no more entertaining or evocative source book. Where else would you discover that every time the lights went out on a thirties Tube train underground someone would start making 'animal noises'? Or that a common pastime of the age was to shout 'Beaver!' at men with beards?

So it's 11 p.m. on 12 May 1937, and you're at Leicester Square Tube. Mind out: 'As we go up the escalator we are amused to see a young man, hugging a soda-water siphon, come sliding down the belt of the banister; as he comes in contact with a lamp-stand on the slide the bottle is broken, and he sails on his way merrily, too drunk to mind anything.' Outside you see a crowd dancing arm in arm and singing 'Knees Up Mother Brown'; you discreetly ease open your notebook and write 'They appear to be working people.' You cross into the square, where a man with 'brown uneven hair, blue coat and bowler worn at an angle' is operating a three-card trick: 'he asks you to select the queen, turns the cards over and when you draw the queen it is an eight. He sells the trick to a young boy who shows you how easy it is . . . later he gives the boy a cigarette. At next pitch, man is chaining partner prior to release act . . . as he takes the collection he says he is a white man (this with much feeling) and points to Union Jack above. He says it covers four corners of the universe and it does not matter if you are yellow or white or black, if you are British you are a sportsman and expect a fair wage for your work . . .'

It starts raining; you take cover in a pub doorway. 'On way out push against somebody, say "Sorry" and hear "That's all right, dearie, don't be in such a hurry." Look round and in spite of lack of make-up and neat well-cut coat, realise I am being quite nicely accosted by a prostitute, quiet-voiced, good accent, etc. Ask why she's out so late – or so early? – and she says business is not so good as it might be. Before she can decide whether I'm a potential client, I cut across the road and into Underground station.'

Feeling an impulsive burst of empathy for those men with notebooks, and trying not to think too much about that dearie business, I'd been seized with inspiration. Looking at the board, and then at the map, Vic and Marge's yellow-set game plan had suddenly seemed obvious. A movie in Leicester Square, a cocktail in the Café de Paris on Coventry Street, and to round off a romantic evening, what better than a . . . well, a night at the Ritz down the end of Piccadilly. It was an inviting schedule, and one that with a bit of planning I could replicate faithfully. As faithfully, anyway, as Victor probably managed to. A night at the Ritz, I soon discovered, starts at £305. Bed was out; I'd settle for breakfast. The restaurant opened at 7 and I'd arranged to meet my friend Ian there on the dot. I was going to do Leicester Square, Coventry Street and Piccadilly in a single through-the-night burst. I was going out to paint the yellows red.

Throughout my suburban upbringing I'd only rarely been Up West past midnight, and never until the small hours were starting to get big again. Excited by my belated debut as a twenty-four-hour party person, I was also inevitably trepidatious. The incompatibility of the three venues presented a sartorial dilemma: I would have to hang about Leicester Square, presumably in the company of noisily tanked-up students, before being granted entrance to a club that sounded as if it might not let me in without a top hat. And the schedule was, by my standards at least, wildly ambitious: these days I only stay up all night for general elections, and as a father of three, access to the powdered stimulants most often associated with nocturnal stamina was not as straight-forward as it might have once been.

Compromises, in short, were inevitable, but slipping a pack of guarana chewing gum into the pocket of my black velvet trousers I hoped I'd made the right call. As night began to fall, though, so did a steady drizzle, and, gathering my family together by the front door, that potentially voguish ensemble was set off with an old raincoat stuffed full of possibly relevant bits of paper. 'I'm going out now,' I announced bravely, 'and I'm not coming back until tomorrow.' (I wish I'd remembered this ten minutes later when I bought that day return.)

Extended to distant new suburbs west and north in 1933, the Piccadilly line is probably the most thirties of all. And because

London is the way it is, through a combination of sloth, economy and nostalgia much of that period ambience lingers on. The bench upon which I planted my lustrously trousered fundament at Hammersmith station bore the patina of seventy years, and the next stop down, Barons Court, was protected from the October elements by a rural-branch-line platform canopy with those scallopy wooden overhangs. Half the 'next train' indicators at this end of the line look like they've been torn off the front of a bus with wooden wheels.

My carriage was the standard refurbished seventies job, but as recently as 1988 the Piccadilly was still running scarlet thirties units with maple-wood floors and woollen moquette seating that together with the soft downlighting and underfoot carpet of fag ends imbued my journeys to school with the louche ambience of a slightly seedy cocktail bar at closing time. At least our Tube trains still have proper sprung and upholstered seating, unlike the buttock-bullying plastic benches favoured by most other European mass-transit operators. That's got to be up in the top one hundred reasons to live in London, probably somewhere in the mid-seventies between Andy's Kebabs on Turnham Green and the view of Battersea Power Station at dusk.

Just before we dived underground, I looked up at a mansion block and noticed the ceilings of the apartments within flickering with the reason why the train was almost empty at 7 p.m., and why those super cinemas aren't so super any more. Televisions first appeared in London's shops the same year as Monopoly, under slogans that read 'Hear – *and see!* Complete darkness IS NOT NECESSARY'. And though in fact complete darkness *was* all you'd have been able to watch a lot of the time – the BBC inaugurated the world's first programme schedule in 1936, but even twenty years later was putting out only four hours of telly a day – the writing was on the screen. Once video had killed the radio star, he got stuck into the cinema, the art of urban promenading and – yes – even board games.

Interestingly, however, no one seemed to have passed this on to Leicester Square. On an unpromisingly moist-aired Thursday in October, the only pedestrianised street on the Monopoly board was jammed with human traffic, a burger-breathed, busker-bellowing melee which could only be traversed via extensive weaving and excuse-mes. Hopping neatly over a puddle of beery vomit, I began to realise that most of the entertainment was very much of the old school. The teenagers around, nearly all of them Asian, were at least one sheet to the wind, with a vocal minority who'd certainly have known what to do if you'd handed them a soda siphon at the top of an escalator. Two million E tablets are necked every week in Britain, and the only way the brewers have been able to lure back the youth market has been by working up new variations on the oldest drug: viz., alcopops. And with London's pubs charging up to £3.10 a pint, landlords in earnest pursuit of the young pound have been obliged to appeal to what the industry calls 'volume drinkers' (10 per cent of us – I'm taking you with me – are responsible for 60 per cent of the nation's total alcohol intake) by slashing prices. West End happy hours now run all evening, often in bars where the music is so loud that the only point of opening your mouth is to pour a Bacardi Breezer into it (or several out of it).

A silent Donald Pleasence in a funeral suit came up and pressed a leaflet into my hand; I looked at its cover and read: 'This world is heading for a terrible day.' Leicester Square was still clearly seen as a playground for souls who needed saving, but I'd so much rather have been invited to the more wonderful days detailed on the nightclub flyers being pressed upon everyone else. With a start I realised Donald had singled me out for redemption because, like him and unlike anyone in a generous radius who didn't have numbers on their epaulettes, I was over the age of nineteen, alone and sober.

And in fact wearing a tie, which had seemed a prerequisite for the Café de Paris and the Ritz, but in being liberally decorated with *Magic Roundabout* flowers and teamed with those black velvet trousers was now achieving the precise opposite of the intended social camouflage. A phalanx of bare-midriffed girls nudged each other and made loud bursting sounds as they passed, and I suddenly recalled my French O level exam, and the picture story which ended with a boy in a flamboyantly cut three-piece suit wilting in humiliation before a dance floor of jeering cap-sleeved peers. Absently folding a £1 pizza slice into my mouth outside the Odeon, a huge gobbet of oiled matter slopped straight from chin to tie; as a tribute to the reckless stridency of design it looked comfortably at home.

I'd chosen the Odeon partly because it's one of the last London cinemas not to have been chopped and sliced into a dozen mini screens which make watching a big new release like going to your mate's house to watch the football – the main screen capacity is 1,612 and there's still a price difference between stalls and royal circle – and partly because in an earlier life it had been the Alhambra. It's almost impossible to overstate the cinema's dominance of London's social life in the thirties: over half of all Londoners went once a week and over a quarter twice or more. There were 4,967 cinemas in the country, and in 1937 London's studios turned out two hundred films.

Even more dislocated than is usual after watching huge things happen in a big dark room – by opting for *Moulin Rouge*, the leg I'd tried to plant in 1936 had just been yanked back another forty years – I blinked out into a jarring brashness that at 11 o'clock was noticeably diminished. Very drunk girls stared grimly ahead as they ploughed towards the Underground with the off-balance determination of a sailor crossing the deck of a storm-tossed ship; boys in T-shirts tried slightly too hard to pretend they weren't cold as they followed. Most people's evenings were coming to an end whereas mine – consult watch, stifle sigh, feel age – was just beginning. 'You wanna show some fucking RESPECT!' shrieked a female voice close behind, and though everyone else around summoned a derisive chorus of 'Oooooooooh!' I couldn't restrain a reflex squeak of distress. If I couldn't handle a lairy schoolgirl at 11 p.m., what hope for the considerably more colourful characters I was certain to encounter in the eight hours ahead?

The beep-beep of reversing dustcarts announced that the binmen were coming on duty just as the entertainers were clocking off, a black dwarf packing up her unicycle and one of those bronze-robot types shuffling towards the Tube station and what at this hour would certainly be an especially stimulating journey home. Nothing substantial had changed in sixty-four years: I didn't see an escapologist, but on another night I might have; and though the three-card tricksters have been cleared off the streets in recent years there were a couple of guys running the old 'funny bike' scam.

As a late-night spectator sport, only an extended on-foot police pursuit runs this close. First a bloke – usually, as here, a native of the Turko-Balkan regions who hasn't spent quite enough time in north-western Europe to decode the correlation between moustache–bulk and homosexuality – scratches two chalk lines 8 feet apart on the pavement before riding a small and slightly odd-looking bicycle between them, shouting as he does so that if anyone give him one pound and do this, he give them ten pound cash money. Then a lot of men – drunk men – queue up, pay up, saddle up and fall over. The equation I'd begun to dread was rewardingly inverted: I was having a good time, and other people were getting hurt.

Working people still lived around Leicester Square in the thirties – there was a big grammar school on the south-eastern corner – and, even more arrestingly, they actually worked here too. Thurston's at No. 45 knocked up billiard tables, there was a beer bottler's at No. 36 and smaller enterprises around the square turned out umbrellas, chocolates and musical instruments. Feeling another pang of melancholy that here, as everywhere in central London, all such romantic manufacturing endeavours had been shoved aside by the bronzed-glass, security-desked likes of The Communications Building, I walked past an All Bar One and glumly beheld staff bringing out the binliners and switching the lights off. It wasn't even half-eleven. Despite the grumblings of Westminster Council, Leicester Square just isn't the twenty-four-hour party it was in the thirties, when the snack bars and restaurants started serving breakfast at midnight.

People could feast their eyes and stuff their faces in Leicester Square, but if you found yourself a few gins short of an escalator luge challenge and it was gone 10.30, then the only place to get them down your neck was one space along. It might not mean much to anyone now, but then more than any other street on the board the inclusion of Coventry Street is a reflection of the Monopoly era.

Knocked up ten years after Leicester Square and named in honour of Charles II's Secretary of State (first name Henry), Coventry Street wasted even less time than its quadrilateral neighbour in sacrificing prestige for profit. Gambling clubs appeared immediately, soon followed by the sort of restaurants and theatres that would later have Victorians huffing that 'the bad character of the place is at least two centuries old'.

Claustrophobically sandwiched between Leicester Square and Piccadilly Circus, Coventry Street seemed incapable of resisting the West End status quo, but somehow, in the twenties, it managed to make a name for itself as the venue for a slightly higher class night out, one that would stand it in good stead when Vic and Marge promoted it above Leicester Square in the yellow-set hierarchy.

Even the Lyons Corner House on Coventry Street stood a cut above its ubiquitous brethren: opened in 1907 it was the size of a department store, boasting acres of gilt and marble and a stupendous and still globally unrivalled dining capacity of 4,500 – not so much the chain's flagship as its aircraft carrier. Scott's restaurant next door could claim a pan-European reputation for its fish dishes (despite sharing premises, as I noted from a contemporary photo, with the intriguing Universities Toilet Club), and the Prince of Wales Theatre opposite resisted the pressure to dumb down by becoming a cinema (it was at the Royal Variety Performance there in 1963 that John Lennon trotted out his jewellery-rattling putdown).

But Coventry Street's reputation was founded, almost exclusively, on what one contemporary commentator called 'a determination to drink out of hours'. Draconian licensing laws imposed during the First World War to stop munitions workers sidling off to the pub were still ruthlessly enforced (as in fact they largely are today, most particularly in terms of 11 o'clock closing), and those stricken with unslakeable nocturnal thirsts were forced to patronise obscure venues that through some arcane loophole were exempt from the legislation – they formed railway clubs and got drunk on trains, or drama clubs and got drunk in theatres.

Although there was no shortage of pubs, a certain sort of Londoner wouldn't be seen dead going into one, or rather would be if he tried to. Pubs were for working men, with spittoons and sawdust, and remained fiercely territorial: it was common to ask a man not where he lived but which pub he drank at. Strangers, particularly of the hoity-toity sort, were not welcome. Besides, many pubs didn't serve anything but beer – the landlords couldn't afford the more expensive spirits licence – and toffs simply wouldn't consider what even one of George Orwell's more sympathetic upper-class creations called 'filthy common ale'. (Having said that, as the decade wore on it became fashionable amongst the elite to affect an ironic enthusiasm for working-class culture: in 1937, a record year for dartboard sales, our old Queen Mum was photographed on the oche alongside her husband, and the year after the Duke and Duchess of Kent were seen doing the Lambeth Walk, oi.)

The first so-called 'night-clubs' sprang up in the early twenties, catering for the new craze in cocktail drinking, denounced by medical authorities in an age before lager and blackcurrant as 'the most reprehensible form of alcoholic abuse'. People danced the Charleston; some kind soul guaranteed future generations endless trite amusement by choreographing the Black Bottom. But those early clubs had to stop serving at 10 p.m., and for the era's unusually devoted drinkers that was many hours too early. When you bear in mind that this latter group included the Prince of Wales, Rudolph Valentino and any other number of persuasively rich notables, you will understand the temptation to bend the rules. As well as the old gin-out-of-teapots ruse, clubs organised 'bottle parties', ostensibly private gatherings with a notional 'host', whose 'invited guests' were in reality anyone prepared to pay . . . sorry, to 'help out with the expenses'. Memorable features of such occasions included 'the semi-nude cabaret and the frankly lewd song'. The rewards were prodigious but so were the penalties: Mrs Meyrick, a respectably middle-aged club-owner whose three daughters all married into the peerage, was twice convicted and spent over two years in prison – in true Monopoly style, she continued running her empire from behind bars.

Opened in 1924, the Café de Paris on Coventry Street somehow managed to tread that fine line between excitement and respectability, and trod it with such agility that it soon established itself as the dominant club of its era – the master key, no less, that unlocks the mystery of Coventry Street's appearance on the board.

To succeed in those days it was vital to secure the patronage of the 'Upper Three Thousand', a group we may safely define as the stupidly rich good-time aristos who dominated the social scene much as today's *Hello!*-class celebs. The Café's Danish manager Martin Poulsen was a friend of Edward, the errant Prince of Wales, and to secure his majesty's crucial long-term patronage packed the club with game lovelies on the night of that first royal visit. 'Oh, God!' said one young dancing girl on being told that the Prince wished to meet her, 'What do I say to him?' '"Yes, sir" or "No, sir",' said Poulsen, 'but "Yes, sir" for preference.'

Edward came three times a month thereafter, and once the Upper Three Thousand followed so did their celebrity cohorts. Noël Coward was a regular, and Fred Astaire, Charlie Chaplin, assorted Churchills and Kennedys. Cole Porter gave 'Miss Otis Regrets' its first public airing on the Café de Paris's tiny stage. Stockbrokers had phones installed by their tables so they could trade on the New York exchange after the London markets had closed; a bandleader once eavesdropped and made a fortune of his own. So generous were the tips that the Café's doormen actually had to pay the management £10 a week to work there.

Inevitably, the high jinks at the Café were the highest and jinkiest in town. Someone would dot sugar lumps with drops of coffee and shoot craps. Huge sums were wagered on cab races down Piccadilly. Poulsen was an ex-Olympic gymnast and walked across the dance floor on his hands when he was in a good mood; the King of Spain would turn up with a butterfly net full of oranges and give them out to people he liked the look of. Edward and Mrs Simpson met there often, as indeed did the Queen Mum and her future husband: though the gossip columnists, forbidden to advertise, could only refer to it as a 'supper restaurant in Coventry Street', the Café's society nickname was 'the bower of love'.

If the Leicester Square riff-raff fancied a peek inside the Café, they could forget it. Strictly evening dress only, and no rabble was the order of the day: even Vic and Marge would have had to have smiled particularly nicely. As indeed did I, in a telephonic sense, when I'd called up the Café de Paris earlier in the day to secure a place on the guest list.

The unusual ease with which I succeeded owed much to the unshakeable conviction the duty manageress had somehow acquired during our conversation that I was out scouting locations for a new and apparently lucrative London clubland edition of Monopoly. Any determination to disabuse her of this worrisome delusion evaporated when a substantial doorman guarding the Café's unremarkable entrance interrupted my explanatory mumblings with an eager, which is to say terrifying, beam. 'Oh, yes *indeed*! Mr Mon-o-poly!' he boomed, in the manner of an unusually strident master of ceremonies at a world title fight. Then, in a different but perhaps more unsettling voice, he bent towards me and with his bow tie almost in my mouth whispered, 'Go on, make us Mayfair. *Go on.*'

Exhausted by the ensuing exchange of false laughter I stumbled down the steps and into the club's hot, loud darkness. 'Busy night tonight,' bellowed a freckled man with a New-World accent and a curly plastic wire sticking out of a device in his ear. He said my name, and then his, which I couldn't quite hear as we shook hands. We were at the open end of a horseshoe balcony curved snugly around and above a dance floor half-filled with tables; an eclectic assortment of hearty revellers were eating, and a lot more were jiggling energetically about in front of an iron-throated songstress at the low stage before them. Her backing band abruptly climaxed and in the following seconds of calm we had our conversation.

'Busy night,' I repeated.

'Yeah,' he confirmed, scanning the crowd beneath with a practised eye. 'I reckon about 450 out of a seven-one-five capacity.'

'Not bad for a Thursday.'

'Well, you know,' he said, in what I took as a wry tone, 'Thursday is the new Friday.'

As soon as the theatrical chortle warbled idiotically out of my mouth I realised this had not been a joke. 'Yes!' I said, failing to mould counterfeit amusement into genuine enthusiasm. 'That's *exactly* what . . . what has happened. To Thursday. In relation to Friday.'

He directed a short, sharp look at my face, then at my tie, before continuing more circumspectly. 'Yeah . . . Friday is a bit . . . east goes west.' Actually, I'm not sure if he did say precisely that, because halfway through his sentence the band struck mightily up once more. Just as well, as craning uncertainly towards his moving mouth I could just detect little wisps of compromising banter, a 'prestige spot on the board' here and a 'licensing deal' there. I nodded a lot, letting my lower lip sag into an expression of benign confusion that I somehow hoped would say, 'Though of obscure but pivotal importance in regards to this clubland Monopoly venture, I'm both a bit stupid and spinelessly corruptible.' You may imagine how this expression developed when I found myself, a short number of seconds later, sitting at a table for one on the VIP balcony, the Prince of Wales balcony, watching froth subside in the champagne flute before me. Bring on the semi-nude cabaret; let the frankly lewd songs commence.

From here it was simple to imagine the Café in its heyday – almost impossible not to. There were still chandeliers; still champagne. And velvet sofas, white linen and live music, and an audience that blended the Upper Three Thousand with the middling millions. The PA was squawking on about medical students and a twenty-first birthday; alongside me, a family of four I'd seen emerging from a spanking new Roller out front were having the time of their lives, the dad drinking Veuve Clicquot straight from the bottle while his wife and twentyish sons linked arms and did the cancan. I don't think I have ever seen so many people having such fun on a Thursday – certainly not since Frank Dobson tried to pick a fight with Ken Livingstone on *Question Time*.

Ol' iron-throat made way for a fashionably cheesy medley of seventies TV theme tunes and Shirley Bassey numbers, and I sat back in my armchair, velvet sliding softly against velvet, glass tilted suavely towards lips. My trousers felt at home, and so at last did I. Only then did I look up and realise something important about where I was sitting.

The outbreak of war hardly checked the Café's debonair stride. Poulsen bought 25,000 bottles of champagne as an indication of his confidence, and even in 1940 was able to offer his patrons oysters and caviar. His nightclub advertised itself as 'the safest and gayest restaurant – twenty feet below ground', and when the air-raid sirens started the Upper Three Thousand ran in: it was their equivalent of sheltering in the Tube.

I have to say, however, that my research revealed an establishment which even in its early days had seemed marinaded in ill fate. Café regulars were always overdosing in toilets or fatally involving themselves in unlikely boating accidents. Car crashes, plane crashes, hotel fires . . . one pissed-up millionaire was kicked out of the Café after throwing plates off the balcony and shot himself when he got home. And it wasn't just the human toll. How's this for an account of contemporary priorities: 'A terrible accident . . . almost £80,000-worth of jewellery scattered all over the road, much of it never being recovered. Prince Mdivani was killed.'

When you design your club as an exact copy of the restaurant on the *Lusitania* you should probably expect trouble, and at 9.50 on 8 March 1941 it came. The bomb dropped in through the plaster and glass above and glanced off the first balcony table on the left – my table, in fact – before exploding. The club was packed and eighty-four people, including Poulsen, were killed in what was to be one of the West End's most devastating Blitz tragedies. But accounts of the immediate aftermath offer an interesting insight in the Blitz spirit: let into the Café at last, the riff-raff exacted a rather unsavoury revenge by stripping the dead and wounded of their valuables. One man had £60 looted from his blood-soaked trousers; the cufflinks were pinched off Poulsen's corpse. Taxi drivers commandeered to ferry the wounded to hospital berated their prone passengers for bleeding on the seats, and survivors reported a man kneeling down by the heads of the dying and hissing 'Are you prepared to meet your God?' in their ears.

Eventually patched together the Café reopened after the war – the Goons, Tony Hancock and Shirley Bassey honed their acts on its tiny stage – but all clubs fall out of fashion, and with that dicky-bow dress code still in place it was never going to make it to the sixties. The Queen chose it for her coming-out party, and so very nearly did Liberace, who in 1956 almost had his trousers pulled off by students in the street outside, but in 1957 they bowed to the inevitable and mothballed the Café as a part-time venue for private functions.

As you will have gathered, however, it is now reopened, and I can recommend you include a visit to the Café de Paris on the Monopoly tour of London you've no doubt already begun to plan. I've no idea how much it costs to get in or what a drink will set you back, but that doesn't matter – there's got to be some mileage in the Clubland Cluedo gambit.

They were playing the *Wonder Woman* theme when a waitress who I'd noticed examining me for some time marched confidently up. I raised my empty champagne glass and jiggled it promptly; her facial response indicated this to be an inappropriate course of action. 'Sorry,' she said, sounding anything but, 'all these tables are reserved.'

Almost managing not to bleat in panic I told her that it was absolutely fine, a statement she inevitably found wanting. 'But I'm a corporate guest on a courtesy fact-finding visit,' I elaborated. 'One of your senior colleagues invited me to this table.'

'Which one?' she asked, and fruitlessly scanning the dark sea of heads for one to point at I knew the game was up.

'Some Australian bloke with wires coming out of his ears.'

Stubbornly unintrigued, she raised her eyebrows at someone in the purply gloom beyond. It would have been about this time that I recalled how the Café de Paris waiters effected their 'flying wedge' expulsion technique: an irresistible phalanx of half a dozen propelling obstreperous guests smartly across the balcony floor and down a secret rear staircase.

The waitress motioned to the door, and with my powers of resistance conspicuously sapped by this recollection I cravenly collected my belongings. What were the options? Dig myself deeper into the already echoingly cavernous Clubland Monopoly hole I'd excavated, or take this opportunity to be forcibly hauled out of it?

Perhaps it was for the best, in any case. Despite the unwieldy gob-full of chewable stimulants I had been steadily accumulating, the sofa was beginning to feel rather too comfortable for a man only halfway through his mission: Cole Porter, I thought, probably wouldn't have complained about getting no kick from guarana.

I sloped up the stairs followed by wisps of dry ice, slipped past the bouncer and with my ears as confused by the sudden hissy silence as my eyes had been coming out of the cinema I gave the rest of Coventry Street a wistful once-over. It didn't take long. The Prince of Wales Theatre's streaky, portholed superstructure imparted the look of a recently raised shipwreck; what had been the Civil Service Co-Operative Society was now a TGI Friday, and looking at my watch I saw that the phrase behind those cursed initials had indeed applied for over an hour and a half.

A Starbucks, an Aberdeen Steak House, a KFC – the only catering establishment that didn't have its chairs on the tables was McDonald's, and only then because they were bolted to the floor. A bureau de change (actually there were two, but you have a go at the plural); Churchill Souvenirs; a Sock Shop. I've never understood why Sock Shops exist at all, and especially why they did so with such bewildering ubiquity during the chain's mid-eighties boom. I'm as well acquainted as anyone with lurid tabloid tales of ruinous yuppie excess, but can't seem to recall any sordid confessionals headlined 'My Novelty Anklewear Hell'.

Sock Shop occupied part of what had been Scott's restaurant, but next door a far grimmer mutation had taken place. Consulting my directory with a sigh so loud it caused a street sweeper to look up from his broom, I noted that what had once been the world's largest restaurant, the acceptable face of fast food, the first Lyons Corner House was now – and what spittled loathing this still causes me – Planet Hollywood. I would draw the attention of those unfamiliar with Planet Hollywood to the following nouns: 'Sylvester Stallone'; 'buffalo wings'. I don't really have the stomach, nor in fact the libel insurance, to explain in further detail why Planet Hollywood might easily be the very worst thing in the world.

I'd banked on emerging from the Café de Paris, elegantly wasted, at around 3 a.m., but even though I was a couple of hours early Coventry Street had already gone to bed. A limo driver was polishing his windscreen; blokes with Stanley knives were kneeling in front of newsstands cutting open bundles of tomorrow's – today's – papers. People who'd drunk their fares home were queuing outside the banks down Haymarket, and for the first time I appreciated how the cashpoint has revolutionised late-night urban culture.

But every silver lining has a cloud, and of the unrightful beneficiaries of this revolution none is more disagreeably irksome than the pirate minicab. By the time I'd made it to the drunks shuffling about Eros I had already been hailed by half a dozen deftly subtle toots and whistles and small inquiring yelps, each delivered with such innocence that I was invariably lured over to see what the kerb-crawling driver wanted. Directions? The time? Hot water and towels? But no. What they always wanted, of course, was up to £50 of my money in return for a circumlocutory tour of the western suburbs in an uninsured Toyota Corolla with one headlight and a leaking sack of chickpeas on the back seat. If I had – let's see – shaved the head of every driver who beckoned me in this infuriating fashion in the ensuing weeks I could have, I don't know, made St Paul's a wig.

The pace picked up as the street flared out into Piccadilly Circus. As I fumbled and flapped my notebook into a pocket a cocky gaggle of Asian girls passed. 'Working at this time of night?' chirped the nearest, and though it didn't seem a devastating one-liner they all giggled like Barbara Windsor. I nodded indulgently; a second wind was blowing me towards the neon signs.

Though I shouldn't really have dawdled at Piccadilly Circus, a separate entity to Piccadilly and strictly speaking peripheral to my journey, it seemed the best bet for some night-on-the-tiles action. A bloke in a Huggy Bear hat was sidling up to passers-by and hissing a suggestion their reactions betrayed as comically risqué, and while wondering if I wanted to hear what it was two beardily Orwellian men of the road, one with bare and blackened feet, invited me to share a bottle that had at some earlier stage in its life contained Lilt. 'Go on, you handsome devil,' drawled the one with shoes on, winking laboriously. And yet even as I backed swiftly away towards the buffed and bleached French Renaissance edifice of the Criterion theatre and restaurant, it was already becoming clear that the Piccadilly Circus of today no longer offered the reckless revelry which once defined it.

'Man and girl begin to undress in front of Eros statue, man has taken off his shirt and girl pulled up dress when police stop them,' wrote a thwarted Mass Observer on that night in 1937; later on, surrendering to a boisterous crowd, a policeman with a megaphone shouted, 'Ladies and gentlemen, the Circus is yours.' Despite being relentlessly circled by buses and Bentleys – these days it's only half a roundabout – Eros was where you went by day for a bunch of roses from the famously grumpy old flower sellers, and by night for the company of the more accommodating women who made Piccadilly Circus a focal point of pre-war London whoredom. 'THE CENTRE OF THE WORLD' screamed the banner slung across the London Pavilion, taking its cue from the only slightly less ambitious slogans flashing around it.

'A monstrous exhibition of vulgarity,' scolded the *Architects' Journal* in 1924 with reference to the circus, 'yet country cousins come and gawp with astonishment and even admiration at this degrading spectacle.' Our friend Harold Clunn was no less strident ten years later: 'A reproach to the metropolis,' he called it, 'which would not be tolerated, for instance, in Berlin.' Anything that's not tolerated in Berlin, you might think – especially in the 1930s – has got to be worth encouraging. Particularly because the phenomenon under discussion was not compulsory public masturbation or pro-celebrity badger baiting, but illuminated advertisements.

The first electrically lit hoardings appeared in Piccadilly Circus in 1893, and by the time neon arrived in the thirties, almost every edifice around its circumference was already plastered ground to rafters with slogans and logos. 'For your throat's sake smoke Craven A'; 'Persil oxygen eats up the dirt' – you could say what you wanted, and say it wherever you wanted to. It wasn't just Piccadilly Circus: every major London thoroughfare hosted an unruly jostle of billboards and hoardings; every bus bristled with strident slogans. Look into the capital's heavens on any clear and calm summer's day in the thirties and you'd be presented with the fluffy evidence of the sky-writer's art. One Old Kent Roader recalled a squadron of biplanes tagging the entire south London firmament with a chain of mile-wide OXOs.

Most creative energy, though, went into the promotion of health and hygiene. The discovery of vitamins in 1912 had kick-started an industry founded on the public's hope that all manner of conditions could be remedied by a pill or tonic, particularly as this presented an economic alternative to the often prohibitive cost of healthcare in the pre-NHS era (it's no accident that half the Community Chest penalties are related to medical bills). When you wanted to shift laxative pills in the twenties, you stuck your brand-name under the slogan 'Civilisation's curse can be conquered'; Horlicks wasn't just a nice bedtime drink but a cure for 'night starvation'. The genre reached its joyous zenith with a campaign for Scott's loo paper: concerned surgeons bend over a patient on the operating table above the catchline '. . . *and the trouble began with harsh toilet tissue*'.

By the thirties this medical paranoia had evolved into a rather dubious Nazi-style obsession with national wholesomeness. In 1936 the King and Queen attended a huge Festival of Youth at Wembley, watching massed displays by the Women's League of Health and Beauty and thirty other hiking, cycling and gymnastic organisations. *The Times* correspondent all but burst into a chorus of 'Tomorrow Belongs To Me'. 'The young people were clad as for the day,' he frothed, 'and in their flimsy array they marched forth to greet the sun and to gambol in its radiance.' It could so easily have led to a ruthlessly inhuman quest for a British master race, but in the event we got the Community Chest beauty contest and a complex about personal hygiene. In common with Elvis and my parents, the phrase 'BO' is the same age as Monopoly, coined in a campaign to promote Lifebuoy soap. 'Why is he always alone?' hissed a snide billboard for Listerine, before answering its own question: 'HALITOSIS IS RUINING HIS CAREER.'

No one seemed to mind any of this, but what they did mind was neon illumination. 'Evil red and blue . . . a frightful corpselight,' shuddered George Orwell; Harold Clunn pompously decried neon's vanguard role in 'the uglification of the Capital of the Empire'. Well, you can call me a country cousin if you like, but I love neon adverts. In my ideal urban residence there would be at least one room ethereally lit by a restless animated slogan flashing and buzzing outside the window.

There is something childishly appealing about those luridly over-coloured sixties postcards of Piccadilly Circus, the painfully yellow Wrigley's Juicy Fruit arrow, the gaudy striptease of those disappearing wavy Coke lines. Whenever we had foreign visitors my father used to drive them up to town for an after-dark sightseeing trip, and I always went along for Piccadilly Circus and those great walls of colour. It was like being in the title credits for the sort of film which would end with a blearily smiling dollybird slowly disappearing down a cobbled mews on the back of a milk float. It was a part of Swinging London that still swung.

Looking up and about me at the large, dark gaps in what used to be a glorious arena of light, it was clear that if Messrs Orwell and Clunn were around today they'd have to go spleen-venting elsewhere. There was a glib McDonald's arch, a half-hearted Coke roundel and the pixellated simulacrum of Martin Clunes puckering horribly up to a cup of Nescafé. The electric tickertape that had enthralled the crowd on Mass Observation day had been superseded by a puny digital readout so transfixed by the temperature in Caracas that it couldn't talk about anything else. And that was it.

Piccadilly Circus at night used to be like standing inside a giant pinball machine with three balls on the go and Roger Daltrey battering the flippers. Now it's like watching a kid over the road turn his PlayStation on. More than anywhere else in London, Piccadilly Circus represented the boisterous commercialised may-hem that was and still is the capital's defining feature – cluttered, unplanned, perhaps slightly seedy, but as unavoidably alluring as a free funfair. It brought out the country cousin in all of us.

It's all rather a shame. People – tourists or anyone else – come to Piccadilly Circus to stand dwarfed beneath buzzing towers of electrically charged gas, their faces lit by glowing molecules and childish glee. Without the gaudy vigour, the place has no unique selling point. Like the Criterion's, the Trocadero's stuccoed exterior has been stripped of hoardings and banners, but if people want to see a nice clean building with columns on the front, they can walk down the road and check out Buckingham Palace. I can only supposed it's all to do with this Florentine-style piazza fixation, the concept that anything that brash, that flash is by definition an offence against . . . well, against what, precisely? Let's get this straight: the Trocadero does not house a museum of rare antiquities, or a children's hospice, or the tomb of Queen Victoria.

No. The Trocadero houses Madame Tussaud's Rock Circus.

'I'll fuck you over! BASTARD!'

When you're alone after midnight there's nothing worse than hearing precisely that sort of terrible bellow slur raggedly out behind you. On the other hand, when you hazard a nervy half-glance backwards and note that it is being directed up at the digitised leer of Martin Clunes, there's nothing better. I had a look up at the illuminated billboard, and was certain I saw that famously fleshy lower lip jabber with poorly restrained fury and frustration. Clunes was taking it, but he couldn't dish it out.

'You want a real fucking up? I'll fucking fuck you up!'

The relevant orator was clearly a straggler from an after-office drink that had taken a drastic wrong turn, his untucked shirt flapping beneath unbuttoned jacket, tie at half-mast. He was red of hair, redder of face, with an empty pint glass in one fist and an abused McDonald's bag in the other. Hardly a figure to arouse the envy of fellow pedestrians, but watching his right foot comfortably fail to connect with a litter bin I knew that here was a man doing what I should have been, the roaring drunk's roaring drunk, off on a solo debauch. It was nearly 2 o'clock and I'd managed a single glass of champagne; time, perhaps, to accept that I might have paced myself a little too conservatively. In sadly muted homage I flicked a quick V sign at Martin Clunes and undid the top button of my shirt.

'Men Behaving . . . FUCKLY!'

I could still hear him at it as I set off into the classy darkness of Piccadilly. Before me the facing ranks of regal buildings – the Deco might of Simpson's, the balconied magnificence of the Meridien Hotel – tapered distantly to a point a mile away. Any road in London that for more than 200 yards resists the temptation to flail about like a tortured earthworm is very likely Roman; Piccadilly did indeed once resound to the massed slap of sandal on flagstone as legionaries set off towards the road's far-flung terminus, possibly muttering to each other 'Silchester?'.

The one-way stream of taxis speeding towards me out of the gloom somehow suggested that everyone else was heading to the light at the end of the tunnel whereas I was off to, well, to Silchester, but having experienced the empty and emasculated thrills of the Circus I knew the tunnel would be more fun than the light. Besides, I've always held a torch for Piccadilly. I think it's the name more than anything. Just as Coventry Street and Leicester Square both slump from the lips with as much élan as anywhere inadvertently twinned with a decaying centre of Midlands industry, so Piccadilly sparks excitingly off the tongue like space dust. It is at once urbane and inane; so suave, yet so silly.

If you don't know how it got the name, don't waste your time guessing. What happened was that in the early seventeenth century the land near what is now the Circus was bought and developed by a tailor who had made a fortune from the manufacture of pickadills – spiked metal collars employed to support the elaborate ruffs popular at the time. See what I mean? It's like a risibly transparent false definition in *Call My Bluff*.

As the fields along the ancient road disappeared beneath grand mansions, so repeated attempts were made to endow the street with a more appropriately stately name. For a few years it was Portugal Street, honouring the nationality of Charles II's missus, but Piccadilly was just too good to waste and by the end of the eighteenth century it had stuck fast. Dozens of dukes and earls built or acquired large and plush residences all the way up to Hyde Park Corner – for a hundred years until the 1850s, Piccadilly was the grandest address in London.

It hasn't slipped far. Distanced from the slums and rookeries gathered around and within the City's square mile, Piccadilly was able to avoid the fate of Leicester Square. It was bordered by royal Green Park; the air was clean – the nobs stayed put. Even when shopkeepers inevitably moved in, they were of the fancier variety: Swan and Edgar, the bookseller Hatchard's, Fortnum and Mason. Alight here for gilt candelabras and sugared swan beaks only, please; next stop, some bird whipping bunnies out of her chuff. Interesting, then, that less than a minute after entering Piccadilly proper I had been mistaken for a newspaper vendor and seen a tramp's penis. A blow to my preconceptions, but not a fatal one, and confident that these were exceptions to the Piccadilly rule on I strode, along broad and sparsely populated pavements, nosing into the window of J.C. Cording, tweedy shirewear kings of long standing, and getting lightly sprinkled by an unseen hand watering the Meridien Hotel's lofty window boxes.

Partly due no doubt to its unforgettably foolish name, Piccadilly's fame is global. I well remember a Soviet border guard happily trilling 'Peeka-deal-ee, Peeka-deal-ee' over mine and Birna's passports as his mate stripped bare our Saab's door panels, and when in 1992 Hasbro released European Union Monopoly, Piccadilly was one of the three streets selected for the UK's entry, along with Park Lane and Oxford Street (we made it as the red set; no prizes for guessing who got up early and laid their towels across the dark blues). Global fame attracts global companies, in particular airline offices, and, in Piccadilly's case, Japanese retailers. For a solid 100 yards the windows promised slim pickings to anyone whose shopping lists didn't feature a large plastic Boeing or spinach-flavoured lollipops.

Then came a great rush of vintage Piccadilly – the alluring old 'bachelor chambers' of Albany, through whose sentry-boxed entrance have passed men-about-town from Lord Byron to Terence Stamp; the columns and courtyards of Burlington House, last of the Piccadilly mansions and home to the Royal Academy; the somewhat overbearingly twee Burlington Arcade, its chocolate-box Regency booths gated shut at night and thronged by day with cashmere-hungry Japanese tourists and silly looking warders known unfortunately as Beadles.

It was gone 3 now. Looking ahead along the cultured frontages and the expansive pavements laid at their feet, I realised what it was that set Piccadilly apart – though so definitively British that it had been the childhood home of our present monarch, the street was also somehow uniquely Continental. Piccadilly is one of the few places in London where the hotels and shops convincingly swank it up big time, perhaps the only street built on a style and scale to warrant an Italianesque twilight promenade. Line Piccadilly with trees and you'd have a boulevard, I thought, and give me a silver-topped cane and some spats and you'd have a boulevardier. You can still feel a chipper dandy strolling down Piccadilly at night, just as you can down Pall Mall by day.

On cue a silver Aston Martin pulled up at a casino over the road and collected a towering blonde in black. As it throbbed gracefully away, four seventy-year-olds in immaculate evening dress strode merrily past with arms linked, blowing cigar smoke lustily up to the streetlights. Piccadilly's party was almost over, and though I'd predictably arrived too late to gatecrash, what a party it must have been. I wasn't nearly as surprised as I might have expected when moments later a gold-lipsticked transvestite with improbably prodigious knocker padding and a huge cold sore wiggled to a halt right in front of me.

'Happy evening,' he announced in unplaceable Eurotrash, and after a forthright wink embarked on a candid up-and-down sartorial assessment. 'Trouser . . . gay, jacket-coat . . . boring, oh, and thees, thees . . .'

With painted features puckered in a cheerily impertinent parody of disgust he waggled the luminous fingertips of one hand across his own throat area while directing his gaze at mine. He was of course passing defamatory judgement on my tie, but because those fingers occasionally waggled towards his own lower lip I felt justified in nodding with priestly concern and helpfully finishing the sentence.

'This cold sore?'

'Eh?'

'That mark on your face – the very large red one,' I said, smiling gently. After my King's Cross experience this was a mere bagatelle. He looked at me carefully, then with camp malice sparkling in his eyes opened up again.

'You are . . . coat-pizza homo-trouser man.'

For a while we stood there, toe to stiletto, jovially damning each other's appearance. Old-lady tights, old-man coat, Dana International's mum, Sacha Distel's son . . . if he remembered the word for tie I'd had it, but to his evident frustration it never came to him.

'OK, OK,' I said, holding up a stop-this-nonsense hand, then pressing it against my chest. 'Handsome devil,' I concluded, before boldly transferring the hand to the yielding mass of his chest. 'Spot-face lady-boy.' I tried to walk past but he was never going to let me have the last word.

'Is very ugly,' he barked. 'Next!' And after a winsome pout he poked a tongue through those gold lips and wiggled off.

Oddly delighted to be playing even a bit part in this peculiar late-night production, I marched smartly on with a wide smile. Something important had happened: I was getting a funny feeling inside of me, just walking up and down. And yet though this was London, at the same time it was not London as I knew it. It was somehow like being on holiday. Striding past the shambolic Iran Air offices, clearly feeling the effects of that *fatwah* on office cleaners, I wasn't even troubled to glance across at the Ritz's invitingly fairy-lit Frenchiness and ponder that I still had – let's see – three and a half hours to kill before they'd let me in for breakfast.

Past the Ritz everything got quieter: I was into that short hour of sleep London snatches between the departure of those who keep the city up past its bedtime and the arrival of those waking it for the new day. But then from here down to Hyde Park Corner, Piccadilly was traditionally seen but not heard, Green Park and its distantly bleating sheep backing one pavement and aristocratic residences set regally back from the other.

The Piccadilly palaces held out longer than most. Last to go was Devonshire House, the opulent ducal residence where the fêted Georgiana entertained Charles James Fox and the Prince of Wales, where later Dickens performed comedies for Queen Victoria, where footmen with solid silver epaulettes ferried guests through the gates. Looking up at the Devonshire House that replaced it in 1921 I surveyed what Harold Clunn described as 'a very stately edifice built in the American style . . . and erected in the record time of less than two years'.

I think Harold's praise damns this structure more effectively than any criticism. I promise not to do this too often – try to mourn the loss of every fine old building in London and you'll end up with a loyalty card at Sackcloth Supplies – but there is something particularly poignant about this case.

No one's crying for the Duke of Devonshire – he flogged the place to the developers for £1 million, enough in 1921 not just to keep the wolf from the door, but to have the hapless beast dragged howling over a distant horizon by his tail. It isn't even that the old Devonshire House could have been preserved as another Royal Academy or museum or something – although of course it could have – or even that the new Devonshire House is in any way evil or hideous. Actually, it's just boring: a car showroom with what looks like a six-floor telephone exchange on top. It adds nothing to London, but doesn't in itself take much away.

What upset me was a photograph I'd seen of the old mansion in mid-demolition. Partly because of the rubble chute smashed so eagerly through its two-hundred-year-old portico, but mainly because of the proud hoarding that informed passers-by of the 'MAGNIFICENT building to be erected on this site – SHOPS, RESTAURANTS AND FLATS'. I read that and thought: they really didn't have a clue.

From just before Monopoly's birthday until the game was almost old enough to blag early retirement, a lot of important people in London allowed some extraordinarily wrongheaded things to occur. How could anyone genuinely have imagined the new Devonshire House would be an improvement on the old? And yet they clearly did – why else keep the same name? Out with the old, in with the new: that was all that mattered. Everything had been happening so fast up to the thirties – Londoners who were born into a horse-drawn city without electricity or telephones or automatic doors on the Tube were now utterly in the thrall of technology and whatever might be considered progress. There was a genuine feeling that machines were helping mankind build a Utopia, and if the new Devonshire House had lifts and entryphones and car showrooms on the ground floor then the destruction of its predecessor represented a bold step in the right direction. Greed and incompetence were unfortunate enough, but there was something particularly heartbreaking about this catastrophically misjudged idealism.

Over the road and behind the magnificent gates that are all that remain of the old Devonshire House, Green Park looked dark and haunted, and the grand buildings further along – most notably the famous headquarters of the club familiarly known after the directions on its driveway gateposts as the In and Out – were unaccountably abandoned and in a state of what you might call cultivated neglect. The next day I discovered that the mothballed In and Out and its broken-windowed neighbours were acquired in 2000 for £50 million by an obscure Syrian with even obscurer motives: facts that demand an outburst, if only I hadn't just finished one.

The road splayed into a four-laner, then a sixer, with the two in the middle diving beneath Hyde Park Corner. Old man Clunn had got his way, and thus Piccadilly died away into gyratory desolation. It was no place for boulevardiers. No place for anyone, in fact, except perhaps traction-engine drivers looking for somewhere to do a U-turn. An owl hooted from over in Hyde Park; a rustle alerted me to a subway entrance where a homeless sleeper lay, perilously mummified in plastic sheeting like a pod in *Invasion of the Bodysnatchers*. I turned and, I'm afraid, ran.

It was unfair to expect that pizza slice – which, let's face it, had already done a lot of work – to cope with this level of enhanced activity, and slowing to a shuffle back up Piccadilly I started to feel as if my body might have started feeding off its own muscle tissue. But dawn was at last hesitantly poking up at the corners of Green Park, and there were more people about: orange-jacketed Tube workers trooping down the station stairs; a man with a 5-litre bucket of B&Q emulsion beside him propping up a bus stop. It was a rare and rewarding insight into the oddness of other people's daily routines – rare because I now realised I'd never once been up in the centre of town at this time, and rewarding because I wouldn't have to ever again. At least not for another four chapters.

Focusing laboriously on my watch I saw that I was still an hour and a half early; there was nothing to do but keep walking, back up the other side of the street to the Circus. Past Egyptian Hall, now that nation's tourist office but in an earlier incarnation an extra-ordinarily eccentric palace of entertainment where mountaineers recreated the ascent of Mont Blanc and 800,000 Londoners filed in to see Napoleon's state coach. More of those irksome, dull and obscure commercial amalgamations – SalomonSmithBarney; HDP International; the Bond-villainesque Corporate Executive Board – in Edwardian blocks that once accommodated the National Sulphuric Acid Association, ladies' blouse maker Mrs Rosa Kennard, Titanine Aeroplane Dope and John Robertson & Son whisky merchants. What an office party they'd have thrown at Christmas (best go easy on the punch, though).

But the further I walked up Piccadilly, the more its commercial past and present converged. An ancient chemist's shop the size of a washbag had its walls stacked floor to ceiling with Resolve and Timotei and anything else you'd find at Superdrug, along with plenty you wouldn't: pomades, natural sponges, even an 'engraving service on brushes'. The black, bow-fronted windows of Hatchard's look as if they'd be happier stocked with pickadills, and the staff of my favourite London bookshop retain a similarly old-fashioned sense of customer service: they always know what they're talking about, and more crucially what you're talking about.

Hatchard's has been in Piccadilly for two hundred years, and Fortnum and Mason for almost a hundred more. Both seemed winningly reluctant to embrace unappealing commercial developments that may have taken place in the interim: I'm delighted, for instance, that neither is willing to open beyond 6.30, which frankly is as late as anyone should be out shopping for anything except drugs, sex or diesel.

I've probably got a few Christmases left before glacé fruit starts creeping on to my present wish-list, but even so there's something undeniably delightful about Fortnum's, an establishment which has cultivated its Regency air so successfully that I was astonished to discover the present building dates only from the mid-twenties, and that the quaint little mechanical models of Mr Fortnum and Mr Mason who on the hour turn to each other above the entrance and bow or faint or drop their trousers or something were in fact slightly younger than me.

Nosing up to one of the store's dramatically downlit displays I decided it was somehow reassuring that even in the twenty-first century someone was being employed to design and painstakingly assemble a tiny scale model of the Potala Palace in Lhasa, encrusting it with lychees and tinned wild asparagus tips in extra virgin olive oil before balancing the whole ensemble on a stuffed camel's back in a shop window. In an only slightly ridiculous way it seemed a fitting memorial to all London's absent craftspeople, the cobblers and seamstresses and portmanteau makers who only a generation ago, even along Piccadilly, had hammered and hummed and stitched a living.

Under more favourable circumstances I would have maintained my detailed vigil, dutifully checking each building against my 1933 directory. As it was, having passed my third Starbucks in apparently as many minutes I switched the camera in my brain from high-resolution video mode to grainy screen grabs. I forgot to check out Lord Peter Wimsey's hypothetical residence at 110A; similarly overlooked was 145, the Duke of York's home when in 1936 he was declared Britain's third king in a year, and where Princesses Elizabeth and Margaret were raised and educated. I snagged my hair in the wisteria recklessly tumbling down from the gardens around St James's Church, Piccadilly's oldest building ('beautiful and convenient' to its architect, the usually modest Christopher Wren; 'rather ugly' to Harold Clunn), and gawped blankly at the dawn workers trundling purposefully about the Circus and Leicester Square like after-hour functionaries at a theme park: men in overalls with spirit levels over their shoulders; bouncers sweeping up rustling mountains of club flyers; phone-box disinfectors sluicing away the tramp juice.

The taxis all had their orange lights on now, driven by men who had made the trade-off: less traffic on the back roads, more vomit on the back seat. Their targets were the knots of hardcore revellers, still getting cheeky with seen-it-all sergeants, still yabbering to commendably tolerant friends on their mobiles: this was Friday morning, for heaven's sakes, and it wasn't even 6 a.m.

'*Big Issue*,' sang a cheery young crusty as I headed back for the Ritz. 'Only a quid with two free staples!' I turned towards him; he scanned me up and down – trenchcoat, notebook and all – and his face went south. 'You a . . . *copper*?' he whispered in horror, answering the question himself by wheeling away up Regent Street. From Groovy Dad finalist at the school disco to hard-faced beggar-beater in two short years: how cruel one's mid-thirties can be.

If only he'd seen me an hour later, unshaven and haggard and blinking under the Ritz chandeliers, street-soiled mac buttoned up to my neck. In 1938 a hundred unemployed protestors invaded the Ritz's grill room and demanded tea; I hoped they were ready for a one-man reconstruction. 'Are you sure you don't want me to check that in for you?' asked Ian after he'd established it really was me, but aware that the coat's subsequent retrieval from some lickspittle bellboy in a pillbox hat would set me back rather more than its value I dully shook my head.

One such jockey-sized sneerer strutted past our table, and as he did so I caught sight of us in one of the many mirrored panels arranged along the dining room's towering marbled flanks. Ian was the immaculate but eccentric philanthropist; I the overawed God-bless-yer bench-dweller he'd taken pity upon during his morning constitutional through Green Park. 'You're a true gent, so you are, governor,' I croaked as my £20.50 plate of eggs on toast was laid silently before me. And he was as well. I've just realised I never even offered to pay.

Around us early-bird businessmen loudly caught their worms as pinafored maids criss-crossed bearing salvers of melon balls and flowers so aggressively colourful they looked plastic. 'Fourth quarter's looking pretty fruity,' bellowed the power-breakfasting pinstripe alongside us. 'Yuh, well, I guess you could say we've got an allergy to tax,' came the smugly drawled reply.

'This is a favourite place for head-hunters,' said Ian, and he nodded towards a slightly less appalling pair conniving over their kedgeree. 'They come here before work for shady little meetings.'

Where were all the hungover Hanovers, the puppy-pampering prima donnas, the wayward Waddington womanisers? Had the Ritz, too, capitulated so totally to the character-corroding bland-nesses of the corporate dollar? But my higher functions were shutting down one by one, and conversational output was now available only via an intermittent read-only memory. 'Opened in 1906, the Ritz is the oldest steel-framed building in Britain,' I mumbled, wordlessly upending Ian's leftover salmon into the plate-space recently vacated by my eggs, 'and it was opened in 1906.'

As a man whose considerable business success can at least be partly attributed to never, ever going to sleep, Ian might at this point have felt justified in picking up the vase on our table and introducing its contents to my sallow, stubbled face. Instead he nodded kindly, and, accepting the time for talk was at an end, bent down to withdraw something of mine from his briefcase, something that due to the incompatibility of angular backpacks and nights on the town I had been unwilling to burden myself with.

As discreetly as was possible on a small table crowded with polished and starched dining accessories and any tiny particles of food I had omitted to cram into my filthy gullet, he laid the board flat, placed my motor on Piccadilly and proffered the dice. I shrugged and flicked a tired and bloated gesture of concession.

'I'll roll,' he said with an understanding nod. It was a four. Toc-toc-toc-toc. Community Chest.

'No cards,' I muttered.

He held an index finger aloft, raised his eyebrows and bent back down towards his briefcase. 'Cards,' he said, holding a pink pack towards me. 'I thought I'd bring everything along just in case.' There was a pause while I dozily updated my mental checklist of secrets for business success: 1) Don't sleep. (1.1) Bring everything along just in case. Oh, and (1.2) less egg and pizza on tie. In fact (1.3) new tie.

I took the top card, and seeing the bars didn't need to read it. But Ian did anyway. 'Go To Jail,' he said, loudly enough to shut up our horrid neighbours in mid-bray. 'Move directly to jail, do not p—'

'Wait!' I barked, shocked into action. 'I wasn't on Piccadilly. I was on Leicester Square.'

Ian's thwarted glower did not last long. 'Leicester Square, yeah?' Toc-toc-toc-toc, all the way to the finger-raised cop.

CHAPTER 7

Go To Jail

'Timothy Sebastian Perris Moore, sir!'

When a man whose uniform is accessorised by a medievally proportioned bunch of keys asks your name, you don't fanny about. You give him your name, your whole name, and nothing but your name, and you don't think about the consequences of its more curious components. At least not until two dozen of his surrounding colleagues are bent double, slapping hard surfaces, clutching stomachs and exhibiting other well-catalogued symptoms of advanced amusement.

'Tim . . . Moore?' I whimpered superfluously into the uproar. Four minutes into my stretch in Pentonville and the short, sharp shocks had started already.

I'd chosen Pentonville as my prison because it shared a name with a street on the board, because it was the oldest prison in London and because my neighbour Bernie's dad had worked there as a probation officer in the seventies and told me it was like

Porridge. It still is, in a way. 'A local nick for local people,' quipped the female officer who'd been nominated to show me around while her colleagues in Pentonville's Audit Unit recovered their composure. 'Eleven hundred-odd inmates, 90 per cent of them from north London. Fair number in their thirties and forties – one guy in his seventies, in here on a robbery charge. Mostly thieves and druggies.' Placed in crime's full spectrum, her indulgent tone suggested, such offenders had done no worse than roll three doubles on the trot.

We walked down some stairs and up a corridor; at the end she unlocked a huge barred gate and let it slam behind us with a great Norman Stanley Fletcher clunk. Into my nose filtered that sheltered-housing smell of reheated leftovers spiced up with a splash of TCP. Into my ears an unintelligible chorus of clinked trays and slammed gates and truncated building-site yells. Radiating around me were five passages, in which loitered dozens of men in grey sweatshirts and jogging pants. One was the spitting image of the sallow and thin-faced Monopoly-nick weasel; another had only one leg. And above me were four more floors of the same. I might be Just Visiting, but it had stopped feeling like it.

Pentonville hadn't looked like a prison from the outside. For a start it wasn't discreetly marooned amidst misty heathland as most of its institutional brethren are wont to be, even in London, but uncomfortably slotted slap between the busily bus-laned Caledonian Road and a tight grid of Victorian terraces. And there'd been graffiti on the almost decorative white wall out front, which along with a note in the car park disclaiming responsibility for loss from or damage to vehicles left there hardly suggested the slavish fixation with security that I'd idly imagined to be a prison's defining characteristic. Gazing up at the main building's stuccoed arches and pediments I was reminded of a Victorian seat of learning or provincial railway terminus. But then Pentonville was different: a Model Prison, the first in Britain whose intention was to reform its inmates.

Erected in 1842, Pentonville was a bold departure from the capital's usual filthy, raucous dungeons. For the first time prisoners were to be kept in single cells, each with a hand basin and lavatory. The cells were arranged in wings that fanned out like spokes from a central hub, within which a handful of officers could effectively monitor hundreds of inmates. It was clean and light. Within years, Pentonville was the blueprint for new prisons from Germany to Australia and the USA.

But this was 1842, remember, and the rehabilitation regime was never going to involve the construction of matchstick cathedrals or correspondence courses in O-level Spanish. Prisoners were kept in their solitary cells for twenty-three hours a day, with meals pushed through hatches. Most cells were fitted with a crank that pushed paddles through sand, a hard-labour device invented at Pentonville that produced nothing more useful than fatigued agony. A large bell announced the start and end of labour – all speech was forbidden, and officers even wore special overshoes to maintain the tomb-like silence intended to force inmates to reflect upon the error of their ways. It was soul-destroying, and it was supposed to be. Let out for their hour of fresh air, prisoners were escorted individually around by officers, and had to wear slitted, visored hoods that prevented them from seeing the face of any official or fellow inmate. In chapel they were herded into solitary boxes like veal-calf stalls. All they'd have seen during a typical eighteen-month sentence were their feet; all they'd have heard was that bell and their own breathing.

Oddly, on their day of release many prisoners seemed rather overawed by the outside world. Some whimpered for cotton wool to stop up their ears. Others were struck dumb. But the Victorians thought of everything and in 1851 opened the Middlesex County Pauper Lunatic Asylum – Europe's largest mental hospital – just up the road.

Britain still loves imprisoning its citizens. Almost 75,000 of us are inside – more, as a proportion of national population, than any EU country except Portugal (and you thought their only crime was Mateus Rosé). We're 50 per cent up on France, and a third ahead of Italy. Even Turkey and China can't match us. You can consider this a shocking blight, or as carrying on a proud tradition. At Pentonville they are of the latter school of thought.

'Look there – you can still see where the food hatches were.' We'd started our tour up on the semi-deserted 'fives' – the fifth floor – and my guide was keen to highlight any evidence of Pentonville's heritage. She didn't have to try too hard. That bell was still there by the chief warder's office. Everything was cast iron and glazed brick. In 2001 a tuberculosis outbreak affected fourteen inmates and visiting relatives. And by the phones I'd seen a Samaritans poster.

'Yeah,' she said, clanking open another of the fifty-odd gates and doors we'd pass through in the hours ahead. 'See that in there?' We were back down on the twos, passing a door with a wired-glass inspection panel. 'That's what we call The Bubble. Eight suicidals, sort of keeping an eye on each other.' Through the glass I could see the end of a bed, and on it a pair of restlessly twitching legs.

'Watch out, mate – nonce alert.' The voice came from behind, warning me of the heavily guarded group filing towards us: clad in distinctive burgundy tracksuits, a genuinely loathsome parade of every pervert cliché, from shiftily leering embodiment of human evil to slack-jawed gentle giant. What was I doing here? When I'd asked the Home Office for permission to visit Pentonville I'd expected nothing more than a ruminative stroll round the perimeter walls with a brogue-wearing architectural historian. And here I was clinging to the nylon shirt-tails of a strident Miss Mackay as she casually nodded at a confinement cell whose occupant's behavioural excesses regularly warranted the close attention of anything up to six officers. 'Sex case fruitcake,' came her blithe assessment.

'Is he board of visitors, Miss? Oi, mate, you board of visitors?'

This time I turned round, thereby breaking Bernie's dad's golden rule. 'Never catch a prisoner's eye,' were his enigmatic parting words to me, and afterwards I'd eagerly run through the hideous consequences that might have spawned this adage: nose-splitting head butts, baptism by phlegm, Romany curses. Now I was about to find out.

'No,' I croaked feebly in the direction of a youthful inmate carrying a tray with bits of stew on it. But it was too late. 'I haven't had a visit for two months,' he started as we walked up the iron stairs past another web of anti-jump netting. 'And the food's a *joke*, man. Look at this!' I supposed he was waving his tray at me but my guide had already led us away. She sucked her teeth knowingly, raised a finger in mock admonishment and as I rather thought she might said, 'Never let an inmate catch your eye.'

'They've had my phone card off me an' all!' came the distant wail before a door slammed behind us and everything went quiet.

'Are, um, drugs a problem at all?' I asked as we stamped up through the darkness to the main work hall.

'Massive. *Massive*,' she replied with feeling. 'Used to hide them up the bum' – this with a faint air of nostalgia – 'but these days it's an under-the-foreskin job. And I'm not going there.'

She glanced at me wryly and for a short but throat-punchingly vivid second seemed poised to order me to Go There, to pass the rest of the afternoon in an inspection cell with a queue of trouserless lags thrusting their unwashed loins at my Marigolds. 'Got something here, miss,' I'd announce cravenly, my voice quavering with self-disgust. Over she'd stride, before stooping down with a shake of the head and a weary tut. 'How do we distinguish cannabis resin from the by-products of physical neglect, Moore?' And with my brittle features crumpling, I'd mumble, 'Using the nose, miss.'

The work hall was a huge and dingy loft room, the kind of place where by rights an escape committee should have secreted its homemade glider. Instead it was cluttered with disordered rows of Formica tables, upon which, it was difficult not to notice as we entered, lay the recumbent forms of a great many young men in grey tracksuits. A Radio Rentals era telly displaying the silent face of Rodney Trotter dangled unwatched from the rafters.

'It's not always like this,' piped up one of the two officers seated behind a huge old desk at the front, like public school prefects monitoring detention. None of her charges reacted to her words or our presence. 'Just that we've got no work to do now.' Her colleague drew my attention to the floor, which I now noticed was liberally strewn with small foam discs. Correctly sensing that this spectacle raised many more questions than it answered, my guiding guard said, 'All the inflight headsets come here from Virgin Atlantic. The inmates take off the old ear covers and put on new ones.' She turned to the desk. 'How many d'you normally do a month?'

'Three hundred thousand. But since September 11 we're down to 80,000.'

It was oddly intriguing to discover that the next hands that would finger my foamies after I'd handed them back to the stewardess were those of a north London larcenist. 'How much do they get?' I asked soon after as we wandered past a glazed door behind which a woman in plaits was failing to keep the attention of her computer-skills class, one of whom had a towel draped over his head.

'Two fifty.'

'An hour?'

An incredulous gurn. 'A *week*.'

I was completely lost now, but at the same time becoming slightly more at home. It was somehow heartening to hear the officers address each other, tongue half in cheek, as 'Mister Harris' or 'Miss Evesham', in cosy *Porridge* fashion. I even began to strike up a rapport with my guide, who it turned out was a relative newcomer to the screw game, having been ideally groomed for the profession by spells in the Army and as a pub landlady. 'I needed a challenge,' she said, as if it had been a toss-up between learning to windsurf and physically overpowering sex case fruitcakes. 'But first time I come in here, I looked up at them five floors and thought, fuck.'

Feeling a common bond at last, we moved on to what was clearly the conversational staple for both prisoners and guards. 'Morale is absolutely godawful. The hours are ridiculous, and the money . . . d'you know we only get sixteen grand? Join the Met and you get twenty-five for doing a similar job. And everything's geared towards the inmates – say or do anything they don't like and you're up before the number-one governor for abuse or excessive force. And don't get me started on the paperwork.'

Was the discovery that prison was a bit shit really such a shocking epiphany for inmates and their guards alike? Just as Bernie's dad had tried to warn me about one side of this equation, so my friend Ian had alerted me to the other. He'd done some research on prisons and had been appalled at the absenteeism rate: the average prison officer takes three weeks off sick every year.

We went outside and, shadowed between the perimeter walls and the warehouse cages of A wing, I managed to get her talking about something else. 'Yeah, we've had the odd escape. Got an E-man now who's always at it – he just tried to get a pass out to his mum's funeral. Checked it out and she died three years ago. Now, if you ever saw a prisoner in this area . . .' – we were now at the foot of a huge, white wall topped with razor wire – 'the shit would really hit the fan.'

Men were ambling about the exercise yard – it was only 11.40 and they'd already had lunch – and I passed close enough to the wire to hear one mumble to another, 'Just hitch a caravan on the back and you're away.' I was still contemplating the possible criminal implications of this comment when we rounded the corner and were presented by a square of lovingly tended lawn framed by neat flower beds.

'The prisoners' garden?'

'You could say that, I suppose, because it's actually where, um . . .' She tailed off, and instinctively I understood. Here before us, beneath this turfed patch smaller than a suburban back yard, lay – or, more likely given its modest dimensions, stood – the bodies of 120 executed criminals. I suppose my expression must have given it away. 'It's not something you really want to gossip about when you work here,' she said, closing the discussion and leading us back indoors.

But I'm afraid I'd wanted to linger. If there was one thing that set the Monopoly era's penal system apart from today's, it wasn't the cat or the crank or the birch but the death penalty. After the infamous Newgate Prison was demolished in 1902 its gallows were removed to Pentonville: 'The finest scaffold in the whole country,' reminisced their regular operator Harry Pierrepoint, 'being fitted to hang three persons side by side.' Thereafter the model prison that had been designed as the bold new face of criminal correction became the capital's capital punishment capital.

More criminals were executed at Pentonville in the twentieth century than at any other British prison. Doctor Hawley Harvey Crippen lay under that lawn, buried along with a photograph of the mistress he had quicklimed his wife for, and the serial necrophile John Reginald Halliday Christie, and umpteen notorious others I seem to know slightly too much about. (A particularly disquieting revelation was that when the police finally apprehended Christie he gave his name as – help me, Mummy – John Waddington.) There were six German spies, and a handful of Great War traitors. For sixteen years until their exhumation the lawn had covered the bones of Timothy Evans, whose execution for two murders later attributed to Christie led to a posthumous pardon and ultimately won the argument for the abolitionists.

By the thirties few British prisons had a permanent scaffold, but Pentonville was happy to help out with a gallows-to-go delivery service. Its proximity to the unrivalled transport connections of King's Cross made Pentonville the natural choice to hold the 'hanging kit' that was sent by train around the country to facilitate provincial death sentences: despatched along with the flat-pack gallows was an 'execution box' containing two ropes (one new; one used), a white hood and straps to pinion the . . . the, er . . . it's difficult not to say 'victim', really. Just as it's easy to imagine why Pentonville's staff and prisoners would rather not dwell on that corner by the north-eastern wall and its 120 dead lifers. A hundred and twenty people who had been killed for killing perhaps 150 more – that's an awful lot of bad karma for one lawn. It was too much to take in then and it still is now.

The last execution at Pentonville took place on 6 July 1961; the old condemned cell, where Crippen and Christie and all spent their final hours, was later converted, Bernie's father had bitterly informed me, into the probation officers' staff room. But Britain's last set of working gallows, over the Thames at Wandsworth, wasn't dismantled until 1995.

'Next time, Mr Moore, bring some ID with you and I won't have to ask about your . . . Sebastian Paris.' I was back in the Audit Unit with the bullet-headed Mitchell brother who had signed me in, and what should have been an exchange of parting pleasantries had taken on the air of an ill-tempered parole-board interview.

'Next time? Not at my age,' I mumbled dismissively.

I'd noted during our earlier encounter that he was the sort of man you wouldn't want to see angry, and now he was angry.

'You'd be surprised, Mr Moore,' came the coldly ominous reply; then, horribly, its deliverer stood up behind his desk and jabbed the small space between our faces with a Prison Service Biro. 'Now you've seen it, let's hope you won't be back.'

I walked out into Caledonian Road feeling hollow and harrowed. It had been my intention to amble about the neighbourhood, putting the prison into the context of its uncomfortably close urban surroundings. But then it had also been my intention to get the board out and jovially inveigle an officer into having three shots at throwing a double. Instead I marched very briskly into the nearby train station without once looking back. In a thirties' London jail there were degrees of punishment: hard labour, the birch, being hung by the neck until you were dead. It was good that these were things of the past. Now all we had was degrees of time – how much you did depended on what you'd done. It occurred to me as I sat on a damp platform bench that in spending even half a morning in prison I had just experienced the very worst punishment that society can now inflict on its members. And then, shocked at how quickly I'd been infected by all that whining self-pity, I whipped the board out on to the bench, clacked my car discourteously over the prisoner's face and rolled. 'Double three!' I yelped, not at that stage having noticed the young mother piloting a pushchair past me. It was a proper Monopoly break-out.

CHAPTER 8

The Oranges

BOW ST
CITY OF WESTMINSTER

MARLBOROUGH ST
CITY OF WESTMINSTER

VINE ST
CITY OF WESTMINSTER

Ask a Monopoly player for his favourite set and he'll say, 'Well, the Mayfair one.' Ask a *serious* Monopoly player for his favourite set and he'll say, 'Get away from my title deeds! Away! Cheat! Rent! Mum!' But soon afterwards, when he's pinioned under your knees having houses stuffed up his nose, he'll reluctantly splutter, 'The oranges.' He'll never tell you why, though, not even when with a coldly vicious *Weiss Engel* gleam in your eye you convey a hotel slowly towards his left nostril. So I will.

That there exists a handsome overlap between Monopoly obsessives and modem-married statistical analysts should come as no surprise. I am particularly indebted to a man who identified himself only as 'Chris' for the website in which he dissects in more detail than one might have thought feasible the bounteous data generated by his computer model of a 250-turn game of Monopoly.

By individual location, Jail is by far and away the most

commonly landed-upon square, claiming four times as many victims as any other on the board; as Chris himself explains, this is due to 'the number of mechanisms by which a player can end up there: Go To Jail, Chance and Community Chest cards, and rolling three doubles in a row in addition to simply landing on "Just Visiting"'. One consequence of what I'm sure he'd be happy to hear dubbed The Chris Paradigm is that – and here I'll have to refer you to the previous discussion of dice-digit probabilities – as I had just myself experienced the oranges are the set you're most likely to see your token come to rest upon. So often will people land there, in fact, that despite Vine Street's hotel bill being half Mayfair's, a fully loaded orange set will on average bag £24,619 in a game, compared to £14,835 for the dark blues. And because I can hear someone – perhaps even Chris himself – muttering that for a fair comparison one should pit another three-property set against it, even the fabled greens don't come close, netting just over twenty grand. Additionally, if I may be briefly permitted to out-Chris Chris, this takes no account of comparative development costs: £100 a house for the oranges; £200 for the greens.

(It isn't strictly relevant, but you might like to know that Chris's rundown of set desirability is as follows: orange, red, yellow, green, dark blue, purple, light blue, stations, brown. He has particularly harsh words for the utilities, which between them can expect to yield an insulting £625 over the course of a game. 'As a digression, we might question whether, in this context, they make a valuable addition to the game' is his shockingly heretical verdict. As another digression, Chris, what would you replace them with? What's that? Well, sweet of you to offer, Chris, but perhaps that remarkable archive of powerful adult imagery is best left on your hard drive.)

But the oranges aren't just deceptively unbeatable. They're also unbeatably deceptive. There is, for instance, no such address as Marlborough Street in central London, unless one bothers with an inconsequential alley in South Kensington, which one doesn't. Bow Street we know – round the back of Covent Garden, home of the famous Runners, London's first crime-fighting force. But Vine Street? Three are listed in the central area, all of a dimensional stature one might justifiably dismiss as poxy. And though all the other colour groups on the board share a bond of location or – in the case of the browns – knees-up gorblimeyness, no combination of the aforementioned orange possibilities seemed to turn on any lights.

It's always slightly bothered me. Only when I sat down and stared at the board for so long that the man in Jail's mouth started moving did I get it. Bow Street was the key. It wasn't Marlborough Street, but *Great* Marlborough Street (the first London *A–Z* might have appeared the same year as Monopoly, epically compiled on foot by unsung cartographic heroine Phyllis Pearsall, but Vic and Marge certainly didn't bother checking their choices against the index). And recalling endless Newsroom SouthEast reports on pickpocket gangs, I suddenly knew which was the right Vine Street.

Though it didn't help to explain Vic and Marge's motives – the Atlantic City equivalents, St James Place, Tennessee Avenue and New York Avenue, were as blandly random as any other set on the US board – what linked the oranges was The Law. The Bow Street Runners. Marlborough Street Magistrates Court. Vine Street Police Station. I'd done it the wrong way round. Having done the time, I was now off to do the crime.

Named after its shape, Bow Street merits a low score on the 'now-there's-a-thing' originometer, but in fact grabs a couple of bonus points by being no such shape. Bow Street is about as much of a bow as a piece of All-Bran, and not much longer. Because it was sunny I'd gone up to town on my bike, and it took less than forty seconds to freewheel down it.

Following the now familiar pattern, Bow Street was knocked up in the mid-seventeenth century as lodgings for the rich and famous – the fêted woodcarver Grinling Gibbons lived here – before succumbing to darker temptations. By the 1740s eight pubs were somehow squeezed into it, along with a number of notoriously outré brothels. Years before you could get arrested in Bow Street it was certainly the place to go if you fancied being picked up by the fuzz.

Edmund Curll, fondly described as 'the father of English pornographic publishing', was living at No. 2 when in 1719 he made his name with a translation of the definitive German treatise *The Use of Flogging in Venereal Affairs*. Having tolerated Curll for five years, in 1724 the authorities took exception to *The Nun in Her Smock*, this time a French original. No doubt hoping for the cat o' nine tails but instead sentenced to an hour in the stocks, he imaginatively saved himself a pasting by winning over the tomato-toters with complimentary copies of some of his earlier publications. 'The Unspeakable Curll' was still at it in his early seventies, when to celebrate publication of *The Pleasures of Coition* in 1745 he was discovered 'laying three in a bed at the Pewter Platter Inn'.

Something clearly had to be done about Bow Street, and in the early 1750s the remarkable Henry Fielding – already an acclaimed novelist and playwright – did it by founding the red-coated Runners. No one seems quite certain why they were called that, but it's my guess that as for the first twenty-odd years there were only half a dozen of the poor saps they'd have needed a Benny Hill turn of speed at the very least. Clearly overawed by the magnitude of their task, it's not surprising that having failed to beat the thieves they joined them. So corrupt and dishonest did the Runners become that it took years for their eventual successors, Peel's bobbies, to gain the public's confidence: in 1832 a coroner's jury returned a verdict of justifiable homicide after an unarmed constable was fatally knifed.

I locked the bike up outside the magistrates' court and walked up and down, mainly down, though, because like so many

London roads Bow Street slopes towards the Thames. In the thirties Bow Street was very much a part of Covent Garden Market, where little had changed since the Artful Dodger's days: stout ladies in crumpled old hats sitting outside shelling peas into enamel basins on their knees; a thousand porters with baskets on their heads; horses all over the place. The Foreign Fruit Market opened on to Bow Street and people would still come, as Charles Dickens had, to gawp at the pineapples. Top bananas Fyffes were based in the street, along with eight other exotic fruit brokers and salesmen: three pubs, a couple of banks, cop shop and courtroom – that was your lot.

The pubs remain, two of them – the Globe Tavern and the Marquis of Anglesey – still under the same signs. But the fruiteries have long gone, relocated south of the river with the rest of the market in 1974, and as elsewhere in the locale the restaurants and advertising agencies have moved in. Hilton & Hooper banana importers had given way to Pizza Express and Amalgamated Fruiterers to a many-named operation subtitled Brand Response. Every other passer-by was blethering conspicuously into a hands-free mobile – not, as first it seems, talking to themselves, but certainly talking about themselves. A black-glass Range Rover with the registration '50HO' throbbed by, tailed closely by a menopausal media male on his over-polished Harley-Davidson. All that was left of the old days was the terrific end flank of the Foreign Fruit Market, supporting the foyer of the new Royal Opera House extension like a towering glass and cast-iron Victorian bookend.

Something looked wrong with the grand old police station – which by the thirties had been 'the principal Metropolitan station' for over a century – and as I strolled up to the door I saw what it was. 'CLOSED FOR USUAL POLICE BUSINESS' read a typically tortuous notice affixed to the sturdy panelling. At first reading this seemed to imply that within police were carrying on their usual business, isolated at last from the irksome and sometimes distressing outside world. Then I noticed that all the windows were filthy and that the door had clearly not been opened for many months; presumably the historic station, in common with so many buildings further down the street, would soon be framed in scaffolding and internally gutted for more lucrative commercial use. On this basis, 'CLOSED' would have sufficed, but for an organisation that thrives on lexical overload – how the police must cherish those endless reiterations on the Go To Jail card – this wouldn't have done at all. I wondered if anyone, delighted at last to find a station that so nobly declared itself open for unusual police business, had hammered on the door demanding a topless tug-of-war or a piggyback.

It was a shame about the police station – surveying it from across the street I was reminded of those photographs of a forlorn Devonshire House awaiting demolition – but the magistrates' court next door was what I'd really come for and it was still doing its stuff. A security guard passed all my possessions through an x-ray scanner – the Monopoly board caused him slight but excusable consternation, though not as much as my explanation of its purpose – before directing me to court number 1, where I gathered the only action of the afternoon was taking place.

Number 1 court was packed floor to ceiling with morocco-spined works of legal reference, volumes of the sort I'd seen a trio of bamboozled west London magistrates riffle through when Birna successfully smart-talked her way off a TV-licence rap with the old 'portable monochrome set powered by its own internal batteries' loophole gambit. The magistrate – there was only the one, which surprised me as I thought like drunk footballers they always went around in threes – wore half-moon specs and sat in a high-backed red-leather chair. He was talking, but, from behind the glass screen that gives spectators something to lean against when they're carving 'AFC' on the seat next to them, I couldn't hear a word.

'What's he on about?' I hissed to my only fellow public gallery incumbent, a tiny woman of middle years who I'd assumed was, like me, here for a sit-down and some free theatre.

'It's my son,' she whispered, angling her head towards the rear view of a young male seated in what I consequently deduced was the dock.

With what I can only describe as quiet pride she ran down his rap sheet: possession of a class B drug in Leicester Square, jumping bail, resisting arrest. Taking my lead from her, I smiled and nodded as if informed of an unexpectedly solid across-the-board O level performance. 'Oh,' she said, raising a beige-gloved finger in recollection, 'and, um, carrying a concealed offensive weapon.' She raised her eyebrows teasingly, saving that A in Geography for last. 'A *police baton*.'

Her son was asked to stand, and did so with studied sloth before immediately tilting his thin neck to the requisite 'yeah, whatever' angle. No suit and tie, just a soiled and voluminous green shirt apparently fashioned from a discarded sofa cover. Clearly the last thing he wanted was to get off, but straining my ears I picked up snatches that suggested this might indeed be happening. 'Possession of a small amount of herbal cannabis is hardly . . .' I heard the magistrate say, rounding off with something about 'the public purse to consider'.

The defendant shrugged extravagantly, and without turning to his mother was led away by a Securicor guard. I turned to her in puzzlement; of course, she'd heard everything.

'Remanded for three weeks,' she said brightly, clearly relishing another appearance. I suppose in a tragic way it gave the two some sort of focus for their lives. She tottered happily out, leaving me alone for the next case, the last of the day. This was much better. A man with a very long Eastern European surname was accused of being drunk and disorderly in Dean Street, a charge with a pleasing vaudevillian ring, like a line out of 'Burlington Bertie From Bow'. He was a model of combed and collared contrition, clasping his hands behind him as the clerk or usher or whoever began to read the police evidence. This demeanour was explained when we reached the accused's response to the officer who coaxed him out from a prostrate wheelie bin. 'Shit, shit, fuck it, shit, fucking, shitting, shit,' intoned the clerk, replicating the rhythm and metre of Brian Cant's roll call of the *Trumpton* fire-engine crew with commendable precision.

The defendant was given a £60 fine plus costs. Not a bad result, I calculated, stepping back into the street. In 1935 Orwell's Gordon Comstock had joined a parade of drunk and incapables being processed by the magistrate at the rate of two a minute: his standard £5 fine was almost three times what he earned in a week behind the counter of a second-hand bookshop.

Great Marlborough Street was a ten minute ride away, through the dense Soho lanes and alleys so nearly buried under Harold Clunn's central London expressway. Bow Street was one of those I'd only ever glimpsed in the wing mirrors of the car in front, but I spent three years working at the offices of *Esquire* magazine just down the road from Great Marlborough Street, and consequently chained my bike to a meter there with as smugly proprietorial a bearing as you can summon with your trouser legs stuffed into your socks.

Ah, Liberty, whose staff had learned to usher me so speedily towards the final reduction rack; the back entrance of Marks & Spencer, whose glazed steel doors knew me so well as 'The £1.29 Lunch Man'; and yes, the magistrates' court itself, wherein as a youth I answered a litany of moped misdemeanours with such beatific stoicism that they let me off with two points and a ten-quid fine.

Named in honour of Winston Churchill's antecedent, the first Duke of Marlborough, and more particularly in recognition of his victory over the French at Blenheim, Great Marlborough Street could for many years boast at least five peers among its residents, along with artists, actresses and scientists from Cavendish to Darwin. It was also, in common with two separate addresses in Bond Street, once the central London home of Lord Nelson. By lying in state in Whitehall and making a notable and ongoing contribution to Trafalgar Square, Nelson thereby stakes a decent claim to be the board's dominant historical figure – Monopoly's dead Daddy. He should by rights nab an extra half-point for Piccadilly, where in 1801 Emma gave birth to his illegitimate daughter, though I'm docking that from him for having insisted the child be named Horatia Nelson Nelson.

Only Oliver Cromwell runs the good admiral close, even though his challenge didn't come to life until he was dead. He'd been three years in the ground when Charles II triumphantly reclaimed the throne – and why faff about with street parties and bunting when you could exhume the Great Protector's mummified remains and string them up at the end of Oxford Street? In such a larky carnival atmosphere it was inevitable that Cromwell's head should soon be hacked – one might more accurately say eased – off and stuck on a pole overlooking Whitehall. There it stayed for twenty years, before embarking on a showbiz career that in 1799, more than 130 years after his death, saw it on display in a museum of curiosities in Bond Street. It's a wonder Hasbro looked any further when they pondered those designs for a new Monopoly token (though as the head's three subsequent owners all met sudden deaths, perhaps it's just as well they didn't).

Once a street of genteel residents, all Great Marlborough Street's original houses are gone, the last dubiously vanishing less than ten years ago to make way for the six storeys of green glass and white plastic that house the headquarters of Sony Music Entertainment. This and a pleasingly shabby old record shop ('Choose any 25 LPs for £10') aside there were no extant traces of the street's Tin Pan Alley days: looking through the Gothic windows of what since 1896 had been the London College of Music I was presented with the novel spectacle of dozens of young women in Barbie nurse outfits buffing each other's nails. I went in, inhaled acetone vapours and was politely informed by the reassuringly unbuffed receptionist that for the last two years this had been the London College of Beauty Therapy. From high-brow to eye-brow.

There was no evidence of the old Philip Morris factory that spawned the world's most widely recognised cigarette brand, but the rag trade was still maintaining at least one Marlborough Street tradition, if only in an administrative and retail sense. What had in the thirties been only slightly glorified sweatshops were now painfully small and painfully trendy fashion company offices, and I spent a very short amount of time in a shop called Uth – sorry, UTH – selling 'menswear for girls' in a challenging environment where breeze blocks and amoeba-shaped sofas stood on a bare concrete floor emblazoned with slogans such as 'if it's high street, it's not us' and 'if you're tempted to compromise, don't'.

Taking my lead from this latter maxim, I herded the sneering, androgynous staff into a cubicle and ceremonially torched every last pair of thirty-quid camouflage knickers on the pavement outside. I can't think of the last time a retail outlet which didn't sell Disney merchandise or tinned shortbread boiled my innards with such furious wrath. In fact, just to teach it a lesson I'm going to call it a boutique. A unisex boutique.

Two poncy hairdressers; bell-plates labelled 'modo', 'e-dreams' and 'Electric Dog' before expanses of etched glass and brushed aluminium; an ad agency receptionist sipping Volvic at a pulpit marooned on a sea of planed maple. But just as Great Marlborough Street seems certain to disappear up its own arse, along comes the junction with Carnaby Street and pulls it feet first back into the daylight.

I suppose the reason every two-wheeled courier in London congregates at the western end of what they might easily call GMS is the presence of one of the last free public conveniences in town. It's an odd sight, though, all those smutty faces and roll-up fags imparting an atmosphere more redolent of a colliery shift-change. But standing over the road, blinking as the sun speared dramatically through a gap in the scurrying clouds, I was quickly diverted by a neighbouring spectacle: one of my very favourite London structures, the splendidly eccentric Liberty building.

Seeking to expand his successful oriental goods emporium on Regent Street in the early yeas of the last century, Arthur Liberty was frustrated by a conservative landlord who routinely vetoed any architectural flamboyance. Because this landlord was the King of England, there wasn't much Arthur could do. Instead, he bought up the properties behind his store along Great Marlborough Street and, allowing free reign to his pent-up frustrations, in 1925 replaced them with an edifice as stately yet unhinged as George III tucking into a tasty hearth rug. From the gilded galleon weather vane via the handmade roof tiles, mullioned windows and fussily galleried balconies to the third-storey bridge that connects it to the Regent Street store, Liberty's Great Marlborough Street annexe isn't so much the acceptable face of mock Tudor as its boss-eyed clown mask. It's wattle and daub and darkened wood; it's black and white and lead all over. But to appreciate the inspired lunacy, you have to go inside.

Launched in 1805, the Royal Navy man-o'-war HMS *Hindustan*'s maiden voyage took her to the East Indies; later, after a brief spell as a store ship anchored off Portugal, she sailed to New South Wales, returning via the Mediterranean in 1819. Renamed the *Dolphin* she served another fourteen years as a storage vessel, this time at Chatham, before seeing out her days down the Thames at Woolwich as the prison hulk *Justitia*. HMS *Impregnable*'s story began seven years after the *Hindustan*'s, but quickly made up for lost time. She landed Austrian troops in Italy during the campaign that ended with Waterloo, and a year later was involved in an idiotically ill-advised attack on Algiers (my, we put it about a bit back in those days) which cost the lives of midshipman John Hawkins, along with thirty-seven of her seamen, ten marines and two boys. So ravaged was the *Impregnable* that the bill for hull repairs alone topped £10,000; every mast was shattered, every sail shredded. After a spell as a guard ship at Plymouth she was pensioned off as a training vessel at Chatham, being finally decommissioned in 1862.

Have you got all that? Good. Now follow me as we wander through Liberty's low-ceilinged labyrinth of dark stairways and panelling, through the stained-glass doorways to the public school assembly hall that serves as the millinery department. Now, sliding between two scarily lipsticked old duchesses fighting over a £500 scarf, we approach one of the stout but somehow crudely fashioned timber uprights that, far above, support beams of similar design. The surface of each, we note, running our eyes and fingers over their sculpted and pitted surfaces, is regularly marked by the planed-off rumps of vast dowels, tenons and mortices, features associated with jointing techniques of another age and a very different field of construction. And, as concerned but compassionate security personnel lead us gently outside one of us – oh dear, I'm rather afraid it's you – collars a Burberry-clad browser and in a panicky wayward falsetto hisses, 'Blood-stained boats – don't you see, you do see it, tell me you see it too – it's all made out of blood and boats and the bones of old John Hawkins!'

For the facts are these: measure the length of the store's Great Marlborough Street frontage and you will discover it tallies identically with that of the two aforementioned vessels. Built twenty years after the Ritz became Britain's first steel-framed building, the structural integrity of Liberty's Great Marlborough Street rests entirely upon a prison hulk coming up to its bicentenary and a ship that helped defeat Napoleon and was later blown to bits off the coast of North Africa. Surveying the shop again from the other side of the road I actually shook my head in disbelief: perhaps no story reveals more vividly what an inspirationally eccentric city London can be.

Just as well, because having paused briefly to admire a more conventional twenties masterpiece, the black and yellow granite mausoleum that is Ideal House, I ambled to a halt in front of the magistrates' court – which as ever I'd been saving for last – and realised I wouldn't be hearing any stories there. A man in a yellow hard hat stamped dustily past me up the steps and opened the stoutly panelled front door; before it slammed shut I glimpsed deconstructional activity whose profundity could not have made it more starkly clear: Marlborough Street magistrates' court had heard its last case. It was the end of a legal connection that had endured unbroken since the first police station opened its doors on to the Great Marlborough Street pavement in 1793.

In fact, the link went back further: in 1786, on the site where the court's disembowelled remains stood before me, Joshua Brookes had opened a museum whose most popular gallery displayed the bodies of executed criminals. The court opened next door nine years later, and soon acquired a salacious celebrity of its own. It was here that Gladstone gave evidence against a man who had attempted to blackmail him after seeing the then chancellor talking to a prostitute near Leicester Square; here also that Oscar Wilde appeared as a defendant in the libel case that proved his undoing.

Continuing this tradition, and perhaps influenced by its proximity to the heart of Swinging London, it was at Marlborough Street magistrates' court that the Establishment chose to take on bad-boy rock 'n' roll. In 1968 Brian Jones was bailed there for possession of cannabis resin and later fined £50; two years later it was Mick Jagger's turn – £200 for the same offence. John Lennon also made an appearance at Marlborough Street in 1970, after the Bond Street gallery in which he had exhibited '14 lithographs detailing intimate and erotic scenes from his honeymoon with Yoko Ono' was charged under the indecency laws. Eight of these images were considered inappropriate for public display (Yoko wasn't in the other six), but the charges were dismissed on a legal technicality. And in 1973, Keith Richards made it a Stones hat-trick when he appeared before the Marlborough Street beaks impressively charged with possession of marijuana, heroin and the tranquilliser Mandrax, as well as a Smith and Wesson revolver and an antique shotgun, both held without licence, and ammunition. Worth a good long stay in that big house with Dr Crippen in the garden, you'd have thought, but somehow Richards got off with a £205 fine.

But what's sadder than the loss of this heritage is the loss of a certain humanity, a character and individualism that coloured the grey streets of London. Almost everywhere I was getting the slight sensation of corners being rounded off, of genuine idiosyncrasy giving way to contrived commercial wackiness. The orange set was no longer where the law met the lawless; the extremes of Monopoly's London seemed to have been snipped off, and I couldn't help feeling we were all somehow the poorer. Where will London get its folklore from when every courtroom is a corporation, every strip club a Starbucks? Marlborough Street magistrates' always had a reputation for the grand and eccentric gesture; on his retirement in the late seventies St John Harmsworth received good luck cards from the many Soho call girls he had dealt with so humanely over the years, and reciprocated by writing off all their outstanding fines – and my later investigations proved this tradition endured to the last.

At the end of the court's final case in 1999, the magistrate Miss Wickham turned to the young man accused of shoplifting in Oxford Street. 'Tomorrow you are twenty-one and you are going to start a new life,' she said. 'We are also all going to start a new life tomorrow, because this court is closing.' Mark Gavin Jones was given an absolute discharge, and the officials filed out for the last time.

There's something endearingly bijou about thoroughfares so diminutive that their names had to be drastically abbreviated on my *A–Z* – R Op Ac for Royal Opera Arcade, B H1 Sc for, I dunno, Brown Hole Scouts – and seeing the relevant cul-de-sac near Piccadilly labelled Vin S I'd known to expect a stubby affair. The grand extent of that stubbiness, however, only became apparent as I wheeled my bike up a passage that smelt of mislaid Chinese takeaways and was presented at its conclusion by a road shorter than Whitehall's width, one rudely stopped in its tracks by the deadest of dead ends.

Cowering at the foot of the huge buildings whose unlovely rear aspects engulfed it on three sides, Vine Street was not so much a runt as a rectum, a back passage, a workman's crack poking out round the back of Piccadilly's fancy façades. Along one side were the grimy sit-upons of Egypt Air, an Abbey National and a sushi restaurant so shy it displayed no menu and bore a sign only in Japanese, but the dominant structure was the Meridien, its muscular hindquarters draped with pigeon-netting, its back doors stacked with old barrels of vegetable oil. A man came out from under a doorway labelled 'Meridien – Welcome to Work' carrying two fire extinguishers like the proud new father of twins; he laid them tenderly in the back of a red van and reversed out, leaving me and Vine Street alone together.

No one's sure how Vine Street earned its name – possibly something to do with a Roman era vineyard – but then few can have bothered to ask. The only story the street had in its locker (admittedly it's a cracker) concerns the encounter that took place there between Frantisek Kotzwara and Susannah Hill on 2 September 1791. Then sixty-one, Kotzwara was one of Europe's greatest double bassists and the noted composer of fantasias with a military bent – *The Siege of Quebec*; *The Battle of Prague*. Bohemian by birth and nature, he was a regular in the bagnios and fleshpots of Georgian London, and on the night in question found himself in the company of the aforementioned sex worker at her room at No. 5 Vine Street.

Nothing if not a gentleman, Kotzwara suggested a meal before the main business of the evening, furnishing Susannah with two bob for a substantial and well-lubricated spread of victuals. Some people like to round off a good meal with a smoke or a snooze, but Kotzwara was made of different stuff. 'After a dinner of ham, beef, porter and brandy,' read one studiously sober account, 'he asked her to cut off his genitals.' Perhaps unwilling to bite the hand that fed her, as it were, Hill refused, but interestingly agreed to assist Kotzwara in fastening a ligature first round the doorknob and thence his neck. Five minutes later, the kneeling, trouserless maestro eagerly conducted himself to a breathlessly memorable finale – tantalisingly uncertain, even at the end, whether he was coming or going. Arrested and charged with murder, Hill was acquitted after the judge accepted her testimony. The court records were withheld to keep the precise and shocking details from the public domain, but the case still remains a landmark for suicidally adventurous perverts and bored law students alike.

My 1933 directory's assessment of Vine Street read, *in toto*: No. 13 – Man in the Moon public house; No. 10 – Police Station. The first – now the slightly ponced-up Swallow Street Bar – still offered refreshment to the many students and stag-night young bucks who set off around London on Monopoly pub crawls, but the second had gone. Now I was here I remembered, and not that many years ago, shepherding a distressed pickpocketing victim from Piccadilly Circus Tube station up to Vine Street police station. But the steps I'd led her up then were now topped with a sign identifying this as the headquarters of Red Media. A young man in a white T-shirt came out down the steps and lit up a fag; I asked with what Red Media concerned itself and he flatly replied, 'Graphics.'

I was still none the wiser as to why Vic and Marge had considered it so important to include a law-themed set: possibly, as with the motoring fines, a private joke based on bitter experience; more probably a reflection of the period's fixation with crime and its detection, a fixation that saw the publication of whodunit novels running at almost one a day and remains the only possible explanation for the abysmal Cluedo's rampant success. But now it didn't matter, and the only mystery left to solve was what currently linked the set. Great Marlborough Street had lost its court and Vine Street its cop shop; by the same token, Bow Street was already one down with one to go. All I could think to characterise the oranges in twenty-first-century London was that, alone amongst the Monopoly groups, its three streets couldn't muster a single McDonald's between them.

'This used to be a police station, though, didn't it?' I said, eliciting a skyward expulsion of smoke and, after a long gap, a two-tone hum of reluctant assent. 'So are the, er, cells still down there?'

If graphic designers were happy to line their Apple Macs along walls that for many generations had rung with the ragged cries of apprehended felons, then maybe there really was something in the absurd scheme I'd been reading about to convert Pentonville and London's other Victorian prisons into desirable loft-style accommodation.

He surveyed me sourly. 'What do you think?'

'I think . . . well, do you know, I think I'm falling in love with you, you splendid little man,' I said, in the manner of one astride an alloy-framed racing bicycle facing an adversary with a nicotine habit and undone shoelaces.

It was a fitting farewell exchange. Vine Street had more cause than any other to get down on its little orange knees and thank heaven for its miraculous inclusion on over forty million game boards, a presence that had made it famous from Aberdeen to Auckland. But instead it looked ugly and ungrateful, as surly and bitter as the man who now dismissed me with a wristy gesture more practised and insouciant than any professionally delivered by Mr Kotzwara's service provider in her pomp. Frankly, you expect a lot better from not just the premium property in a group, but holder of the Chris Award for Lucrative Probability. In the thirties Vine Street was where you came if you'd been caught pissing or puking or doing other drunk stuff. Now it was where you came to do that self-same stuff if you didn't want to get caught.

I pedalled down to Piccadilly, then turned up Regent Street to the junction with Oxford Circus, where I dismounted feeling rather thwarted. Because there was a big picture of a policeman on the board, and because of the London game's particular devotion to crime and the fighting thereof, I'd been planning to spend at least one day on the beat with the Vine Street coppers: pushing electric vehicles off bridges, taking kickbacks from vice kings, enticing my neighbours at a Soho urinal into an incriminating display of indecency. Withdrawing the board and resting it on an unmanned newsstand, I atoned as best I could, waving cheerfully but rather self-consciously up at the towering black lollipop that I knew to contain a police CCTV camera. I rolled a four, but clacking my racing car from Bow Street to Free Parking accepted an unannounced encore was required. I rolled again, waiting for a Tannoyed boom of 'WE SAW THAT, MOORE' to thunder from some unseen emergency-service loudspeaker. A five and a three took me to Water Works. And a very long car journey the next weekend took me to the Crossness Sludge-Powered Generator.

CHAPTER 9

Water Works

Conceived at the height of the cholera epidemics that ravaged London in the mid-nineteenth century, the capital's drainage system is a typically Victorian triumph. Joseph Bazalgette, encouraged by the hands-on civil-engineering enthusiasm of Prince Albert, oversaw the creation of 1,300 miles of new sewers, along with pumping stations, drainage reservoirs and the creation of the Embankment to narrow the Thames and so speed the river's flow as it sluiced away the bountiful unpleasantness.

The scheme took thirty years and swallowed enormous sums of public money – the Embankment alone cost a million quid. So extensive were the necessary gradient-related preparations that the cartographical department it spawned later evolved into the Ordnance Survey. But the Victorians never thought in the short term: by the twenties, London's fifty-year-old sewerage system was being single-handedly credited for a 'remarkably low death rate never surpassed by any other capital city'. Continental visitors might still complain about the smoke, but few European cities in the Monopoly age could match the quality of London's drinking water. Scratch and sniff a wall in many French or Italian cities and even today you'll release a pungently medieval waft. Over-engineered and under-praised, almost 150 years on Bazalgette's network is still heroically keeping London's waste out of sight and mind.

Out of sight, at least, until it reaches the rather too evocatively named Outfall Works way out east at Beckton, and, on the opposite bank, Crossness. Here, until 1998, was enacted a daily ritual that emphasised perhaps more graphically than one might wish the extent to which subsequent London authorities had failed to build on the Victorians' impressive platform. Pulling up at the quayside, a fleet of vessels were filled to the gunwales with thousands of gallons of 'residual solid waste matter' – London's sludge, in the marginally more acceptable industry shorthand – and despatched down the Thames estuary towards the aptly dismal Black Deep. Here, the Thames Water Authority vessels unceremoniously flushed their tanks – four million tons annually, over 80 per cent of the UK's total marine effluent discharge.

This cavalier disregard for the maxim about shitting on your own doorstep would surely be cheerily ongoing had Brussels not called a halt, an intervention that surely more than atones for any regulation on the shape of bananas. After bumping my car through an excitingly awful wasteland of burnt-out Transit vans and flytippings, I finally came upon the EU's creation. Up it rose across the once malaria-infested Plumstead Marshes, a curvaceous, crested wave of glass and anodised aluminium, a slice of Sydney Opera House: in Crossness did Eurocrats a stately poo-furnace decree.

Built at a cost of £125 million, the Crossness Sludge-Powered Generator and its sister over at Beckton squeeze, compress and dry the ordure from four million households into what I'm afraid are known as sludge cakes, before torching the lot in a turbine-equipped incinerator. From a Monopoly perspective it had seemed ideal – with each incinerator generating 8.6 megawatts, here were the utilities combined: Electric Company and Water Works under one roof. Pay ten times the total on the dice and move on. Fast.

Regrettably, I could only gaze from a distance at the little dustbin-diameter chimney that seemed far too modest for the appalling enormity of its task. The SPG was open to the public today, but I'd been snootily informed by the relevant woman at Thames Water two days before that there wasn't room on their visitors' list. 'Not even the *reserves*,' she said snidely, in a tone hardly compatible with a tour round even the most modish crapatorium. Switching to Plan B, I drove back past the horses roaming wildly across sewage scented tussocks, through the Thamesmead estate whose doomed and desolate malls and marinas formed the backdrop of Stanley Kubrick's *A Clockwork Orange*, along the kind of lightly rubbled, under-trafficked roads where fathers teach their teenage daughters to drive. Opened by the Prince of Wales in 1865 and ever since the whiffy end of Bazalgette's line, here was the Crossness Southern Outfall Works, mother of the SPG and London's now-defunct cathedral of sewage.

'There *is* a bit of a smell,' said one tidy old chap to another as the pair divided up their sandwiches on a discarded, rusting boiler panel driven through with rivet-heads the size of halved coconuts. Behind them stood the majestic if rather careworn Beam Engine House, within whose colourful and decoratively arched Romanesque walls stood four mighty rotative beam engines, in their malodorous pomp the world's largest, each capable of pumping over six tons of raw sewage in a single stroke.

There *was* a bit of a smell; when the freshening wind blew back across a neighbouring field of open sewage-farm drums, it reached the high-heaven end of the odour spectrum. But by satisfying both an infantile fascination with bodily waste and a juvenile enthusiasm for the restoration of steam-powered machinery, Crossness held an irresistible lure for Londoners of a certain age (old) and a certain sex (male). Open Day at the Beam Engine House meant what it said; not my number one choice, perhaps, but better than an afternoon with those great big number twos at the hoity-toity SPG. As Marie Antoinette might have said in different yet oddly intriguing circumstances: let them burn sludge cakes.

'See, the Victorians weren't squeamish about any of this,' said a man in a flat cap, one of the members of the trust which since 1985 has been toiling to restore the engines to their harlequin-hued, poo-pumping Victorian prime. I'd been following him and a small group of fellow visitors around the winningly forthright exhibition he and his colleagues had constructed in the room backing on to the pump chamber; at the end of his extended arm, and more precisely at the tip of his pipe's gently smoking mouthpiece, was an etching of Edward, Prince of Wales, being escorted through a specially candle-lit underground chamber.

'So what happened in there?' someone asked, diverting my attention from a 1935 photograph depicting horse-drawn ploughs lifting spuds in a nearby corner of Plumstead Marshes.

'It's the subterranean reservoir,' he said. 'Six and a half acres; twenty-five million gallon dirty-water capacity.' I'd already read enough captions to know what dirty water meant. He nodded at the floor. 'Still down there now.'

I suppose it was just possible to imagine the present Windsors being proudly shown about an enormous underground pit hours before it was filled to the filthy brim with their subjects' lurkers and floaters. But it was substantially more difficult to picture any current royal settling down at the head of a five-hundred-seat banquet in the Beam Engine House, as Edward had done later that day in 1865, and baldly ludicrous to entertain the possibility that even Prince Charles would honour the surrounding engines' prodigious appetite for untreated ordure by proudly unveiling plaques that named two of them after his parents and the others after himself and his sister.

How things had changed by 1968, when seeking civic endorse-ment for their new £500,000 Crossness-based sludge-dumping vessel the Thames Water Authority was reduced to contacting the Mayor and Mayoress of Hounslow. As a resident of this distant London borough, I felt a twinge of betrayal looking at the photographs of the MV *Hounslow*'s launch ceremony: moments earlier, our guide had explained with the aid of an enormous map that the Crossness catchment area in fact ended at Chiswick Bridge, just shy of the Hounslow boundary. This had greatly excited a man from Putney, delighted to be assured that he had indeed made a small personal contribution to the outside stench, but I could not begin to understand why the *Hounslow* should in the most grotesquely literal manner have been forced to carry the can for something its borough hadn't done.

'A moot point now in any case,' said the guide, moving us towards a definitive display of cistern history. 'It was sold to the Ghanaians last year. They're using it as a water carrier.' Everyone went quiet after that, except one man who made a horrid tongue-swallowing noise before blundering straight outside. I expect he'd just returned from a holiday in West Africa.

The Thames was considered 'a fine, health-giving river' in the thirties. A bold statement given that not a single fish had managed to survive in its waters for eight years (salmon finally returned after a century and a half's absence in 1974) but an accurate one when assessed relatively against the river's immediate previous history. For the first thirty years of Crossness's operation, the ghastly contents of its reservoir were discharged directly into the Thames out front at high tide: particularly unfortunate for the passengers of the pleasure steamer *Princess Alice* when on 3 September 1878 her captain chose that precise location to collide with a coal ship. Within minutes 640 had drowned in what remains the worst Thames disaster. 'They weren't so much swimming as going through the motions,' said a boatman returning from the rescue operation, showcasing the Londoner's ability to raise a smile in unhelpful circumstances.

Hard hats were donned and our group filed into the Beam

Engine House. Around us, fitfully repainted in their original golds and scarlets, soared cast-iron grilles decorated with lilies and garlands and the proud acronym of the Metropolitan Board of Works. Industrial faucets just like the one on the Monopoly board jutted rustily through a bulkhead; up in the rafters a trapped pigeon fluttered into panic. Sending submarine echoes off the underfoot metalwork we gingerly crossed lattice walkways to peer 40 feet up to the huge 50-ton beams and 10 feet down to the bottom of their engines' improbably diametered flywheels. Around me men with hairy earholes and pale-blue cardigans nodded quietly to themselves. They were thinking: boiler pressure 150 lb/sq in; 5,000 tons per annum coal consumption. I was thinking: Prince of Wales dinner party; 6¼ tons of crap per stroke.

There was a click and a hum which wavered tremulously as a brave but clearly overawed electric motor tilted the beam of the most restored engine almost imperceptibly upwards. Everyone tried to look impressed – even the pair of panda-eyed Goths I was intrigued to note had joined us – but it was a feeble parody. I squinted up and imagined hobnailed workmen clattering up and down the grid-iron stairs clutching arm-sized spanners as the four mighty engines hissed and creaked and the beams rose and fell, rose and fell, 50 tons of James Watt & Co. of Birmingham's finest forced up to the distant gables and down again every six seconds, every day for seventy years. In its prime the Beam Engine House was as definitively British as the SPG was approximately Scandinavian.

Just before the war the steam engines were replaced by diesel pumps, but those beamed behemoths were recalled for a heroic last hurrah to bail out London during the floods of 1953. Then the workmen left and the vandals and thieves moved in, stripping away the brass fittings and smashing the arched windows. The chimney, a gloriously ornate Blackpool Tower of sturdy yet fanciful multicoloured brickwork, had stood 208 feet above the marshes: it was still one of the tallest structures south of the river when demolished in 1956. Crossness remains an enormous site – like the gas flares in the Persian Gulf and the Great Wall of China you could probably see its huge field of open sewage drums from space – but the improbable glamour the Victorians worked so hard to build has gone.

Back outside in my car, I drove around the Beam Engine House peering up at the columnettes along its walls. Each was topped with a decorative block, most of them patterned but one, our pipe-puffing guide had told us, carved into a representation of Joseph Bazalgette's head. I gave up after two laps, thwarted by a wind-whipped drizzle which smudged out the detail. A shame, as I'd wanted to pay personal tribute to the stupendous tenacity of a man whose personal contribution to everyday London life remains unequalled (except perhaps by his great-great-grandson, the executive producer of *Big Brother*).

As chief architect of the Metropolitan Board of Works, Joseph Bazalgette personally designed three bridges over the Thames – two of them, Hammersmith and Battersea, still extant – and in creating Shaftesbury Avenue and Charing Cross Road was the father of two of the three prominent West End thoroughfares (the other being Tottenham Court Road) whose omission from the Monopoly board it is most difficult to justify. (In fact, I'd also like to include Haymarket, if only to reveal that Ho Chi Minh once worked in a restaurant there.) Most vitally, of course, without Bazalgette's inspiration and tireless endeavour the London Monopoly board would be a square short – the Water wouldn't Work. We might not all get on a Tube train every morning, or take a midnight stroll down Piccadilly, or browse for headscarves amidst the timbers of an ancient man-o'-war, but pending a radical overhaul of human physiology every Londoner should long continue to thank Joseph Bazalgette many times a day. Though this side of Chiswick Bridge, obviously, we couldn't give a shit.

CHAPTER 10

The (Other) Stations

I could never quite be doing with the stations – you couldn't Harold Clunn them over with plastic hotels and no matter what their supporters claim you never, ever got all four. In a game that was about wild speculation, about staking it all in the hope of enormous reward, investing in stations was like opening up a Post Office savings account. When you snapped up Trafalgar Square you'd greedily scan down the rent tariffs and think, 'Blooding buggery-poop!' (It's OK – you're nine.) 'This only cost me £240 and soon it's going to be paying out £1,100!' With a station you'd glumly verify that the very best case scenario consisted of getting your money back. Then you'd swap it with your sister. My sister always used to hoard stations, and when you swapped one with her for anything except a utility it was difficult – impossible – not to wiggle your fingers in her face while whooping the special whoop that traditionally accompanies an abuse of gullibility.

But one soon grows out of such mindlessly vindictive behaviour, and entering middle age I surveyed the stations anew. This time, what struck me was not their tediously monochromatic title deeds, or the plodding linearity of their rent increases, but this: what the ugly, naked man is Fenchurch Street doing there? Trumping even Vine Street and Northumberland Avenue, three of the four stations showcase Vic and Marge at their most wilfully obscure. If Les Dennis introduced 'A railway terminus in London' as a round in *Family Fortunes* and filched his answers off the Monopoly board, there'd be a lot of those negatory electronic donkey noises before anyone got Liverpool Street or Marylebone, let alone Fenchurch Street. 'We'll go for Paddington, Les.' Our survey said . . .' *Eey-ore!* 'Er . . . Waterloo?' *Eey-ore!* 'Euston? Victoria? Charing Cross?' *Eey-ore! Eey-ore! Eey-ore!*

The truth, as anyone with a pre-1948 board will tell you, is that the four stations are the London terminuses of a single company – the London and North Eastern Railway. As with the orange 'law' set, of course, this answer merely substitutes one 'why?' for another, one starker and rather more profound. Quite why Victor Watson nurtured this bizarrely partisan bond to the LNER we are unlikely now to know. Yes, LNER ran King's Cross and Leeds and the trains he took between the two. Yes, it was one of the dominant railway companies of the era, and, as numerous speed records attested, the most glamorous. I have even seen it seriously suggested that the choice reflected London-born Victor's desire to build bridges between the capital and his adopted Yorkshire (his family moved from Brixton to Leeds when Vic was an infant).

But none of this seemed wholly satisfactory, and having pulled over on the way home from Crossness and got the board out and landed on Chance, and been assessed for street repairs, and drawn again and been despatched on a GO-passing, £200-collecting trip to Marylebone Station, and thought for a bit, I realised that to get any useful sense of what the three remaining stations had to say for themselves I'd have to visit them all. Each for the first time. In the same day.

Marylebone's previous role in my life had been restricted to humorously exploiting the tortured arcanities of its pronunciation when provincial relatives plopped their token there – a torment I would later have cause to regret while spending three university years in a city with a suburb called Penistone, and not finding out until the end of the third what I should have been saying to avoid the bus conductress's slaps. Anyway, the name isn't an Anglicisation of Marie-la-Bonne – a popular misconception – but can be attributed to the church built there in 1400 and dedicated to Mary by the bourne, the Ty Bourne being a stream running from what is now Regent's Park down to the Thames. The last mainline London terminus to be built, Marylebone's financers at the Great Central Railway spent so much cash placating the well-heeled nimby brigade up the line at St John's Wood – they had to build a huge tunnel under the outfield at Lords – that there wasn't much left for the station itself. Opened in 1899, it retains a fetching red-brick, low-key air, boldly eschewing a traditional presence on one of the nearby bustling thoroughfares in favour of an address whose ambience is encapsulated in its name: Melcombe Place. If you'd slept through the suburbs, waking with a start as your train shrieked to a halt at one of Marylebone's four modest platforms you might feel rather disorientated. You might in fact think, 'Buttocks – I'm in Lincoln.' If St Pancras is the cathedral of the railway age, Marylebone is its church hall.

The tiling along the Underground platform was venerably Edwardian, and the warm Tube air blowing me up the squeaking, clanking wooden-staired escalator to the mainline station timelessly scented. Were you aware that the distinctive smell of the Underground is largely that of human skin dust? And that although 40,000 tons of cosmic powder falls to earth from space every year, a third of all our atmospheric dust is generated by a single dried-up lake in Chad?

I don't often find such inconsequentialities sidling unbidden out of some forgotten vault in my mind at eleven o'clock in the morning, but Marylebone's tranquillity seemed almost to demand idle rumination. It was like Christmas Day: I counted ten different outlets where you could buy a cappuccino and between them they could only muster seven customers. Mighty expresses once pulled out of Marylebone bound for Manchester and Sheffield, but these days it's served only by foolishly puny Sprinter-style affairs that get bullied by real trains if they go out past the green belt on their own. When film director Richard Lester needed to commandeer a mainline London station for the Beatlemania chase scenes in *A Hard Day's Night*, Marylebone was the only feasible option. The station manager probably thought it would be nice to fill the place up for a change.

Everything about the station recalled a slower, gentler age. The Great Central's acronym looked down on a florist, a proper stripy-poled barber's and a cobbler; stubbornly flouting current trends in railwayspeak the announcements were addressed to 'passengers' rather than 'customers'. Decorating a wall near the side exit was a rewarding illustrated history of the station, which quoted a speaker at the opening banquet pondering that 'when our Queen came to the throne London had not one rail terminus; her reign has now seen the opening of the last'. It was as if the Victorians knew even at the time that their successors would make a bit of a mess of the capital.

If commuters from the swish new Metroland suburbs fanning distantly north-west out of London kept Marylebone alive, then City workers from the older and tattier Essex feeder towns of Shoeburyness and Pitsea did the same for Fenchurch Street. I had never, ever been to Fenchurch Street and without a very detailed map I'd still be looking for it now. Hopelessly disorientated walking there from Tower Hill Tube, I'd ended up at the Monument – which at least gives me the opportunity to explain that the Pudding Lane where the Fire of London famously began derived its name not from anything toothsomely catering-based but a medieval slang term for the turds that perennially clogged its open gutters.

Fenchurch Street might be the oldest address on the board – the first part of the name is probably derived from the Latin word for 'hay' sold at an adjacent market, and remains of what would have been the largest Roman forum north of the Alps have been recently excavated here – but brick-for-brick its current buildings are certainly the newest. Ever since those forum days Fenchurch Street has been close to the heart of the capital's business district, and for the City of London authorities historical sentiment is rarely a match for what they might call hard commercial sense but most of us prefer to describe as ugly, naked greed.

London's first skyscraper went up here in 1957 – a fragile fourteen-storey affair with the sort of balconies the Beatles looked over on those blue and red compilation album covers. Since then the developers have been far too busy looking up to look back. From behind hoardings on all sides issued the empty-vessel clunks and apocalyptic booms of serious construction; the atmospheric cement dust made your nostrils twitch and hard hats outnumbered pinstripes in streets around.

No one sleeps in Fenchurch Street any more, so no one's likely to complain about the noise or the claustrophobia of a life lived in shadows. And, rather more oddly, fewer people work here than at the dawn of the Monopoly era: since 1935, the daytime population of the City's Square Mile has fallen from half a million to a quarter. Computerisation has wiped out the financial sweatshops where rows of clerks toiled at manual calculators like those old bus-conductor ticket machines. This begs the question: what is the point of all these new blocks? And the answer, I'm happy to speculate wildly, is shallow corporate vanity: a lust for unoccupied vertical space which one might call Atrium Culture.

I only really mind because the glazed cliffs that this culture has spawned are just so desperately dull. They're not tall enough to be impressive in a Manhattan sense – only in a fairly lump pea-souper would these boys get to scrape any sky – and are just so unremittingly . . . well, you know, square. Show someone a picture of Liberty's or St Pancras or even Pentonville Prison and they'll have something reasonably animated to say about it: these are edifices that provoke thought. Show someone a picture of one of Fenchurch Street's prominent structures and they'll gaze at it intently waiting for something unexpected to leap out from the photograph – a three-dimensional image of a camel race, perhaps – and when it doesn't they'll bleakly mumble, 'It is twenty-three storeys high. Can you let go now?'

I read, with heart sinking, an A4 'site progress report' gaffer-taped to one hoarding which read, 'Work will proceed quickly now due to the repetitive nature of the panelling.' Gosh! I can't wait to see that place when it's finished. Though, actually, they don't want you to. You don't cover something in mirrors if you want anyone to look at it. When you look in the mirror, you don't look *at* it. Anything in the vicinity that dared to be different was sat on or crowded out by what the architect Richard Rogers has described as 'arguably the ugliest group of modern buildings in London'. The Tower of London could only manage a fleeting, wobbly reflection in some bronze-mirrored repetitive panel, and the graceful, low entrance arch of Fenchurch Street station was aggressively hemmed in by great flanks of louvred glass and concrete.

Twice bombed by Zeppelins in the First World War and overhauled in 1935, the station was given another facelift in 1987. Perhaps that isn't quite the *mot juste*. Many drastic procedures are carried out in the quest for eternal youth, but to my knowledge no pioneering physician has yet been brave enough to push back the boundaries of surgical rejuvenation by stoving his patients' features in with a Le Creuset frying pan. For once inside that graceful arch, Fenchurch Street is transformed before your eyes into the changing room in an Austin Allegro-era leisure centre, with stroboscopically flickering fluorescent tubes and tiles the colour of breakfast cereal leftovers sloughing across the floor and halfway up the walls.

After Marylebone's airy gentility it was all very disappointing. So modest are the vertical and horizontal dimensions of the upstairs concourse at Fenchurch Street that when the announcer spoke it was like being addressed by a wrathful God whose all-seeing eye had fallen upon signalling problems outside Leigh-on-Sea. The route out to Southend has for years been nicknamed the Misery line, and though this may largely be down to delays and overcrowding, the ambience of its London terminus can hardly have helped. I suppose I wouldn't have minded so much were it not for Fenchurch Street's lengthy heritage. For over a thousand years this had been the very heart of the capital – deep under my feet lay a seam of charcoal marking Boadicea's fiery revolt in AD 60, and the street names around told their own long stories: Seething Lane, Crutched Friars, French Ordinary Court. The little runt of a road out at the front of the station was actually called London Street.

My intention had been to stay for the rush hour, clinging on to a ticket collector as a human tide of 28,000 mauve-shirted, power-suited City boys and girls threatened to carry us off through the barriers and away to Shoeburyness. But it didn't happen: the City isn't the 9–5 place it was in the early Monopoly age, and a lot of those 28,000 would be at their desks until well after 6. Five o'clock came and went, and at quarter past so did I.

Only one platform shy of the combined total run up by the other three Monopoly stations, Liverpool Street was almost over-bearingly thronged by the time I got there. Guards were blowing whistles, electric trolleys beep-beep-beeped through the crowds, a phone rang to the tune of 'I'm Forever Blowing Bubbles'.

Named after a road named after a Prime Minister, Liverpool Street was the largest London terminus when it opened in 1874, its lofty, Gothic frontages dominating the spindly medieval taverns and houses around. The station's integral hotel, the Great Eastern, boasted a glass-domed restaurant and a secret platform where trains delivered sea water to fill its marine swimming baths. Here was a building which had some front, and then some more.

From the last war onwards, however, Liverpool Street languished in neglect, acquiring a squalid and rather seamy reputation; Ian, my friend from the Ritz, recalls visiting the bar of the Great Eastern in the early eighties and finding it peopled with ramshackle ladies of the night and lairy wideboys necking Double Diamond. Even the late MP Tom Driberg, whose fondness for toilet sex with big soldiers hardly marks him down as a pernickety fusspot, damned the station as 'a hell hole'.

Now, though, the Great Eastern (once the site of Bethlehem Royal Hospital, the original Bedlam) is a poncily minimalist Conran venture, and the station behind it has been lavishly made over. Standing where the Tube station opens into the concourse I craned my neck back and gazed up at the soaring iron arches and fancy brickwork; the latter gleamed as if varnished and the former had been regally repainted in their multicoloured Victorian livery.

I uncraned my neck and immediately wished I hadn't. Floating uneasily right across the concourse was a sort of aerial corridor of curved chrome and Perspex, as harmoniously attuned to its surroundings as a bouncy castle in the aisle of Westminster Abbey. Along it were arranged a parade of small retail concessions, largely catering for the sorry-I'm-late-love market: florists, jewellers and, for the drunken, tardy husband keen to make a bad situation worse, a Sock Shop. Propped up at one end was a garish confectionery trolley, and seeing this emblazoned 'Sweet Chariot' I made a face like the scorer of a flamboyantly improbable own goal.

With most of the trains hidden behind that chrome walkway, it was suddenly difficult to identify this as a station. In a way it isn't. More so than any of the other Monopoly stations, in fact more so than any other London station, Liverpool Street has moved boldly beyond its original brief – that tired concept of a building where people got to catch trains. The figures seem ridiculous, and yet if they were to be trusted I'd be one of the twenty-five million annual visitors who walk into Liverpool Street with no intention of leaving it on a train. Add on the one hundred million who arrive with every such intention, but inevitably have to hang about for a bit waiting for this hope to become a reality, and Liverpool Street is apparently able to offer retailers twice as many potential consumers as Heathrow Airport. Soon, we're told, there'll be a Marks & Spencer, upmarket fashion retailers and, amongst many other dining options, a slice-to-go operation run by Pizza Express called – and you might want to put any breakable items out of reach at this point – Pizza Express Express.

Any hair-tearing commuters reading Railtrack's commercial manager boast to the *Evening Standard* about the retail benefit associated with 'dwell times of up to thirty-three minutes' could be forgiven for lashing him nude to the Sweet Chariot, though with any luck he's enjoying some professional dwell time of his own these days. Retail sales at London's stations rose 70 per cent in the three years after 1997 and at the time of Railtrack's demise contributed 13 per cent of the company's total revenue. The Costa Coffee outlet at Waterloo is the chain's third busiest in Europe; Body Shop's Euston branch generates more sales per square foot than any other across the globe. Passengers, it seems, have finally succumbed to the indoctrinating argot of the post-privatised railways and become customers. I don't know about you, but it makes me want to push quite large things over.

You know things are bad when the government's own ministers cheerfully admit that Britain's railways are now the worst in Europe. A possibly meaningless but certainly eye-catching statistic reveals that in 2000 passengers on the London

Underground wasted the equivalent of 6,735 years in delays caused by deteriorating service: more dwell time than even the most odiously cynical commercial manager would know how to exploit.

It isn't hard to see why. Britain spends only 0.6 per cent of its gross domestic product on transport investment, half the comparable figure for Germany, France and Italy. With subsidies the lowest in Europe, fares are inevitably the highest: travelling on public transport in London costs commuters an average of 71p a mile, double the going rate in Paris or Berlin and four times more than Rome.

With trains managing the impressive feat of being both expensive and crap, London's commuters continue, in desperation, to take to their cars. In 2001, the number of train journeys undertaken in the Greater London area fell by 1.4 million; in the two decades before, car use in Britain rose by 52 per cent – more than any other comparable EU country. Congestion increases – a quarter of our major roads are jammed for at least an hour a day – and air quality declines. It has been estimated that 1,600 Londoners die prematurely as a result of atmospheric pollution every year, over 90 per cent of it generated by road vehicles.

The bottom-line statistic most relevant to those of us not personally affected by a pollution-related fatality is that British workers now spend an average forty-six minutes a day commuting to work, the highest figure in Europe. The solution is a reasonably straightforward one: London's bus fares have been pegged back in recent years – a one-day pass is half the Tube equivalent's £4 – and after decades of decline passenger numbers are now consequently at their highest since 1975. To meet demand, drivers are being recruited from as far away as China.

How different it all was back in the pre-Monopoly era: it's hard to imagine today's bureaucrats drafting a Cheap Trains Act as they did in 1883. In 1931 Herbert Morrison, then known as

Minister of Transport and now as Peter Mandelson's granddad, introduced the bill that amalgamated the capital's Underground trains, trams, coaches and buses into the London Passenger Transport Board. Morrison understood that London's burgeoning growth and economic importance made a unified transport policy essential, and with a constitution modelled on the BBC's, what became known as London Transport quickly transformed the capital's mass-transit system into the world's greatest.

Almost everything that made it so occurred under the pre-war aegis of the clearly godlike LPTB chief executive Frank Pick: Harry Beck's wonderful 1933 Underground map, inspired by wiring diagrams and now the standard blueprint for urban transit networks around the world; the preparation of six Tube extensions and more than fifty additional stations, most of them blissfully happy marriages of form and function designed by the belatedly revered Charles Holden; the first trolleybuses and double-deckers distinguishable only by people you really wouldn't want to be stuck in a lift with from the Routemasters that still ply the West End today. A 1935 photograph of rush hour at Aldwych featured in a recent history of London's transport is pertinently captioned 'No bus in this picture is older than five years'.

I don't think there's really any need to detail the extent to which it's all gone wrong since. Though perhaps it's worth mentioning that the chapter following that in which those Aldwych buses appear is titled 'Public Transport in Decline – The Car is King 1945–70'. The railways had once dominated and even defined London – 100,000 Londoners were displaced to make way for the main lines that speared in as close to the centre as they could get, and the huge terminuses they sprouted when they got there. Though rail travel had lost some of its novelty by the thirties, the big stations were still the capital's epic structures: they had been built to demand respect, and they were still getting it. But then came cars and planes, and suddenly trains were just another way of getting about, and a rather old-fashioned one at that.

Once this happened, the stations began to seem rather overblown. Marylebone had reaped the benefits of its obscurity and been almost accidentally overlooked by the developers, but Fenchurch Street was an irrelevant and rather ugly little insect cowering beneath many pairs of surrounding concrete boots. And at Liverpool Street, which had once stood so impressively above its neighbours, those boots had come crashing down. Towering but somehow stocky, the £1.8 billion Broadgate office development loomed not just around the station but directly over it, its gracelessly bland beige and green bulk stamping right on to platforms 11–18.

Round the back, with the spindly cast-iron arcs of the station canopy like an opened ribcage between the feet of two startlingly oppressive blocks of granite and glass, I stood glumly in the flayingly bitter wind that tall buildings always seem to generate. Inside the concourse the trains were presented as an afterthought behind the retail barricades, and outside the station itself lay prostrate and defeated, not just bitten by the hand that fed it but almost swallowed whole. On the rent-per-square-foot scale, Liverpool Street had more than justified that berth between Bond Street and Park Lane, just as King's Cross had cemented its position as the board's lowliest station. In human terms, however, the frigid urban cityscape around me offered nothing to enrich the soul or stir the senses. Gabbyland's grubby vigour might be too grubby for some, but this place left a far worse taste in the mouth. Though Gabby's toothbrush would probably beg to differ.

CHAPTER 11

Mr Monopoly

I went to school with Phil Grabsky. He was in the year above and I believe he served as an assistant patrol leader in our Scout troop; I additionally believe that the torch whose batteries I covertly replaced with a banana in the woods in Stoke Poges, a torch whose consequent inutility precipitated a terrible nocturnal stumble into an earth latrine, may have borne a strip of Dymo tape identifying its owner as P. Grabsky. Though because I left the 34th Hammersmith after a record-breakingly diminutive period of service, of course I can't be certain.

But the man I had arranged to meet at a café outside Liverpool Street station was not Phil Grabsky. He was Mike Grabsky. A cheery chap in his mid-forties, with the sort of competent, engaging air of a television DIY pundit, Mike is Britain's most successful Monopoly player. The one-time holder of more regional and national titles than he can accurately recall, he had also represented his country at the global championships often enough to refer to them as 'the worlds'. Mike's day job, undertaken for a foreign bank in one of the Broadgate towers rearing sombrely over our bracing outdoor table, involves the design and maintenance of risk-management computer systems. Deep into the realm of Chris, one can only assume that this work involves much the same mathematical prowess as his extra-mural activities.

Mike's life-defining interest in Monopoly can be traced to his encounter with a book of game-winning tips when he was twelve. Only in 1984, however, did he go public. That year the *Evening Standard* ran a competition to win fifty places in its inaugural London Monopoly championship; using friends' names and addresses, Mike procured no fewer than ten of them. With the field stuffed full of wilfully incompetent stooges, victory was a formality.

'It's just the perfect board game,' offered Mike when I asked him to explain his obsession. 'Brokering deals, money management – it's all useful in later life. There's enough luck involved to allow kids to beat their dads, and enough skill so that if you want you can take it up to another level.'

The moment most of us came to that fork in the Monopoly road, with one branch signposted 'Another Level' and the other 'What Do You Mean, I Can't Put a Hotel On My Station?' was when we got to the bit in the rules about auctions. Everyone was distantly aware that if someone landed on an unowned property and didn't buy it, the bank was supposed to flog it off to the highest bidder. A Mike-style cousin might even have cajoled you into trying it out, covertly snaffling up the orange set for a tenner a throw before luring you into a £1,473 bid for Electric Company. Thereafter auctions would be pigeon-holed along with mortgage interest and the rule about being able to buy houses out of turn in the 'Sod That' file.

By this token, it was no surprise to hear that Mike's family stopped playing him years ago. His social acquaintances would have been warned off by the primer on Monopoly tactics Mike has submitted for publication, and more particularly its title: *How to Bankrupt Your Friends In Under An Hour*. And he doesn't get much joy out of his work colleagues these days either, after a group of them made the mistake of humorously belittling his extra-curricular triumphs.

'I said, OK – give us a game and I'll beat you all ten times in a row.'

And, um, did you?

'No. I did it twelve times.'

Mike's homely features were now beginning to harden into an approximation of religious fanaticism, the bug-eyed, clench-jawed monomania that marks out a competitor determined to dominate his chosen field. His passion for the game is almost boundless: one minute fiercely eulogising my friend Victor Watson as 'a man who believed in the purity of Monopoly', and the next, to my unbridled satisfaction, roundly belittling Gyles Brandreth. 'He turns up at the worlds in this silly Monopoly jumper saying he's the European champion. We all watched him play and . . . well, let's just say I didn't pick up any tips.'

Mike's dream is to run a real-estate company named Monopoly Properties, starting with a flat above an Old Kent Road shop and expanding sequentially around the board. He has replaced many of the screen icons on his company's computer network with images of Uncle Pennybags. When a championship overlapped with the holiday of a lifetime his wife had spent years organising for them, he packed her off to Malaysia alone. 'That was brave of you,' I said. He seemed surprised by the suggestion. 'Not as brave as buying the green set in a three-player game.'

A world final is played with real money, and with $16,500 up for grabs (the bank's total reserves, apparently), gamesmanship in the qualifying heats is intense. One Japanese player stands up throughout, barking out bids and prospective deals like an old-school broker on the trading floor. The early rounds have a ninety-minute time limit, and are vulnerable to tactical time-wasting: proposing ludicrous exchanges, mortgaging and unmortgaging properties. No commercial advantage is spurned. 'I once had a fairly serious, er, bank error in my favour,' Mike confessed, with a wink that suggested neither contemporaneous admission or subsequent remorse.

Ask Mike the longest game he's played and he'll tell you about the shortest: 'A whole table of pros bankrupted in forty-three minutes.' Make no mistake – tournament Monopoly is pitilessly gladiatorial, a dog-eat-battleship conflict. Weaknesses are seized upon: when a player is in trouble, you first dispirit them with insultingly low offers for their stricken property empire, then play the nice cop next turn and invariably snap it up for just a few quid more. You play on people's emotions by whispering that another competitor has been trying to rip them off, or appealing openly for an all-board alliance against the current leader. 'But in the early stages at least you've got to be liked – never propose the first deal or you'll be marked down as the hustler, the man to beat.'

Mike, however, likes to be the man to beat, and not just with dice in one hand and a tiny iron in the other. During the course of our chat it emerged that in 1991, his *annus mirabilis*, Mike won an unlikely treble: the South-East Monopoly championship, the UK backgammon crown and – are you ready for this? – the national Cluedo title.

'Backgammon,' he philosophised expansively, 'is a little like Monopoly – easy to learn, hard to master.'

'Yeah, but Cluedo's rubbish,' I blurted impulsively. Mike looked at me, hard, before slowly draining his cup. Then he sat back in his aluminium chair and cracked a big, lazy smile, a smile that said, 'No, son: *losing* is rubbish.'

In a way, I wasn't learning anything new about the game itself: what made Monopoly good – its intolerance of caution or charity, its brazen yet hard-headed ruthlessness – were the same attributes that made Mike good at Monopoly. Already cold, it was now starting to darken. I changed tack.

'An affinity with the streets on the board?' Mike repeated dubiously. Mad Monopoly Mike had gone; mild-mannered marquetry Mike was back. 'What, me personally?'

I suppose his games are too intense to permit any idle ruminations on the history behind those title deeds. Did he then have any thoughts on whether London had improved since the game's debut?

He did, but it took him a while to find them. 'Um . . . cinemas, theatres, galleries . . . although I suppose they had those back then.' I nodded. 'Public transport – that must be better now.' I grimaced slightly and shook my head. He shrugged cheerfully. 'Well . . . you're asking the wrong person. I've got a place in Brighton.' He paused. 'That's the difference. People can't afford to live in London now.'

That certainly was *a* difference. The average price of a three-bed London semi at the start of the thirties was £700 – the equivalent of about £20,000 today. Turn up at a twenty-first-century estate agent with that in your pocket and you'd find yourself £358,000 short. In 1935 one of those new suburban dream homes could be yours for as little as 8/11 a week – only a shilling more than a Monopoly set cost. Monopoly now sells for £19.99; even the weekly rent on a horrid bedsit in Tooting is over three times that, and assuming you somehow wangled a 100 per cent mortgage on that aforementioned semi the repayments under the Monopoly Price Index would set you back twenty-six sets a week. For a half of all Londoners, including nurses, teachers, firemen and others engaged in similarly useful professions, home ownership simply isn't an option.

Nothing brings Londoners together like a discussion of accommodation costs. We were still on the topic when, having first requested his permission, I placed the board on the chair next to us – it was too big for our hubcap-sized table – and handed Britain's greatest ever Monopoly player the dice. I dropped my car on Marylebone; he scuttered the dice across the board's centre with a practised flick, talking as he did so.

'I mean, some of the prices out in west London are just ridiculous. My brother Philip was telling me that . . .'

'Sorry?' My fingers froze over the token; he had rolled a nine but suddenly it didn't matter.

'My brother was telling . . .'

'Philip Grabsky,' I intoned robotically. 'Philip Grabsky of west London.'

'That's right,' said Mike, carefully.

My face felt wrong, and I tried to make it look different. 'Can I ask you something, Mike?' I said, the chumminess sounding woefully fragile.

'OK.' Jaw clenched, eyes hard and unblinking: Monopoly Mike had returned, and now leaned forward with his hands on the table, preparing to rise and leave.

'Would Philip be an older brother?'

'Younger.' He scanned me quickly. 'About your age.'

I nodded very slowly, seven or eight times.

CHAPTER 12

The Reds

STRAND	FLEET ST
CITY OF WESTMINSTER	CITY OF LONDON

TRAFALGAR SQ
CITY OF WESTMINSTER

I didn't remember about Mike's nine until the following morning; such was my easy familiarity with the board I didn't need to open it to know where his throw had taken me.

Nowhere else on the board so perfectly embodies London's civic dithering as Trafalgar Square. In 1829 the royal stables of King's Mews and the less grand buildings around were demolished as part of John Nash's Charing Cross Improvement Scheme; Nash was the first architect to throw his hat in the ring, but he died soon after and the vacant space was quickly knee-deep in toppers and stovepipes.

First they couldn't agree on the name – the initial working title was William the Fourth's Square – and having finally settled on Trafalgar, they couldn't agree on how to honour the admiral mortally wounded during that famous victory over the French and Spanish fleets south of Cadiz in 1805. The competition for a new Nelson Monument wasn't even held until 1839, and the one hundred-odd entries were all so poor they had to hold a second. One proposed a pyramid, another a prodigious globe held aloft above a lake by the figures of Fame, Neptune, Victory and Britannia and topped by the man himself. The largest of the several column suggestions was a 218-foot monster of cast iron, and though most stuck Horatio on top, James Hakewill put him at the bottom, explaining 'it was improper for a mere subject, however heroic, to look down on royalty'.

William Railton supplied the winning design, but the public hated it. His column was called 'a monstrous nine-pin', and a Commons Select Committee declared it 'undesirable'. But no one could agree an alternative, and work began by default. Finally, fourteen years after the space for it was cleared and thirty-eight after he died at Trafalgar, the 17-foot image of Nelson was bolted to the top of 145 feet of fluted granite. Around its base were bronze bas-reliefs of his victories, cheekily cast from melted-down French cannons captured therein.

That was a start, but the issue of what to do with the vast space behind remained. The original scheme had been to fill it with a grand new home for the Royal Academy, but now people were talking about a coliseum. The chief architect, Charles Barry, still wanted to bin the newly erected column and place a more modest group of statues in the middle of the square. In the end, though, they agreed on the fountains, but it took a further two years to complete them and when the water was turned on they leaked. It would be another quarter of a century – long enough to become a staple London joke – before those famous lions were put in place (six times over budget), and an additional fifty-eight years until the square was properly paved.

Nothing, however, illustrates Trafalgar Square's sloth-like development quite so perfectly as the epically drawn-out saga of its corner statues. Generals Napier and Havelock commandeered the southern corners in a whippet-like eight years, but the statue on the north-eastern plinth – George IV on horseback – was intended for Marble Arch (which itself, of course, was intended for Buckingham Palace) and erected at Trafalgar Square only as a stopgap. Over a century on, that gap hasn't been stopped.

Most notoriously, the debate over what to put on the opposite north-west plinth has rumbled tediously on for more than 150 years. In 1936 someone proposed a statue of Cecil Rhodes; in 1947, George III; the year after, William IV. In 1950 there were moves for a monument celebrating merchant seamen, and in 1964 they very nearly decided on Winston Churchill. And every few years thereafter some quango has discussed and laboriously rejected all other suggestions: Air Chief Marshal Lord Trenchard in 1965, Lord Mountbatten in 1979, Canada's war dead in 1988, Lord Kitchener in 1993. Only in 2001 was it finally agreed, again more or less by default, that the vacant north-western corner should serve as a rolling exhibition of contemporary art, its sculptures regularly changed; currently the plinth supports Rachel Whiteread's transparent resin replica of itself. As an artistic impression of something disappearing up its own arse this could hardly have been more aptly located.

The centre of London, the point from which all distances to the capital are measured, is actually Charing Cross, 100 yards west up the Strand, but walking up out of the Tube subway it's impossible not to be struck with the impression that this is it, the city's hub, with Nelson and his huge exclamation mark like a You Are Here arrow spearing down from on high. To your left, at the end of Whitehall's stately procession, rises the famous clock tower of the mother of parliaments; turn 90 degrees to the right and through Admiralty Arch lies the distant regal mass of Buckingham Palace. In a city starved of grandly sweeping vistas, Trafalgar Square manages two. It is the only place in London where you can stand with your feet on the ground and survey the seats of both monarchy and government.

I thought about this as I patiently circumnavigated the square's outer perimeter under scurrying grey clouds, a circuit which required sixteen minutes and the road-safety input of no less than fourteen illuminated green men. Trafalgar Square's history, I recognised, has largely been shaped by this symbolic centrality. Londoners have gathered here to protest their grievances against the state and to celebrate its triumphs and anniversaries; for decades they came here too to seek its mercy. By the 1880s more than 400 people were sleeping rough in the square every night, fed and clothed by charity volunteers; as late as Orwell's time it was still the default option for London's short-term homeless.

In the street-party age Trafalgar Square's bunting rarely gathered dust. A photograph I'd seen of the 1910 Coronation parade shows Nelson's Column done up like a maypole, fulsomely bedecked with flags, flowers and ribbons. In 1918 the victory celebrations got rather out of hand: if you look harder than I clearly did you can still see scorch marks on the column's base where 'Dominion soldiers' burned down a watchman's hut.

The authorities' phobic response to any public gathering in the square can be traced to its sporadic 150-year history of attracting protestors. Even in the square's planning stages they'd been worried. In 1848 thousands of Chartists assembled in Trafalgar Square, and in 1887 an estimated crowd of 20,000 unemployed men and youths were expelled from the area with such robustness by a force comprising half of London's policemen that some 1,500 demonstrators were hospitalised. The capital's unemployed were reluctantly allowed to gather at Trafalgar Square every Sunday in the early thirties, and it was regularly thronged with anti-appeasement demonstrators before the war and CND marchers after it. That 1990 poll tax riot might have been the first serious bother the square had seen for over a hundred years, but that didn't stop the immediate imposition of yet more draconian public-order regulations.

I know this because pegging it perilously through the rabid yells and parps of duelling white van men and into the eerily calm square beyond, I found myself presented by a precis of relevant

179

bye-laws affixed to a lamppost. Last updated in 1999, in no fewer than fifty-six clauses these represent as fulsome a definition as you'll find of the college principal's wits-end diktat to his *Animal House* miscreants: No More Fun Of Any Kind. You cannot lie down in the square or even look as if you might be about to. You cannot land a helicopter, which I suppose is fair enough, or carry a kite, which isn't. You cannot even, 'unless acting in accordance with permission given in writing by the Mayor', 'use any apparatus for the transmission, reception, reproduction or amplification of sound, speech or images'. Go into Trafalgar Square with an Instamatic or a Walkman, in other words, and without Ken Livingstone's signed permission you're in contravention of the Greater London Authority Act.

Looking around, it was clear how successful they'd been. Despite being backed on most sides by monolithically sober colonial headquarters largely put up, to his inevitable relish, in the immediate pre-Clunn era, Trafalgar Square in the mid-thirties was a far more diverting location for a promenade. The scarcity of traffic helped, of course, as did the continental border of trees. The main departure, though, looking at my 1935 photo of a square filled with sun and people engaged in many activities subsequently proscribed by the Greater London Authority Act, were the adverts. In 1842, the wooden screens around the half-finished stump of Nelson's Column had been liberally flyposted with For The Benefit of Mr Kite-style circus shows, and the capital's first electrically illuminated hoarding – advertising Vinolia soap – went up here in 1890, beating Piccadilly Circus by three years. As the capital's bull's-eye, it was only natural that Trafalgar Square should attract its bullshit.

But what glorious bollocks the hoardings displayed in the thirties. Could anyone really have taken umbrage at a huge rooftop clock with 'BILE BEANS' writ large across its illuminated face? Or the neighbouring slogan for Zam-buk: 'For all SKIN TROUBLE *rub it in*'? I for one would have had them listed and preserved.

The adverts have all been banished, and now they're trying to eliminate the last and most notorious of Trafalgar Square's anarchic idiosyncrasies. Though here at least, as demonstrated by the youth on a mountain bike joyously pedalling at speed through a panicking flock of thousands, they've come up against resistance. Pigeons first gathered in Trafalgar Square before the column was finished – for such enthusiastic navigators it was an obvious geographic meeting point. By the late Victorian era sentimental Londoners were feeding them oats, and the entrepreneurs soon moved in: feed the birds, tuppence a bag, as the old seed-seller sang in *Mary Poppins*. My sunny thirties photo is generously punctuated with little shadows congregating around stooped silhouettes whose complicated hats mark them out as old ladies, and under the aegis of these dedicated avian custodians Trafalgar Square's post-war pigeon population soared to 60,000.

A reflex terror of the world beyond their beaks is one of the pigeon's defining qualities, but at Trafalgar Square they learned to conquer many of their manifold fears. Coupled with mankind's quest for photographic novelty, this docility assured that as London entered the tourist age the square was to witness some truly hideous tableaux: figures with outstretched arms, their entire upper bodies concealed behind a hundred flapping wings and beaks and deformed pink feet. It was like watching the grotesque public humiliation of failed scarecrows.

In 2000, Mayor Livingstone decided enough was enough, and took away the last birdseed seller's licence. Because this was Britain, the protests rang out shrilly: bill something as 'the biggest and most barbaric pigeon cull the world has ever seen' in any other country and you'd be inundated with ticket requests. Today, the thirty or so members of the Pigeon Alliance distribute up to 100 kilograms of birdseed a day in the square, keeping the population up in the low thousands. Notables rushed to support the cause: celebrity spoonbender Uri Geller, TV writer Carla Lane – the list has ended.

I'd made tentative contact with the Alliance and been told they visited at midday, but the appointed hour came and went with no sign of human activity around the unwatered fountain that accommodated most of the cooing flutterers. An already leaden sky was now browning over with the promise of snow, and above their respective national headquarters the Canadian and South African flags whipped tautly in a stiff, chilled breeze; perhaps the weather had put the pigeon fanciers off.

Two unhappy looking figures in fluorescent bibs were stamping about by the left-hand lions, and reading the legend 'Heritage Warden' emblazoned across their yellow backs I went across for a chat.

'They haven't been turning up that regularly for a while,' said one, a Scotsman, asked to explain the Alliance's absence.

'Pain-in-the-arse nutters,' offered his more forthright female colleague. 'One woman always comes up to me and rants on about pigeons being better than people.'

I expected to hear this hypothesis questioned and was not disappointed. 'I get shat on about twice a week,' she said, bitterly flicking a Doctor Marten at an encroaching bird. 'People say they're rats with wings, but they're not. They're worse.'

The pigeon, it must be said, is not an easy creature to love. He eats fag ends and phlegm. He has fleas and craps in your crisps. He out-rabbits rabbits in the shameless fecundity stakes, breeding six times a year to spawn young who are crapping in your crisps just two weeks after hatching. He is prone to blighting mutations of foot and face, mutations that would inspire pity for any other beast, but breed only further contempt for the mindless, soulless pigeon.

The Scotsman wandered off and for a while my discourse with his colleague turned to the apparently more rewarding aspects of her professional life: directing foreign students to the nearest KFC, breaking up impromptu demonstrations, pulling prostrate pissheads up off the benches, photographing Japanese tourists.

'I've taken more snaps of Trafalgar Square than anyone else alive,' she confided touchingly, simultaneously gesturing half-hearted disapproval at three kids riding on a lion's back. A Norwegian tourist came up to ask where in the square the thanks-for-the-war Christmas tree her countrymen donate to London every year is erected; the warden showed her, then murmured to me that the one Finland gives to Belgium is always bigger. She even let me in for a peek around Britain's smallest police station, a one-man granite-walled cylinder hewn out of a squat, jumped-up bollard. On a shelf I noted a rusty set of meat scales and an enormous pair of cartographical dividers: 'Lost property,' she said, mysteriously.

But spend any time in Trafalgar Square and you will find it impossible to keep pigeons off the verbal agenda for long. Wrinkling her nose in disgusted loathing at a hobbling, beakless freak, she returned to the theme with a gusto whose candour I feel it only proper to alert you to in advance.

'We get dead ones every day, but I won't touch 'em. Leave 'em for the cleaners. Saw one cop it under a taxi this morning,' and here she failed to suppress a smirk, 'head over here, body over there. And the other day . . . well, it shouldn't make me laugh . . .' – but my, how it did – 'a couple of them got their heads tied together with some cassette tape or something and every time one tried to take off, the other sort of . . .'

And because words could never hope to capture the slapstick hilarity of this scene she now began to re-enact it, hopping alarmingly about with one hand circling her own neck and the other round an invisible stooge's. A Mediterranean couple with an open *A–Z* and furrowed brows approached, assessed her performance and backed quietly away. When she had finished the Heritage Warden dried her eyes and told me a story about what happens when a pigeon ingests baking powder. I think you can probably guess how it ends, but for those with inquiring minds and washable carpets I can reveal that crushed Alka-Seltzer apparently works just as well.

She was preparing to distress some other tourists when the sun dropped dramatically below those ominous clouds, spilling a sea of gold in St James's Park, a sea which flooded through Admiralty Arch and up to our lions. It was a staggeringly glorious prospect, and speaking for both of us she shielded her eyes and breathed, 'Fantastic. Isn't that fantastic?' For quite a time we squinted wordlessly into the gilded vista. At length she sighed, 'I know I'm in the wrong job, but . . . look at all that.' And as she spoke she passed an outstretched hand from Buck House to Big Ben and all the burnished history between.

It was a pity about the pigeons, the traffic, the Bile Beans clock and the fountains – drained, apparently, for regrouting, their guano-spattered blue tiles suggested a long-forsaken municipal lido – but however unpromising the scenario Trafalgar Square couldn't keep its majesty to itself for long.

Thanking the warden for our time together I walked back through the square's movingly silent centre, the eye of London's storm. Approaching the middle of the wall behind, the square's northern periphery, I spotted a sort of oversized letterbox trying to glint in the sun. Inside it, as I noticed having walked across, were strips of dulled brass labelled 'Imperial Standards of length at 62° Fahrenheit'; dated 1876, here were the Imperial inch, the Imperial foot and the Imperial yard. My heart swelled to see just how literally London had set the world's standards, and sank only slightly when contemplating the looming obsolescence of every stated unit of measurement. We'd had it, baby, and whatever's happened since you can't take that away from us. Then I looked up at Nelson, and pondered with a slight wince that before the night that was just beginning had ended, I'd be back down the road.

Following the unfocused sprawl of the orange set and the stations, Vic and Marge's procession through the reds was refreshingly straightforward: walk up the Strand from Trafalgar

Square and just after you pass the Law Courts you'll notice the road has become Fleet Street. A whole set without one turning. During that journey, however, you'll pass through more years of history than those spanning any other property group: begun in 1829 and now very nearly finished Trafalgar Square is one of the newest addresses on the board; named after an Anglo-Saxon word meaning 'tidal inlet', Fleet Street is very likely the oldest.

Running from Hampstead to the Thames, the perennially disgusting River Fleet was channelled underground in 1766 and now serves only as a sewer. The river's disappearance did for many of Fleet Street's traditional industries – notably the grotesque and malodorous tanning of animal hides – but alongside the usual taverns, freakshows and brothels (right back in 1339 a resident was charged with 'harbouring prostitutes and sodomites') one survived. William Caxton's protégé Wynkyn de Worde printed his first book in Fleet Street in 1500, by which time Richard Pynson – future Printer to the King – was already knocking out copies of *The Canterbury Tales* and text books for Eton. By the end of the seventeenth century dozens of printers and bookbinders were operating in the area, and in the early eighteenth Fleet Street's first newspaper, the *Daily Courant*, opened its offices there. Two was company when the *Morning Advertiser* set up shop over the road, and a century on the crowd was almost out of control.

Huddled blearily up to the steering wheel, so tired that parallel parking was out of the question, I bumped up on to a wet, black kerb at the top of Fleet Street and stared dully at the clock: 3.50 a.m., the time when all radio newsreaders sound like Lord Haw-Haw and all DJs like Noel Edmonds. Before me the street fell away down what had been the Fleet's valley, then rose up to the softly illuminated St Paul's, dome and shoulders above the offices. A police car screamed past in a blur of noise and light; a trio of binmen watched it without interest as they heaved cardboard computer boxes into their dustcart's jaws.

For some time, give or take the odd delivery driver or rattling, empty night bus, that was it. I'd almost drained my Thermos of caffeine syrup – it's always hard to know how much sugar to put in these things – before the first pedestrians stumbled towards me: a groggy derelict loudly preoccupied with expectoration and two shivering office cleaners in blue nylon housecoats.

I hadn't expected much more. All I'd hoped was to imagine the pre-dawn bustle of newsboys and news vans that until twenty short years ago hummed and clattered and bellowed along both pavements and in between. Today the press is collectively referred to as 'what was once called Fleet Street', but in the thirties the street's fame as the centre of newspaper publishing spread across the globe. To fill the time I opened up the 1933 directory at the appropriate pages and tried totting up Fleet Street's resident titles, but somewhere in the mid-120s, between *Gas World* and the *Sierra Leone Weekly News*, I gave up. Number 67 Fleet Street alone, I noted, housed the offices of twenty-five madly diverse publications, from the *Nottingham Guardian* to the *Malayan Medical Journal*. And though many of these might have been one-man operations, there only for the kudos of a Fleet Street correspondence address, plenty of the national press not only answered their phones here, but compiled, composed and printed the entire paper in the same building. Inside its brooding granite fortress the *Daily Telegraph* housed everything from generators to an in-house foundry. The news came in through the front door in a journalist's notebook, and after a few short but hectic hours in the hands of the men in green eyeshades it rumbled out the back in black and white. It was the same at the *Express* almost next door, and the *Mail* across the road in Tudor Street.

In the days of hot-metal typesetting there was hardly an alternative to these Caxtonian guild-era set-ups, but as soon as digital technology provided one – inevitably both cheaper and boundlessly more flexible – Fleet Street fragmented and dispersed. The *Cat's Friend*, the *Dundee Advertiser* and the *Shoe and Leather Record* might already have moved out, but when the last Fleet Street issue of the *Sunday Express* was loaded into vans outside the paper's splendid Deco premises in 1989 an era officially came to an end.

Perhaps because their city's sprawling vastness made it difficult to satisfy the human instinct to pass stories about by word of mouth, Londoners have always liked their newspapers: they had a daily rag seventy-five years before Parisians got one. Approaching the Monopoly era, however, this affection bloomed into an unsightly national love-in.

In an age when *The Times* still had classified ads on the front three pages and spelt 'economy' with a silent 'o' at the start, British newspapers had plenty to offer the man in the chauffeur-driven Silver Ghost but precious little for his more numerous counterparts outside in the street. The revolution was kick-started in the early twenties by *Daily Mail* proprietor Lord Northcliffe, who more than any other took to heart the wisecrack about how to headline that man versus dog biting competition. Indeed Northcliffe's *Mail*, though then a broadsheet in layout, set the British tabloid agenda for the rest of the century: it was the first paper to run sensationalist 'talking-point' features headed 'The Truth about the Night Clubs' or 'The Riddle of Spiritualism', the first to examine new inventions such as aircraft and television, the first to target women readers. 'Get more names in the paper – the more aristocratic the better,' said Northcliffe with unfortunate prescience. 'Everyone likes reading about people in better circumstances than their own.'

The writing of words had been considered as much a work-manlike trade as their printing – a journalist was expected to have served a long apprenticeship, preferably starting out as a fourteen-year-old postboy – but as airy-fairy young Oxbridge aesthetes found themselves in demand as feature writers, a career in Fleet Street became both fashionable and lucrative. The *Mail*'s gossip columns, typically penned either by arch young lordlings or their Evelyn Waugh-style hangers-on, spawned the first columnists: 'the most feared and courted members of society' in the words of Robert Graves.

Northcliffe's journalists were the first to make their excuses and leave – that 'truth about the nightclubs' story began: 'Women dressed as men, men as women . . . dim lights and drowsy odours.' Our current tabloids' unappealingly hypocritical prurience can also be traced to the twenties – the *Sunday Express* would describe at length a lesbian novel, before its reviewer concluded: 'I would rather give a healthy boy or girl a phial of prussic acid than this book.' There were familiarly idiotic campaigns, too: apparently for a bet, Northcliffe undertook to change the nation's diet within six months and for some time did indeed cajole 'practically everyone' into eating a horrid grey loaf called 'Standard Bread'. The *Daily Mail* even introduced its own hat, a cross between a bowler and a homburg.

By apeing the *Mail*, Lord Beaverbrook's *Daily Express* trebled its readership to a million in just four years. The *Daily Telegraph* grew so plump with advertising that it was said a single issue burnt in a kitchen range would boil a pint kettle. By 1936 almost every home in Britain took a daily paper and half of them an evening one too: there were three evening dailies in London and each had circulations over 500,000. A third of households took two Sunday papers, journals whose combined circulation hit 15.7 million in 1937.

But as more publications crowded into Fleet Street seeking a slice of a large and very tasty pie, so the competition spawned ever more ludicrous circulation wars. If all those rival newspaper bingo wars a few years back got on your wick, be grateful you weren't around in the thirties. The *Mail* hired sky-writing planes to emblazon its name above the Derby Day crowds in letters half a mile high, and more or less bought the aviator Amy Johnson for its own commercial ends. Panicked by the *Express*'s success – the latter would be first through the two million mark – the *Mail* began to offer absurdly inflated competition prizes: it is no accident that the 'You Have Won A Crossword Competition' Chance card should have yielded players a generous £100 – the third most lucrative across both decks.

The thirties was the age of extravagant lotteries – a resident of the Metroland suburb of Pinner won a lion which he kept in his back garden – and the newspapers didn't hold back. In 1931 alone, the *Mail* paid out £125,000 in crossword prizes (over £3 million in today's money), but soon even that wasn't enough. Papers started canvassing door-to-door and giving away an insane variety of free gifts: flannel trousers, mangles, tea sets, the collected works of Dickens.

The era also witnessed the birth of silly season stories, most notably a tedious obsession with the Loch Ness monster that in 1933 dominated the pages of those papers who chose to overlook the election as German chancellor of some Hitler chappie. But if you had to select one story to define British journalism of the age, you could do a lot worse than the one-man media circus of randy Reverend Harold Davidson, rector of Stiffkey – that's what I said – in Norfolk.

Found guilty in 1932 of many acts of unseemliness with young prostitutes, Davidson was defrocked, but chose to appeal and funded his own defence through a number of ill-advised publicity stunts. Fleet Street hacks, invited by the miscreant minister to Blackpool, were scarcely able to believe their luck as he wedged himself into a barrel on the beach and announced an intention to starve himself to death. Charged with attempted suicide he sued the Blackpool authorities for damages and won £382, before delighting the press pack once again with an appearance at a Bank Holiday fair on Hampstead Heath in the company of a dead whale. By the middle of the decade he was touring with circuses, and in the summer of 1937 stopped the Fleet Street presses one last time: that appearance in a threepenny lion-taming sideshow at Skegness was itself worth a tasty news-in-brief slot, but by being mauled to death therein the last century's hottest gospeller guaranteed himself a final front-page splash.

And yet behind all the free trousers and naughty vicars, Fleet Street's political influence was inestimably more potent in those days – and without the need for any 'It Was The *Sun* Wot Won It' braggadocio. The conservative newspapers – as every notable one was – helped table the consensus that shaped London's subsequent make-do-and-mend development, a consensus described thus by Robert Graves in 1939: 'Never to do what the Russians had done and the Germans and Italians were doing – pull the house down and build up from new foundations – but to continue patching and riveting and bracing so long as it would stand.'

When Fleet Street got on its soapbox, the authorities had to listen. The creation of the BBC in 1922 incited fury amongst press barons, convinced their sales would be adversely affected: by way of appeasement, the government forbade its new corporation from broadcasting news before 6 p.m. and anything at all on Sunday morning. When it broadcast live from the Derby the BBC was limited to transmitting the crowd's cheers and the thumping of hooves: for the result you'd have to wait for the evening paper. And if a newspaper could persuade the whole nation to eat grey bread or wear a stupid hat, it could certainly steer their pencils towards a particular cross on the ballot paper. Especially if that cross was theirs: in 1929, the *Express* ran an 'Empire Free Trade Crusade' – a campaign which spawned the little red knight who still adorns its masthead – that saw four Empire Free Trade MPs elected in by-elections. More frightening, in 1935 the *Mail* came out in support of Mosley's Blackshirts: its sister paper the *Sunday Dispatch* offered £1 prizes to readers who sent in postcards explaining, no doubt in fifteen words or fewer, 'Why I Like The Blackshirts'. The habit of ennobling proprietors – the bosses of dailies *Express*, *Mail* and *Telegraph* were all made lords – was a mark of successive governments' desperation to keep them on board.

Yet even at the lofty high-water mark of its global importance, Fleet Street remained little more than a medieval alley: 'A commonplace, dingy thoroughfare one might rightly call Grub Street' wrote *Country Life* in 1922, complaining that New York and Paris housed its newspapers in far grander offices. That was the whole point, of course. Fleet Street sourced its first stories in the poky inns and coffee shops where Dr Johnson had held court, and later its seven pubs were the nation's newsrooms. Overblown, lurid, sensationalist, hysterical – the qualities that defined good pub gossip were also those that sold papers. A good journalist needed his finger on the pulse, and if London was the heart of the Empire nowhere did that heart beat more loudly than Fleet Street. Promenading with Boswell one morning through the bracing, bucolic splendour of Greenwich Park, Dr Johnson turned to his companion and sighed, 'Is this not very fine?'

'Yes, sir,' returned Boswell, 'but not equal to Fleet Street.'

Johnson, who lived a wig's throw from the street and surely had the area in mind when he coined his tired-of-life aphorism, instantly agreed. Fleet Street had always been at the centre of things – it was the only Monopoly street to be torched in the Great Fire – and in the thirties all human life was still there: P.E. Chappuis reflector manufacturers, the London Egg Exchange (swop you two cracked browns for a sunny side up), Bowker & King barge owners, Snow's Sacramental Wine Company, two Lyons Corner Houses, half a dozen jewellers, the Salisbury Hotel, cigar merchants, legal booksellers, fancy drapers, stamp dealers – oh, and as well as the HQ of the World League Against Alcoholism, seven pubs. That was a lot of London for you to get tired of, but if you somehow did indeed fall foul of the good doctor's maxim there was always the British Undertakers' Association at No. 108.

My grandfather worked for the *Daily Telegraph* for thirty-nine years, first as a foreign correspondent and then, for twenty postwar years, as a leader writer in some lofty office within those thick grey walls. Staring up at the huge clock leaning out perilously above me as I stepped out of the car I imagined him sidling gracefully beneath it into work, dapper as ever in his groomed goatee and bespoke three-piece. His journalistic career spanned Fleet Street's golden age: so glamorous that his name was on occasion plastered across double-deckers, so handsomely rewarded that he was able to collect property with Monopoly-like nonchalance.

I was still looking up at the clock when two guys in unbuttoned jackets, ID photo chains round their stubbled necks, emerged wearily from the main entrance and stood in the chilled darkness, rubbing eyes and arching back shoulderblades, until a minicab arrived to take them away. Vibrating with the first of many shivers – buttoning my shirt right up to the neck promoted modest retention of body heat at the expense of suggesting a serious personality disorder – I shuffled over and peered into the reception: though the listed lettering across its façade still read DAILY TELEGRAPH, in the covert fashion I'd begun to expect from London's financial institutions the building now reluctantly identified itself as the offices of Goldman Sachs.

It was the same just up the road at the magnificently megalo-maniac *Express* building, all curved black glass and chrome like a Flash Gordon space station. Inside, a great silver starburst exploded figuratively across the lobby ceiling, and I wondered to what extent its own offices' design had fuelled the paper's tradi-tionally grandiose delusions. Recalling all the larger-than-life characters who had swaggered in through those doors, all those bloody and very public circulation wars plotted out up there by loud men with cigars, it seemed disappointingly feeble that the building's current incumbents couldn't even whisper their names on a bell-plate.

These days there are no long lunches or boozy benders, and nearly all of Fleet Street's restaurants, along with a couple of its pubs, have been replaced by sanitised, globalised, de-alcoholised establishments catering for today's hassled, frazzled office workers: McDonald's, Coffee Republic, a pair of Prêt à Mangers, the inevitable trio of Starbucks. A lean and twitchy youth hunched jerkily past muttering complicated obscenities to the cold pavement – oh look, his shirt was buttoned right up to the neck – and a minicab tout tried to hit on me from the other side of the street.

There were odd traces of the old days – a bell-plate faintly engraved 'Irish Press' but with 'Bridge Security' stickered stridently beneath it; a wall emblazoned with tiles spelling out DUNDEE EVENING TELEGRAPH and PEOPLE'S FRIEND – but many more of even older days. Fleet Street's link with the church goes back 1,500 years, and trying to stamp off the cold up a short alley I found St Brides still at it (its steeple, Wren's tallest, was the inspiration for the first tiered wedding cake). And though Snow's Sacramental Wine might have gone, further down the road were the Churches Conservation Trust and the Protestant Truth Society. And after the priests – to be fair to Goldman Sachs, Freshfields Bruckhaus Deringer and the rest – came the money men: Messrs C. Hoare, hoity-toity Fleet Street bankers since 1672, were still going, as were Coutts in a horrid concrete bunker over the road.

Fleet Street was clinging stubbornly to its history, fighting a rearguard action against the office invasion. Yes, most of the retail outlets sold only service convenience, being places you dashed into on the way to work to drop something off which you dashed into again to pick up on the way home: Mr Minit, Snappy Snaps, a dry cleaner's. But it was heartening to see a few offering products you couldn't blithely stuff in a briefcase without a lot of practice: hedge trimmers, a ceiling fan, an improbably puffed up and reassuringly unfashionable Fred Perry ski jacket.

El Vino's, a wine bar which until legally obliged to in 1982 refused to serve women at all and only recently admitted any wearing trousers, was still pompously and ostentatiously present and incorrect; so too, down an especially tight alley, was the Cheshire Cheese, haunt of Johnson, Voltaire, Dickens and a parrot who on Armistice Night in 1918 pulled a hundred corks on the trot before dropping dead. The landlord had been unable to resist a 'Ye Olde' on the sign, but with a history like that I could just above forgive him.

Even older was Prince Henry's Room – a perfect half-timbered edifice whose robustly ornate five-hundred-year-old interior panelling bears the monogram of the future Henry VIII. Until 1901 its grand façade was completely hidden behind a vast billboard that winningly read,

FORMERLY THE PALACE OF HENRY VIII AND CARDINAL WOLSEY
HAIR CUTTING SALON – BRUSHING BY STEAM POWER.

There was still a ground-floor barbers there in the thirties, in fact, and a still more memorable establishment at No. 153 down the other end of the road. Hairdressers have a well-chronicled weakness for abysmal puns when naming their business, but at Sweeney Todd's of Fleet Street the joke was more forthright: not so much Curl Up and Dye as Curl Up and Die.

I'm sure most of us are familiar with the story of the Demon Barber of Fleet Street, a troubled trichologist who gave his eighteenth-century customers the ultimate shave before mincing them up in the basement for subsequent pastry-packaged resale. He was the only hairdresser for whom Head and Shoulders was a pie filling, the only businessman to appreciate the full scope of the phrase 'tough customer'. Though generally conceded to have been cobblers, his legend is still ghastly enough to linger on in the minds of Londoners, most famously inspiring the Flying Squad's rhyming-slang nickname. And in 1936 it would have been especially *au courant*: that year the fêted film-maker Tod Slaughter finally lived up to his name with a cheerfully candid interpretation of the Sweeney myth.

'It's only a story, sir,' the proprietor of No. 153 would breeze slightly too cheerily, rasping his gleaming razor noisily back and forth across the strop. '*I* certainly won't be slicing you from ear to ear and flogging your guts off under a crust at football matches. Now – plenty off the top?' Gingerbread Cottage Forest Refuge, King Herod's Kindergarten for Boys, the Umbrella Stand Elephant Sanctuary – it's difficult to contrive a more unhappily named commercial venture. Only a London journalist would have found it funny.

Fingers were at work on the celestial dimmer switch, but as dawn became morn it wasn't getting any warmer. When I knocked on the window of the San Marco café the whistling old chap cleaning the espresso filters inside pointed at his watch with an apologetic shrug, and succumbing to one of those panic attacks that are the preserve of the underdressed I linked my rigid fingers behind my vibrating head and, hot wrists pressed to agonisingly frosted ears, hammered waywardly back to the car.

It took fifteen minutes for my shuddering whimpers to peter out, and by then the shelf stackers were flinging cellophane packets about in the sandwich bars. Through one drooping eye I saw the first bus without an 'N' in front of its number deposit a trio of security guards; then my chin slumped gently to my chest before being jerked jarringly aloft by the Radio 4 pips bleeping me back to life.

It was still only 6 a.m., yet the Fleet Street I woke to was logjammed with double-parked taxis, dropping off the serious earners, groomed and jaunty young men and women who bounded eagerly up to their lobby doors. The buzz-click of entryphones resounded up and down the road, and in the midst of an epic yawn I recognised precisely how much I would hate to force myself out of my bed, out of my bath, out of my door at this time every day. And it all seemed so sterile and unproductive, all this yah-ing into phones and scrolling endlessly through columns of coloured digits. Fleet Street's dawn output might once have wrapped that evening's fish and chips, but at least in the interim its black and white had been read all over. The earnings that were so definitively visible then were now invisible, and here were some of the otherwise invisible people who earned them. And here also, ambling towards me with an expression of innocent malice, was a traffic warden. My word they start early up here, I thought, waiting until his knuckles were poised to rap against the passenger window before sparking up the ignition and hanging a terrific *Kojak* U-turn.

Not many London thoroughfares have earned themselves a definite article in common parlance, and most of those have done so by virtue of their destination: the Great West Road is the great road to the west; the City Road terminates at the Square Mile's northern edge; and thoroughfares to forgotten villages, royal monuments or fairgrounds are commemorated in roads Brompton, Charing Cross and Tottenham Court. That old road to Kent is awarded a 'the' by everyone except cartographers and John Waddington, but so is another on the Monopoly board – this one an exception to the destination rule.

I don't know why I'm bothering to try and build up some suspense here because I'm obviously talking about the Strand. Hard as it is to imagine it now, high above the waterline and never closer than 200 yards to the Embankment-narrowed river, the Strand was once a bridle path along the banks of the Thames; its name is derived from the Old Norse word for 'beach'. Just as Fenchurch Street is Roman and Fleet Street Anglo-Saxon, so the Strand is the Monopoly board's resident Viking.

The last Norsemen lingered in the Strand long enough to see the son of King Cnut (and my, how those of us with an unsure touch on the keyboard pine for a return to Canute) buried in the church that is still known as St Clement Danes, but by the twelfth century the street was lined with gracious mansions for almost the entire mile of its length. The Cnuts made way, if you will, for the nobs. For sixteenth-century foreign visitors, the Strand – home to over half a dozen dukes or earls, a whopping 134-foot maypole and, now on your left, ladies and gents, London's most central windmill – became a highlight of the guided tours that began at the Tower of London and ended at Whitehall. The Secretary of State's official residence, next to Northumberland House, became known in Charles II's era as No. 1, the Strand – London's first numbered address.

But – and I know this is going to come as a bludgeoning shock – some time in the early eighteenth century, when the aristos began to move west away from the crime and stench of city centre life, the Strand lowered its sights. Its taverns had always attracted wrong 'uns – the Gunpowder Plot was hatched in a Strand pub – and now their keepers were hiring strippers, or even luring 'buggerantoes' to what were the capital's first gay bars. Playing-car manufacturers set up in the narrow edifices that now crowded the Strand, and muggers battered their victims to its potholed pavements 'at no later hour than eight o'clock at night'. Johnson's mate Boswell picked up most of his many tarts along the Strand, and once shagged one from behind on Westminster Bridge. If he'd kept it going for forty years that 'earth hath not anything to show more fair' ode dedicated by Wordsworth to the relevant Thames-spanning structure would have made an inestimably more captivating O level test.

Still happy-go-lucky but now slightly more wholesome, approaching the Victorian age the Strand became the home of London's first public zoo, opened in fact by the brother of Great Marlborough Street's corpse-o-rama. The Exeter Change menagerie regularly paraded its choicer attractions up and down the Strand, a practice that rebounded in 1826 when an elephant ran amok. The extent of the ensuing panic may be imagined from the beast's subsequent post-mortem, during which surgeons extracted parts of a cannonball, a broken spear tip and no less than 152 bullets.

Shortly after, the street's west end was tarted up as part of the Trafalgar Square makeover, which when finished moved Disraeli to hail the Strand as 'perhaps the finest street in Europe' (yes – there we go again). Charles Lamb went even further, claiming that the street's 'multitude of life' regularly moved him to tears.

But the Strand's golden age was the Edwardian, when as London's premier good-time promenade it boasted restaurants, hotels, pubs and more theatres than any other street in the capital. The ghost Tube station that is now Aldwych was opened in 1907 as Strand, running a special late-night 'Theatre Train' that connected with the main Piccadilly line. More so even than Leicester Square the Strand was London's music-hall mecca, celebrated not only in the verses to 'It's A Long Way to Tipperary' but as the lyrical stamping ground of 'Burlington Bertie', who walked up the Strand with his gloves on his hand, and walked down again with them off. It even made it into a title, commemorated in 'Let's All Go Down The Strand', a number whose immortality is ensured by the popular habit of inserting the phrase 'have a banana' in any pause between lines. Respectful of its heritage and flying fearlessly in the face of current standards of aesthetic acceptability, the Players Theatre on the Strand continues to run a *Good Old Days* vaudeville experience.

My mistake, one whose shocking enormity had come groggily into focus as I shivered out of in-car hibernation, was not experiencing at first hand the Strand's thirties speciality – the huge luxury hotel. I'd booked myself a table at the Savoy for lunch, but how much more civilised to have transformed that Fleet Street sortie into a bracing dawn stroll between long sessions of pampered slumber. Wearily trumping an obstructed van driver's single raised finger with two of my own as I laboriously manoeuvred the car into a meter bay round the back of the Savoy, I realised that by the time parking charges had been accounted for I wouldn't even have saved much.

Recklessly recharged by a queasy surfeit of Charing Cross

station doughnuts, I began my trip down the Strand (have a banana) as Vic and Marge would surely have done, back up at the Trafalgar Square end.

The homely country-town high-street atmosphere that so tickled Disraeli has clearly been diluted by a Clunn-chuffing road widening scheme that during thirty-three years of typically faltering endeavour demolished almost everything on the Strand's southern flank by 1934. It's still easy, though, to take in the motley vigour that made Charles Lamb weep: in the foreground two squat, plump Nash-era towers – in the thirties Barclays but now Jigsaw – bursting like a tart's cleavage from their Georgian bodice; on the distant horizon St Mary-le-Strand, a Baroque needle threaded up between four furious lanes of traffic. And in between, bullied by the beefy office blocks but still holding out, a sort of medley of the Strand's greatest hits: a couple of theatres, a couple of hotels, a couple of pubs.

Assessing the Strand's appeal in the early thirties, Professor C.H. Reilly proved himself a lot cannier than Harold Clunn: 'It is essentially the London we love, and the stream of red omnibuses, taxi-cabs and carts, which congest it as a thoroughfare, all add appropriate life to its multicoloured, many materialed buildings. Even the advertisements with their sprawling lettering by day and the illuminated signs by night can do little damage to a muddled bazaar where you can not only buy clothes and boots of every quality, but have your photograph taken at any time as a Red Indian or cowboy in ready-made fancy dress.' Got that? *At any time*.

A tough act to follow, yet the Strand managed better than I'd expected. In terms of commercial and retail possibilities it runs the gamut, with more variety than any other street on the board. And this street has upheld its traditions better than most, too: of its thirties commercial themes only the fêted trinity of pawn-broking, dentistry and the manufacture of surgical instruments have been swept aside. Half the Strand's six Lyons Corner

Houses are still restaurants, and the Adelphi still projects its on-stage stars up and down the street in lights. Those cartoon Chinamen above the entrance to Twinings, the tea importers who have been paying rates to the borough of Westminster for longer than any other firm, are welcoming in customers as they have since 1706. There are still jewellers, still a Boots – along with pubs, London's only reliable retail constant. Anyone not stupid enough to have packed their innards with fabric-flavoured doughnuts can still enjoy London's finest breakfasts within the extravagantly mahoganied dining halls of Simpson's-in-the-Strand – an establishment so stubbornly British that it banned the word 'menu' in favour of 'bill of fare'. The travel agents and luggage emporia attracted, as with the Northumberland Avenue hotels, by Charing Cross station's boat trains to the Continent maintain a stout presence, and still flying the flag for the dozen or so postage stamp dealers resident along the Strand in the thirties I was charmed and delighted to discover the continued residence of Stanley Gibbons and a less familiar rival.

This wasn't so much because I'm interested in postage stamps – although I'm afraid I vaguely am – but because peering into their windows I noted the extent to which both outlets have diversified into the more broadly fascinating showbiz memorabilia market. Stanley was offering one of Johnny Rotten's mohair scarves for £2,800 – almost what I'd have paid to see it looted by rioting poll-tax anarchists – but between the first-day covers and Penny Blacks over the road was an offer yet more shriekingly irresistible: a set of pewter Dalek salt and pepper shakers, complete with a signed photo of Tom Baker, all for £95.

Yet at the same time it was difficult to avoid the sensation that the Strand has been slightly neutered, that the street has become rather a jack of all the trades it once mastered. The muddled-bazaar/cowboy-photo end of the market has migrated to nearby Covent Garden, and, Dr Who cruet sets aside, most of the retail establishments offered little to the window shopper unmoved by the leisured perusal of staplers or bifocals. And the Gaiety Theatre has been tellingly usurped by the headquarters of Citibank plc.

The Strand's atmosphere, even on the many occasions I've walked along it at night, always seems rather muted and downbeat, and standing at its halfway point, by the messy and turbulent junction with the Aldwych and Waterloo Bridge, I understood why. Behind me, sloping gently down to Trafalgar Square, the Strand's northern side was still a pick-and-mix chorus line of three hundred years of architecture. But facing it across the traffic was the most humourless audience imaginable, a massed row of po-faced blocks. Harold Clunn, trying to pinpoint exactly what it was he despised about London's higgledy-piggledy old frontages, and what he loved about their uniform, monolithic replacements, concluded that 'the new buildings in the Strand made the old ones look as though they wanted a shave'. Regrettably, someone had passed the razor to Sweeney Todd.

I crossed the road deep in thought – an ill-chosen state of mind that elicited a volley of parps – and miraculously found myself in a bucolic oasis. To stand amidst the carefully tended geraniums and pansies in St Mary-le-Strand's horseshoe-shaped and almost horseshoe-sized churchyard is to experience one of London's more arcane pleasures. Its old iron railings enclose the condensed essence of a timelessly rural England, yet lean across that flagstoned path to sample the scent of a fragrant briar rose and if you're not careful a bus might make off to New Cross with any prominent facial features. The only other time I have experienced such a sense of calm amidst chaos was standing on a ledge as a mighty Icelandic waterfall crashed down before me. One might imagine a spitefully mischievous deity – let's call him Harold – plucking up a village church and dropping it in the M25's central reservation.

Certainly not many brave the barrelling one-way onslaught. Inside, with the traffic roar filtered down to a watery hiss, I read that the church only holds three services a week. And the visitors' book, by no means an unwieldy tome, went back eight years.

Back over the road, Somerset House was another rewarding discovery, but this was an oasis of such grand proportions that I couldn't imagine how or why in all the times I'd walked past its gates I'd never once taken the trouble to saunter in. I'd seen it billed as the sole survivor of the Strand's great mansions, but in fact the present stately buildings, arranged around an enormous and – ooooh – windily exposed square, were Britain's first large-scale, purpose-built government offices, erected in the 1780s and for 140 years the headquarters of the Register of Births, Deaths and Marriages. Now home to the Courtauld Institute's rather wonderful art collection, Somerset House is a splendidly agreeable place in almost every way. You can have a cup of coffee in that expansive courtyard, perhaps flicking grains of Demerara sugar at the ice skaters pirouetting across the rink before you, or stroll through the river wing to the terrace overlooking the Thames and enjoy a glass of something cold, refreshing and wart-inducingly overpriced (I did say *almost* every way).

But the Strand is very much a street of two halves, or in fact three thirds, and up from Aldwych it is squeezed into its colonial Establishment phase beneath the clean-shaven, slightly forbidding twenties bulk of the Australian and Indian high commissions and Bush House, now synonymous with the BBC's World Service but built by American tycoon Irving Bush as a vast and extravagantly appointed trade centre.

Hailed at the time as the world's most expensive building, Bush House saw its commercial dream rather soiled by the Depression, and its imposing marble-clad showrooms and leisure facilities were largely empty when the Post Office pension fund acquired the freehold. In 1940 the fund leased Bush House to what was then the BBC's Empire Service: swimming pools and cinemas were converted into studios, and throughout the war the Service cemented a reputation as a trusted broadcaster. Today, with 120 million listeners and programming in thirty-eight languages, it remains one of the few British exports we can all be genuinely proud of – when Radio 5 Live's commentator breaks off during a Saturday afternoon football match to announce that we're now being joined by World Service listeners around the globe, some part of my soul is always stirred.

As well as the colossal sheep's head over its front entrance, the Australian High Commission is otherwise notable for its visa section's opening hours, these being 9a.m.–11a.m. Having posted my c.v. through the doors I circuited the second of the Strand's central reservation places of worship, the heavily shrapnel-pitted RAF church of St Clement Danes, and beheld before me the Strand's third third.

Recently sandblasted back to their late Victorian Gothic splendour, the Law Courts present a grand but suitably stern face to the Strand. I probably could have gone in – any building made up of sixty court rooms and thirty-five million bricks can only be a remarkable one – but it didn't look as much fun as Somerset House, and after eight hours of wind-chilled pedestrian endeavour I somehow lacked the wherewithal to explain my Monopoly board to another bag-searching sobersides. After a quick tour of the engagingly archaic legal alleyways of Middle Temple – an area so ubiquitously peopled by the administrators of law that I passed three unmanned newspaper stands with honesty boxes – I turned on my worn-down heels and headed back.

Turning into Savoy Court and the eponymous hotel's extravagantly chromed Deco entrance, the good news was that I had long since walked off those doughnuts: I'd fed the meter and now it was my turn. The bad news was that because my day had begun in an earlier life, and because the man who led that life was apparently a giant buttock, I had forgotten to wear a tie.

You can't dine at the Savoy without a tie. This is a place that writes its own laws – the hotel's carriage drive, Savoy Court, is the only thoroughfare in Britain in which motorists must keep to the right – and unlike the many-bricked edifice down the road it tolerates no appeal. As the maitre d' glided up to me across the thick lobby carpet I hurriedly cloaked my incriminating neck and chest area with a hand and two photocopied images of the Strand of yesteryear. If I could evade detection long enough to whip a napkin into my collar, and then spend a lot of time minutely examining broad objects – first the menu, then my Monopoly board – I might possibly get away with it.

'Good afternoon,' he announced in cultured tones spiced with the merest hint of Italian.

'Table in the name of Moore,' I grunted, chin to chest.

'Certainly, sir.' The tiniest pause. 'May I offer to lend you one of our ties?'

I smiled like the R. White's secret lemonade drinker caught at the fridge by his wife: a foolish, feeble, don't-hit-me smile. Casually arranged in the heady aftermath of my power breakfast at the Ritz – my free power breakfast at the Ritz – this solo Savoy lunch was now laid bare for what it was: an indulgent, vainglorious pomposity, one for which I was already being punished in more ways than one. Shepherd's pie was listed on the menu outside the Grill Room as the day's speciality, but the pricing of even this utilitarian dish at £18.50 had briefly effected reverse-thrust doughnut action.

Of the grand Strand hotels, the Savoy is the only survivor. The Strand Palace, though still very much alive, had never in fact placed itself in the top tier: part of the J. Lyons Corner House empire, it sought, as did its catering brethren, to offer a wing-collar experience at blue-collar prices. But grand it certainly appeared, at least until a Clunn-style shave in the late sixties: how the proprietors must hate visiting the Victoria and Albert Museum, where the wondrous Deco entrance they discarded so eagerly has been painstakingly reassembled. Today the Strand Palace exudes a sort of Dralon dinner-dance suburbanity: you wouldn't catch the Savoy advertising a £14 carvery on a board out the front.

At the time of its opening in 1896, the Cecil was Europe's largest and most magnificent hotel, with six hundred rooms. Shortly before completion, regrettably, its proprietor went bankrupt and was sentenced to fourteen years in prison – in those days fraud and deception were taken seriously, and suicide was a regularly selected option for tycoons whose empires went belly up. The Cecil never recovered: 'The building was demolished in the record time of sixteen weeks in the autumn of 1930,' recounts Clunn, out-Clunning himself, 'and a magnificent new twelve-storey building crowned by a massive stone clock tower has now been erected on this site by the Shell Mex Company.'

Much as I hate to agree with Harold, I've always been slightly in awe of Shell Mex House. A sort of musclebound Cenotaph with windows, it more or less demands respect from all beholders, still exuding that tremendous arrogance appropriate for the first corporate headquarters in London whose construction costs topped £1 million. Only with hindsight at the weedily parodic commercial structures that Shell Mex House later inspired can its name be taken in vain: if Shell Mex House is Elvis, then the sorry blocks around Fenchurch Street are all Shakin' Stevens.

So anyway it's just the Savoy these days, a hotel which hasn't forgotten that Monsieur Ritz was its first manager and Monsieur Escoffier its first chef, but probably wished no one remembered the night in July 1923 when the Parisian wife of an Egyptian prince expressed her ennui for a marriage characterised by fierce arguments and enforced sodomy by fatally shooting him three times in one of the hotel's grander suites.

Juries might have been tough on business fraud in those days, but they certainly weren't on sodomised wives: accepting her barrister's claim that the gun accidentally went off in her hands (three times?), they acquitted her. As a side issue it was also claimed in the trial that the prince had been enjoying a gay affair with his personal assistant, which I only mention so as to be able to wheel out Stephen Fry's comment on arriving late for a press conference at a grand hotel: 'Sorry, I was just upstairs in my suite – well, that's what I call him, anyway.'

And before I return to my tieless humiliation, I've just got time to get some more retaliation in first: working undercover as a cleaner at the Savoy around the time of my visit, a *Guardian* journalist saw a mouse running into the staff kitchen, and a cockroach, and had to buy her own rubber gloves even though after deductions she was paid £2.69 an hour. Work through the night and she could have put a down-payment on a *feuilleté* of asparagus.

The maitre d' returned with his emergency tie collection, one I shouldn't have been surprised to see characterised by prodigious breadth and an unabashed boldness of design. I selected one that only vaguely resembled a child's hand-drawn copy of a Magic Eye image; he smiled gently, then lowered his gaze in compassion. 'And for the, ah, jacket?'

As he led me cravenly off to the cloakroom I tried not to think that I might actually be paying – paying through the bloodied and broken nose – for this indignity. This was a thought that crystallised as I trudged head down back across the foyer in the attendant's jacket selection, a gold-buttoned, soup-cuffed blazer presumably abandoned in some West End gutter by Sir Les Patterson after an especially clumsy night out.

I shuffled silently into the Grill Room, in no fit state to appreciate that the low-ceilinged velvety chromeness made this comfortably the most thirties ambience I had yet experienced. A waiter settled me behind many items of geometrically aligned crockery, unable to avoid tilting his incredulous leer towards my outfit at an angle that made me feel like an improbably bosomed barmaid at last orders.

When he returned to take my order figures had been wobbling up from the menu as if out of a heat haze: monkfish ragout £28.50, haddock Monte Carlo £27, veal steak with salsify £26.50. 'I think I might have something light . . . maybe . . . maybe just the Welsh rarebit?' What was I doing here, dressed up like a Rotarian tramp in a place where cheese on toast was nine quid, and where that was a bargain?

'Just the Welsh rarebit,' he repeated, endeavouring to bully his features into an approximation of servility but instead looking as if low but increasing voltage was being applied to the soles of his feet. 'Shall I call the sommelier?'

A bray of unsteady laughter burst out to my left; I turned and saw two red-toothed priests gesticulating at each other over a table of half-filled glasses. What was the point? Why order Welsh rarebit from a kitchen whose quest for gastronomic novelty inspired so many notable creations, including two – one of peach, one of toast – that bear the name of Edwardian Savoy regular Dame Nellie Melba?

'This *is* the American Bar, isn't it?' I asked, hardly bothering to sound genuinely confused or surprised.

'I'm afraid not, sir,' replied the waiter in an identical tone. And so five minutes later, relieved of the sartorial accessories not deemed obligatory for those merely intending to get pissed at the Savoy, I was propping up the American Bar – a venue whose already pleasing period ambience seemed substantially more pleasing by the time I'd sucked down the dregs of a Long Island Iced Tea, not so much a cocktail as a minibar in a glass. Mind-messing entertainment for the price of a Welsh rarebit.

The Strand, I pondered, had rather lost its way since the thirties; these days it was more of a bypass than a promenade, a through way to the West End proper, a means to an end rather than an end in itself. But then having been encouraged out through the foyer doors by busy, starch-cuffed hands, it occurred to me that promenading was a dead art. As I reeled light-headedly up Savoy Court I wondered if I might possibly be the first Londoner since Burlington Bertie to have walked up the Strand and down again just for the sake of walking, right across the city's heart from the tip of SW1 to the toe of EC4.

The doorway dossers I'd passed on the way up had now been supplemented by half a dozen others, and stooping into the scaffolded pavement passage I almost tripped up a crusty on crutches appraising a discarded Prêt à Manger sandwich. Peter Ackroyd called the street 'a great thoroughfare of the dis-possessed', and though everyone else around might have been passing through, the Strand's vagrants were clearly going nowhere. When, for the fifth time in half as many minutes I was mumblingly hassled for change, I found myself doing something very unusual. Maybe it was the cocktail, or maybe it was where I'd drunk it, but anyway there I was, squatting down next to a sallow, expressionless youth with the sort of matted dreadlocks that suggested he'd only just learned to request money after years of begging passers-by to smear their chewing gum in his hair. 'This might sound a bit odd,' I said, trying not to let him smell my breath or me his, 'but if you roll these dice I'll give you a quid.'

The tiny change in his expression suggested amused relief – of the many novel transactions proposed to him I imagined this was amongst the least unsavoury. He tilted out a minute shrug and held forth a surprisingly pink palm into which I dropped the dice. A wrist rotated, fingers opened and out clicked a six and a three. 'Cheers,' I said, but preparing to pick up the dice I did the maths: the six would take me from Trafalgar Square to Go To Jail, and the three on to Community Chest.

Blurting an apology, I rooted through the backpack for the cards that since my experience in the Ritz I now took everywhere. I elbowed an ankle and a pedestrian tutted sourly; as I scrabbled out the top pink card my ears were already a matching shade. 'Advance to GO,' I read aloud, before addressing my guest roller again. 'Look – make it two rolls for two quid.'

He almost smiled this time as the dice were picked up and dropped once more, revealing a six that I deduced took me to The Angel. 'Should be two hundred quid,' he said in a dis-armingly soft milkmaid burr. 'You went past GO.'

I allowed myself a horribly patronising laugh as I gathered up dice and cards and got to my feet. 'Should be,' I drawled pompously, reaching into my pocket, 'but I'm afraid it's just the two.'

Only as my fingers scrabbled forlornly for things that jingled did I remember my parking meter's serious change habit. My red ears blanching and that R. White's smile sidling tentatively across my face once more I held out a hand with three coins in it, one of them tiny and silver, none of them gold. And moments later I was jogging past Charing Cross with pungent West Country epithets ringing reedily out behind me.

CHAPTER 13

The Light Blues

THE ANGEL, ISLINGTON
LONDON BOROUGH OF ISLINGTON

EUSTON RD
LONDON BOROUGH OF ST PANCRAS

PENTONVILLE RD
LONDON BOROUGH OF ISLINGTON

Of all the London board's idiosyncrasies, none is more roundly ludicrous than The Angel, Islington. It's a pub, not a street, and it's not even in Islington. At least it wasn't when Vic and Marge stopped there for lunch, having walked up Pentonville Road from King's Cross: in 1823 the *Gentleman's Magazine* reported that the Islington parish had refused to bury a dead beggar found in the street outside the Angel, allowing the parish of Clerkenwell, whose boundary ran just the other side of the pub, to annex it after having undertaken the responsibility themselves. In the thirties Clerkenwell was part of Finsbury, which was amalgamated into the borough of Islington only in 1965. So you see, it should have been The Angel, Finsbury.

In the early seventeenth century an inn with the spread-winged Angel of the Annunciation as its sign was the first staging post out of London on the Great North Road, and when in 1756 the New Road – London's first bypass, you'll recall – was opened, cross-town commuters joined inter-city travellers at its bars. Business boomed when London's first bus was routed past the tavern doors in 1829, and again in 1862 when the Agricultural Hall opened up the road. Rebuilt with the lofty dome that remains a landmark, by 1899 the Angel was serving eight hundred lunches a day, the sort of figure to attract the Lyons Corner House site-seekers, who duly snapped it up in 1922.

The Lyons Corner House dominated thirties London in a far more ubiquitous and all-pervading sense than McDonald's or Starbucks have managed or ever will. They were institutions: almost every street on the Monopoly board had one, and some – Piccadilly, the Strand, Oxford Street – boasted half a dozen or more; by 1939 the chain was operating 260 premises. Many were enormous – if the aforementioned Coventry Street outlet's capacity of 4,500 didn't impress you, perhaps the 1,000 staff employed at the Marble Arch Corner House will – and often palatial. An American visitor was astounded to find what was by rights just a big cafeteria 'decorated after the fashion of a palace ballroom, with immense chandeliers of prismed glass and a balcony furnished in cream and gold'.

The chain employed top architects and designers: Oliver Bernard, creator of that V&A-exhibited Strand Palace doorway, was also responsible for many Corner House interiors. And yet they were truly democratic: Orwell's destitute Gordon Comstock, walking past a Corner House, was met by 'a wave of hot, cake-scented air' and fondly mused that 'you could sit there for nearly an hour. A cup of tea twopence, two buns a penny each.' Nonetheless it was more than good enough for a company director like Victor Watson, and when, on New Year's Eve 1966, George Harrison was refused entry at a poncy nightclub for not wearing a tie, off he went with Eric Clapton to celebrate at the all-welcoming Coventry Street Corner House.

Opened on Piccadilly in 1894 by a firm that had until then operated a chain of tobacconists, the first Lyons Tea Shop represented a social revolution. The Underground had made it possible to travel quickly and cheaply into town, and for the first time middle-class, suburban women began to congregate in the West End from all over London with the idea of spending an afternoon window-shopping along Monopoly's green streets.

But alas! Lunchtime arrives, and madam's options are limited to an expensive and exclusive restaurant whose maitre d' will very probably turn away anyone he doesn't personally recognise, or a pub, where she will knock over a brimming spittoon with her bustle while trying to ward off a drunk encyclopaedia salesman.

Or consider this: madam sagely stuffs her face at home prior to hopping on the Tube, but then, horror of horrors, finds those cups of tea demanding to be let out as she's peeping at the Heinz tins in Fortnum's window. Only recently had London's first female public convenience opened in Camden, and it was still being deliberately run into by cabbies expressing the general outrage at such a concept. In short, when a downtown woman had to go, she had to go to a Lyons.

The Lyons Tea Shops changed middle-class women's lives, as later the larger, cheaper Corner Houses did for the working class. As well as being clean and congenial, they were increasingly grand. People who couldn't entertain at home could buy their friends tea at a Corner House done up like a stately home, and be served like the nobs by a maid in a pinafore (Lyons trademarked their waitresses' nickname, the Nippy, in 1924). The Corner Houses catered for a tea-time culture that Londoners of all classes subscribed to: that famous name out the front, in gold letters on a white background, was a guarantee of value and quality. Soon there were salon orchestras in the larger outlets, and a Corner House became one of the few venues considered respectable for a meeting between young couples, inevitably before going on to the pictures.

The firm was an eager innovator. Lyons' central kitchen at Hammersmith was a mass-catering production line, pre-

preparing cakes and sandwiches and delivering them by van to branches all over London. The Corner House at Throgmorton Street was the world's first underground restaurant, serving Viennese whirls and poached eggs 40 feet below the Bank of England. Most of the West End branches were several restaurants in one: an Egg and Bacon Bar serving all-day breakfasts; a sandwich counter; other departments specialising in cakes or cooked meats. To keep control of the stupendous throughput of staff, customers and buttered scones, the firm was one of the first in Britain to acquire a computer: unable, in 1949, to find any such machine to buy, the Lyons R&D boys sat down and built one themselves, based on a pioneering Cambridge mainframe. I still can't quite get over that.

And yet despite all this, you will be aware from the current absence of Lyons Corner Houses on the nation's high streets that it all went wrong. By the fifties London's youth wanted something a little less prim, a little more boisterous: an espresso bar, perhaps, even if it meant having to listen to Tommy Steele and Cliff Richard. When they went out on a date there were now more romantic options – cosy French bistros or an Italian trattoria – and when they got married they could stay in and watch telly. Lyons saw which way the wind was blowing, or thought it did, and in 1954 introduced the first Wimpy Bars in its West End Corner Houses.

Well, we all know how that turned out. Still clinging to the waitress service and that mindset of genteel Edwardian decorum which had served the firm so stalwartly, every Wimpy burger was delivered to your table by a Nippy along with the knife and fork with which you were to effect its consumption. Unaware that they were rather missing the point of the fast-food revolution, Lyons blindly proceeded to convert many of their outlets into Wimpy Bars. If the name itself, borrowed from a minor *Popeye* character, was unfortunate – wimp meant then what it means now – then the menu was even more tragically deluded.

Take a broad, waxen frankfurter, hew notches all the way up one side and drop it into a deep-fat frier. When charred to an approximation of lightly napalmed flesh withdraw, bend into a tight coil, sling in some onions and stuff and wedge between two halves of a bloated teacake. Note that many of your customers are now leaving, their faces pale and tight; but note too the small group of novelty-hungry schoolboys who remain. They are eager to sample your outré creation, it seems; all that remains is to give it a name. You lift the breaded covering and gaze at the broiled, coiled sausage for inspiration: Frankentwister, you think, or maybe Whirlyburger. Loopolata? But suddenly it comes to you, and nodding in happy self-congratulation you walk up to your youthful clientele, theatrically clear your throat and holding forth Wimpy's new flagship offering grandly announce: 'Gentlemen, I give you the Big Bender.'

And what of Wimpy's Brown Derby, a doughnut confection evidently picked up on a shovel, still steaming, from behind a racehorse? I don't think I've ever read through a Wimpy menu with a straight face or a still stomach.

Of all the London institutions that messed up after the war – the Underground, C&A, homburg manufacturers – none had more to mess up than Lyons. Yet mess it up they did, promptly and utterly. London's last Corner Houses closed in the seventies, and most of the Wimpy Bars were sold off in 1989, reopening soon after as Burger Kings. Along with McDonald's, these did for families what the Corner Houses had done for women: allowed them the freedom and independence to have a day out in town without being tutted at. Yet somehow 303 Wimpy Bars survive around the country, patronised by a doubly doomed clientele of smoking pensioners, 303 waitress-served restaurants where the Benders are forever Big, the Derbies forever Brown.

The Angel Corner House, though, was one of the first to go. It served its last scone in 1959 and after a brief period as a student hostel lay empty for decades until converted into what I saw, standing by a polished black-granite pillar at the foot of the façade's netted scaffolding, to be a branch of the Co-Operative Bank.

Wouldn't it be splendid, I thought, leaning back towards the bad-tempered lunchtime traffic as I tried to trace the meshed silhouette of that famous lofty dome, if someone resurrected and updated the Corner House concept: family-friendly catering for all in grandly regal surroundings. Later I would conclude that labour costs (most of those 1,000 staff at Marble Arch were paid far less than the equivalent of today's minimum wage) and the unfeasibility of luring 4,500 punters into a single restaurant made this unlikely, but at the time I had other concerns – mostly related to the builder's transistor radio which, choosing that moment to work its way through some high-up hole in the scaffold netting, met a traumatic and noisy death perhaps 7 inches in front of me.

Pentonville Road was right there, heading west just past those shards of black plastic and pirouetting Duracells, but instead I walked back north along Upper Street's raised pavements past a staggering succession of coffee shops and cute eateries: eighty-six in all, I learned later, and almost all with outside tables even this late in October. Add in the antique market and a token ethnic veneer – an Indian bedspread shop, a Bengali in a Nehru hat selling peacock feathers outside the Tube – and you have the apotheosis of right-on yuppiedom. The sun came out and within moments everyone around me had whipped on a pair of those bug-eyed sunglasses so *de rigueur* amongst off-duty racing drivers.

This part of Islington, gentrified so ruthlessly in the last twenty years, seems ill at ease in the light blues: in the real world, each of those little fifty-quid houses you line up on The Angel would, according to local estate agents, have set you back £600,000. Perhaps aggrieved that he'd paid nearer the latter figure than the former, a couple of years back a spokesman for the Angel Neighbourhood Forum, inevitably christened Jamie, appealed to

Waddingtons to promote The Angel, Islington, up from the cheap end of the board. 'It's very misleading,' he blethered, no doubt in a shrill yet braying yah. 'People feel it's somewhat derogatory of the area. I mean, places like Whitechapel Road do remain a little questionable.'

Pat Haynes laughed like a drain when I'd told him about that on the phone. A self-described 'local geezer' for almost sixty years, Pat is Islington's longest-serving councillor and a man better placed than most to offer an overview of the set's upheavals; to sing me the blues. Pentonville Road and The Angel – or at least its immediate environs – were the first places on the board I'd visited where people didn't just work or play, but still actually lived. There was a human side to their story which needed a human insight.

Radicalism has been part of Islington's make-up since Tom Paine drew up his Rights of Man while lodging at the Angel. In 1990 Islingtonians played a prominent role in the poll tax revolt, and in 1995 protestors forcibly excluded traffic from what remains one of London's most polluted areas. For years you couldn't walk out of Angel Tube station without being harangued by *Socialist Worker* vendors in elaborately knackered donkey jackets. Walking in through Islington Town Hall's doors – above which the red flag has been hoisted on more than one occasion over the years – it was easy to imagine being intimately examined for telltale signs of imperialist decadence by a humourless conscript in the Haynesian People's Army.

But it shouldn't have been, because Councillor Haynes – as he had been respectfully referred to by every receptionist and security guard I'd spoken to – was both a lovely chap and an almost soundlessly mild-mannered one. 'These days the EU flag is about as radical as we get,' he joked in a sort of parched gasp. That drain he'd laughed like had, in truth, been more of a dripping pipette, and as he ushered me out of his office's old-school disorder into a nearby staff room my ear was already almost in his mouth. Pat's micro-decibelled man-and-boy account of the borough's post-Monopoly history couldn't hope to compete with the resident percolator, let alone the industrial photocopiers behind us. Someone came in with a many-paged report, and after they hit the green button I missed the whole of the 1970s.

Spooling back to the decade of his birth, Pat spoke of a healthy population of blue-collar Islingtonians in poorly remunerated manual jobs: railway workers, print workers, clock makers and, above all, postmen at the huge sorting office in what had been the Agricultural Hall (and is now, inevitably, the Business Design Centre). The noise and filth of the railways had already driven middle-class residents further north in search of a quiet suburb such as Islington had once been, but had also attracted industries; as these in turn began to decline so the population shrank.

Pat had no trouble compiling a lengthy roll call of consequent local casualties: theatres upon whose boards Oscar Wilde had trodden, Pat's old school, cinemas, the pub opposite what he still called 'the Corner House'. 'We knocked down a lot of places we shouldn't,' he said, holding his hand up a lot higher than the current breed of don't-blame-me politicians are ever prepared to.

Labour won control of the London County Council for the first time in 1934, and under Herbert Morrison's leadership embarked on a major rehousing schedule. By 1939 more than 300 acres of London slums were named 'clearance areas', many of them in Islington, which along with the neighbouring boroughs of Finsbury and St Pancras had been declared among the capital's poorest and most overcrowded under the terms of the 1935 Housing Act. Ready as ever with an offensive snobbism, Harold Clunn described Islington's Monopoly-era artisan dwellings being 'as stunted in their proportions as the majority of their inhabitants were wanting in their moral character'.

New low-rise LCC blocks emerged in clusters around the

borough, offering the sort of unfamiliar amenities that spawned Tory jokes about families storing coal in the bath. But even after the war three-quarters of Islington households had no running water, and well into the sixties plenty of families were still living in single rooms in dilapidated nineteenth-century terraces. A leaflet Pat had drawn up for the Islington Fabian Society revealed that as late as 1965, 332,313 'warm baths' were being taken in the borough's five public bath houses each year by residents whose homes lacked such facilities; by 1990 this had fallen to under 9,000. But at the same time Islington's population continued to decline, down by almost 50 per cent during that twenty-five-year period to 165,000.

With the streets literally half-empty, the great street markets started closing down and what Pat sagely referred to as 'useful shops' gave way to the first bistros and antique stalls catering for that pioneering wave of gentrificationists. Morrison's LCC had drawn up the green belt legislation that stopped London's ever-outward suburban expansion, and encouraged by government grants the middle classes returned to tart up Islington's now-desirable old houses. Some sort of class Rubicon was crossed when the Wimpy Bar shut down in the late eighties, ending a position in the front line of tobacco consumption Islington had held since Walter Raleigh lit up on Upper Street.

'It wasn't the first time we'd had the yuppies in,' Pat murmured benignly, betraying no personal bitterness at the middle-class invasion. 'Gentrification happened over a hundred years ago when the clerks set up here because they could walk into the City. As soon as the City revived in the eighties it happened again: three stops down the Tube from Angel and you're at Bank.' It was all cyclical, Pat seemed to be saying. In a few years the haves will become the hads, and Islington's population will once again be depolarised into a borough of have-nots.

With reference to this latter group, Pat spoke of 'the classic inner-city thing': pensioners, single mothers, asylum seekers, a lot of drugs and criminals – 'more than our fair share of both'. Two-thirds of Islingtonians are council tenants and two-thirds of them are on benefits. Perhaps the most telling insight into Islington's condition is that the borough is burdened with the nation's highest proportion of children in care. 'If there is any resentment,' he said, 'it's down to middle-class council-tax whingers who don't want to know that it costs forty grand a year to keep a kid in care.'

Pat drained his coffee and squinted up at the clock. 'Have you ever played Monopoly?' I asked as he rose to bid me farewell. Councillor Haynes chuckled softly, nodding in fond recollection. 'I think the first time,' he began, but then someone a few corridors away turned on a vacuum cleaner and twenty minutes later I was back at the top of Pentonville Road, none the wiser.

Presenting as it did an opportunity to chart the awesome rise and farcical fall of the Corner House, I was indebted to Vic and Marge for their auspicious lunch at the Angel. I could see, however, that it was going to be difficult to generate equal enthusiasm for the road they walked up to get there.

Named after Henry Penton, the landowner on whose grounds it was laid out in the 1770s, Pentonville was one of London's first manufactured suburbs: a new town, in effect, along what was then still called the New Road. In an age when craftsmen and trades-people could still make fortunes, many walking under those filigreed fanlights into Pentonville Road's grand, five-floor residences were organ builders or clock makers. John Betjeman's grandfather, a 'fancy cabinet maker', constructed the first tantalus – 'a case in which spirit bottles may be locked with their contents tantalisingly visible' – in his Pentonville Road residence.

Rescued from Fagin's clutches by Mr Brownlow, Oliver Twist is so astounded by the fragrant splendour of his benefactor's Pentonville surroundings that in Lionel Bart's musical he throws open the window and – capturing the spirit of Dickens if not the precise vocabulary – invites all-comers in song not just to buy the wonderful morning, but have it boxed and wrapped in a ribbon for his extended perusal. For Oliver it represented a virtual voyage right round the early Victorian Monopoly board, from the square after GO to what at that time might easily have been the one before it.

So swift was Pentonville's decline that less than a hundred years on it had been reeled all the way back from dark blue to light. The arrival of London's first penitentiary for fallen women can't have helped, but again it was the opening of the big mainline stations down the road which put the heaviest damper on those what's-yours-worth after-dinner house-price blather-ings. To preserve the road's sense of airy distinction, bye-laws forbade the erection of buildings within 50 feet of the road; but as the well-heeled residents moved on and further out unscrupulous developers filled in those grand front lawns with workshops and retail premises, creating a peculiar street-within-a-street effect that still lingers in places. It was as if having heard the old not-in-my-back-yard rallying cry, some hardfaced landlord had replied – no problem, sunshine: we'll stick it in your front garden. By the time Vic and Marge walked up it the industrial concerns described by Pat Haynes were well entrenched: sheet-metal workers, chandlers, safe manufacturers, asbestos traders, a huge Lilley and Skinner boot factory and at No. 230, what my 1933 directory described as 'Samuel Friedentag, incandescent fittings dealer'. Add in a horse trader, another Corner House and the headquarters of the London Master Bakers' and Confectioners' Protection Society and you have a peerless selection of those concerns most poorly equipped to deal with London's post-war commercial climate.

Established at No. 25 Pentonville Road in the 1860s, in 1933 Thomas S. Jones Ltd stopped manufacturing their famous organs and in desperation began turning out toys; the year after Vic and Marge walked past they closed for good. Once so desirable, this part of the capital – the blue properties are alone on the board in featuring an N in their postcodes – had declined so far by the thirties that Harold Clunn walked through Islington sneering how 'almost anything was good enough for the people of North London'.

And seventy years later the last of Pentonville Road's original arch-windowed townhouses, two-million-quid jobs anywhere else, now wallowed in Withnailesque decay: seven bells on every abused front door and upside-down shopping trolleys in the gardens. Appositely encapsulated in one of my London guides as 'battered reminders' of the district's distant hauteur, these abruptly gave way to a cheerless, post-industrial wasteland as Pentonville Road swooped mournfully down to King's Cross and Hellogabbyspeaking. The lost-cat note on a bus shelter represented a poignant farewell to the living metropolis; thereafter the pavements were as empty as most of the buildings laid along them. Neatly complemented by another trouser-flappingly, hand-clappingly cold and blustery afternoon, it seemed a prospect purged of humanity.

I used to drive up to Pentonville Road with my father to consummate our shared love for the improbable bargain: there was a cheap mirror place, I recall, and a cheap tile warehouse and a paint merchant and a printer equally deserving of that most exhilarating of adjectives. We once drove home from the Pentonville Road – no minor round trip – dangerously cocooned in an enormous sheet of foam rubber, an item whose obscure utility never concerned me at the time, nor even when we moved house thirteen years later and it turned up, still unscathed, in the shed.

Of all Pentonville's noisy commercial concerns – bandsaw makers, tin-box manufacturers, gravel merchants – only a couple of printing firms and garages are still keeping the muted faith. The sole premises still trading under the same name was, once more, a pub – but from the horribly scabbed monarch on its sign to the nuclear winter hanging baskets beneath, the George IV was a hopelessly moribund establishment. All the everything-must-go emporia had apparently kept their eponymous vow, and passing the boarded-up windows I felt the same wistful loss last experienced when noting the demise of the self-styled 'Mr Cheap Potatoes', a greengrocer on Wandsworth Road who'd been around long enough to endow me with a derogatory spousal nickname.

Leaning into the wind-tunnel blast whipping around their ankles, I approached a pair of ungainly coppered-glass office stacks and with a now practised eye immediately detected an absence of vital signs. Walking past the dusty reflective glazings, noting as I did so the browned and wrinkled sheaves of junk mail strewn about mothballed reception areas, I came to what would have been the tradesmen's entrance and beheld two lonely female security personnel eyeing me though a grimy revolving door. It was staggering: these buildings couldn't have been more than twenty years old.

Realising the skeleton staff would have plotted my progress up to and around their establishment on CCTV I hoisted a nothing-to-hide wave; moments later I was being reluctantly informed that the blocks were the property of NatWest and the Royal Bank of Scotland – 'and they're both coming back any day now'. Naturally this was patent cobblers – I felt like a telephone salesman being told the kitchen had just burst into flames – but by shepherding away a potential squatter they were just doing their job. So close to the street people of King's Cross, though, it seemed a preposterous waste of roofs over heads: you could put up 1,000 vagrants in each of these buildings. Yes, they might wee in the pot plants and race each other up and down the corridors in typists' chairs, but so what? Only twenty years old they might be, but in today's image-obsessed commercial climate no major corporation would contemplate occupying such tired looking premises without a ground-up overhaul.

It was the same at the hulking carcass of the former Girobank headquarters opposite, and a couple of other unidentified blocks, all of them reinforcing the lesson of Pentonville Road, that London was no longer being built to last. The Victorians always had one eye on posterity – consider Bazalgette and his sewers – and there was nothing flimsy about Shell Mex House and those other totalitarian structures that went up in the thirties. But the modern capital was characterised by a sort of cynical built-in obsolescence, and to compare most of its recent edifices with their surviving forefathers is to hold a pair of hand-stitched brogues up against last year's Nikes.

Pentonville Road flattened out as it neared King's Cross, and though there was some life after all that burned out and boarded up death it was hardly radiating good health. The pavements were busy again, but the human traffic had failed its MOT: in 200 yards I notched up five on the begometer.

The streets around The Angel might have been to hell and back, but this end of Pentonville seemed to have lost the return half of its ticket. Despite the regular turnover of residents around Upper Street as the gentrificationists sold up for a plump profit and moved on, a sense of community, of *joie de vivre*, had somehow been maintained; arriving at Pentonville's ramshackle conclusion I felt as if Ralph McTell had just taken me by the hand and led me though the streets of London.

It was all monumentally squalid and woebegone, and as if to remind myself just how bad it had been I turned to look back up towards The Angel. And as I did so, answering a prayer that hadn't even been asked, she presented me with a miracle, a sign that set me off towards home with a kittenish spring in my step and a sense that London's heart was still somehow in the right place. Beyond the empty office blocks and beneath Pentonville Road's lofty, scarred brow, my gaze was interrupted by a distant but still strident legend I had obscurely endeavoured to overlook among the light-industrial ruins: FOAM CUT TO SIZE.

*

Of the many motorcycles that passed as I waited in gusty morning sun at the junction of Euston and Tottenham Court roads, none promised acceptable temporary accommodation for my buttocks. Filthy, scarred courier bikes, wanky executives on over-chromed retro-machines, trainee cabbies dangerously preoccupied with acquiring The Knowledge via route maps clipboarded to their scooter handlebars. There was a particularly bad moment when an L-plated pizza-boy wobbled to an adjacent halt in the bus lane, but frankly I'd merrily have budged up beside his vegetarian hot ones the moment that fearsome black beast throbbed purposefully up to the kerb.

Its first name was Yamaha, though I can't quite remember its second, something stark and brutal slashed across a flank in Gothic Manga, something like Bastard or Fistfuck. The matchingly clothed rider slowly lifted one black glove in recognition, then slapped the other imperatively on the tiny pillion seat behind him. The Pall I'd met at a recent Icelandic Society gathering was a freckled psychiatrist from Reykjavik. The one raising his tinted visor in recognition before me was a leathered contract killer from hell.

I have rather a large skull, larger anyway than Pall's wife, whose helmet I now wedged my head into, thereby extruding its fleshier features through the face slot in a painfully puckered gurn. Attempting intelligible speech through that cat's bottom of a mouth was a challenge, but then with the top half of my ears folded down over their holes I could hardly hear myself try. 'Don't move about,' bellowed Pall as he dropped his visor and turned on the ignition. 'Just sit there like a sack of potatoes.'

Few life forms suffer more consistently awful ends than the potato, and with the exhaust already sautéing my right ankle I could only hope a peeled mash-up didn't lie in store. The purpose of this exercise was to try and hack through the twenty-four-hour logjam that is Euston's Road's defining characteristic: four wheels bad, two wheels good. Before leaving home I'd checked the traffic cameras on the BBC local news, and as ever the one pointed down Euston Road depicted a poorly laid out yet astonishingly popular car park. It was now 9.37 a.m.; the rush hour had long since peaked but the pace was still slurry-like. Perfect.

Only as we barrelled through the back alleys towards Euston Road's western extremity at Great Portland Street, bumping between bollards and briefly traversing a pedestrian zone, did I belatedly remember an enduring truth, one that saw the Royal Navy repelled by a plucky armada of cod trawlers and coastguard vessels, one that sent my sixty-five-year-old father-in-law running – *running* – ahead of me towards the almost perpendicular summit of Reykjavik's nearest mountain: if you're looking for somewhere to throw down a gauntlet, don't choose the feet of an Icelander.

'Just a little creative licence,' came the muffled shout as my head whiplashed back and we roared between a facing set of no-entry roundels. Utterly disoriented and distantly picturing Pall's diploma from the takes-one-to-know-one school of psychiatric diagnosis, it was all I could do to check my watch as we leaned into a sharp right-hander and there before us lay the Euston Road, a mile of fumes and frustration, six lanes of noisy stasis, each separated from the next by a thin corridor of tarmac, one of which we were soon careering through, wing mirrors almost flicking our elbows.

In an era of side-impact airbags and tamper-proof jam-jar safety buttons how could this shriekingly reckless lunacy be permitted? Some of it, of course, was not, but Pall's occasionally cavalier approach to the technicalities of traffic control was by no means the most unsettling aspect of our progress. With my previous experience of motorised two-wheel transport restricted to machines of or below 90cc, I had to fight off a powerful urge to unhook my hands from the grip handle behind my clenched buttocks and clasp them urgently around Pall's leathered waist. I fixed both eyes on my own fisheyed reflection in Pall's polished black helmet, Euston Road's erratic skyline haloed around it as we slalomed through the hot and stagnant aisles of vans and buses.

Pall banked the bike into the mouth of the dual-carriageway underpass, and scything between Transits I caught a flash of the Euston Tower, a startlingly dated construction that has the air of Bratislava's tallest building, circa 1974. Remember the famous early photo of the Beatles leaping joyfully, limbs akimbo, over a ridge of earthy rubble? That's right: it was shot on the bulldozed remains of a venerable community of shops, warehouses and restaurants demolished to make way for that underpass and its surrounding commercial edifices. It took almost the whole of the sixties to knock down all those old buildings, and consulting my 1933 directory while awaiting Pall I'd understood why. There were just so many of them: three pubs, five Italian-run sweetshops, six teashops and dining rooms, three tobacconists, no fewer than fifteen car dealers or garages and perhaps a hundred other concerns from machine-gun manufacturers to a fantastic marble merchant whose statue-stuffed yard I'd seen in a photograph.

And in their place? I'd looked across at the plaza: you could just see how it would have looked in the architect's model, little plastic families enjoying little plastic picnics on little plastic benches, angular HO-gauge executives caught in stiff-legged mid-stride walking away from their Matchbox Ford Zodiacs. But in the cold light of a cold day it was scattered with people supremely ill at ease in their surroundings: an office worker battling with her newspaper in the now-traditional tower-block gale, two postmen shouting out a laboured conversation above the roar of traffic and wind. Around them all the marooned and forsaken sixties buildings were shedding grubby little mosaic tiles and weeping rust from metal panels like dreadnoughts in dry dock. You could only hope that the King's Cross redevelopers had been brought here to see what not to do.

Trailing a huge echo we tore through the dark underpass, below another inscrutably mirrored commercial block, below a parade of low-octane government offices, below the headquarters of the Wellcome Trust, the world's largest charity. As well as dispensing grants for medical research – over a post-traumatic coffee Pall told me his south London psychiatric unit regularly lobbied for funds – the Wellcome Trust is also a benefactor to the arts, and was currently hosting an exhibition of works inspired by the human genome project.

One can only praise the hands-off commitment to free expression that inspires a major pharmaceutical concern to grant so prominent a soapbox to its own critics, for as I'd noted without surprise from an online exhibition catalogue the human genome project is not one fondly revered within the artistic community. 'What is the consequence of evolution becoming a product?' barked a strident note beneath the mock-up of a perfume box labelled 'PROGRESSION'; another exhibit was entitled 'The Spit of God'.

The Euston Road has always nurtured artists. From its base at No. 314, in the late thirties the Euston Road School sought to promote 'a more natural, impressonistic portrayal of everyday life', which would have been a lot easier then than now: predictably enough, that photo showed the Beatles dancing on 314's grave. And Sonia Brownell, who married George Orwell shortly before he died, was known in literary London as the Venus of Euston Road.

London's first women's hospital, a splendid LCC-monogrammed Art Nouveau fire station – buildings I imagined we'd spend long minutes idling in front of were flying through my peripheral vision like those hyperspaced streaks in the Pearl and Dean ad. The Venus of Euston Road, I thought, wistfully mourning a lost age when even an unpromisingly semi-industrial thoroughfare could feature in such a romantic appellation. Clearly Euston Road once had a personality, but whatever it was had long since disappeared in a cloud of diesel particulates. It has been soberly predicted that the street's traffic volume is to treble in the forthcoming decade, and struggling to envision the double-decker taxis and motorcycle-courier pyramids such a reality would necessarily entail I was presented with an apposite reminder of the most widely advocated solution. Jolting to a halt as the gaps between the lanes converged impenetrably together, there beside us, gracefully isolated in a precious sliver of parkland, were Nos 188 and 190, sole survivors of London's first railway terminus: the entrance lodges of Euston Station.

'The greatest public work ever executed in ancient or modern times,' wrote one contemporary of the rail link to Birmingham, yet incredibly, the 112-mile line had been completed from scratch in just four years. Then again, a plaque I later read outside a pub by Great Portland Street told me the New Road had been knocked up in as many months. It only goes to show what you can achieve with engineering determination, compulsory purchase orders and expendable slave labour.

Not that any of this cut much ice with the powers-that-were in the sixties. Euston Station, named in common with the road that runs past it after its ground landlord, the Earl of Euston, had for years been considered antiquated and inadequate – Harold Clunn called it 'shabby and inconvenient'. But it took another epic period of dithering before British Rail elected to break the habit of a lifetime by knocking everything down and starting again.

It was a decision that did more than anything to kick-start the architectural preservation movement. Euston's Great Hall was still the largest waiting room in Britain and comfortably the grandest, boasting a sweeping double staircase and a 60-foot-high coffered ceiling whose extent and ornamentation were rivalled only within Buckingham Palace. But it was the proposed demolition of the arch that welcomed travellers into the terminus, a 70-foot portico supported by what had been the tallest columns in London, that excited most outrage.

One of London's pet landmarks, the Euston Arch was also revered as a fitting monument to the world's first inter-city railway (assuming you forgot about the one between Liverpool and Manchester). No one ever imagined they'd go through with its destruction – even BR's deliberately pessimistic estimate that shifting the arch slightly out of the way would cost £180,000 hardly seemed exorbitant – but in 1963, down it suddenly went along with the Great Hall, 130 years of railway history demolished at a stroke. 'But . . . but that was the largest Greek propylaeum ever constructed,' somebody in a paisley bow tie might easily have whimpered, unaware that even worse was to come. In the same spirit of unwarranted nastiness that saw London's last tram being burnt alive, the arch's constituent stones – despite being numbered with a view to eventual reconstruction – were secretly disposed of like gangland victims, heaved into a lonely, stagnant East End creek known as the Channelsea River.

'Simplicity is the keynote in design of the new Euston,' trumpeted BR in its promotional grand reopening literature, hardly needing to add 'what with it being a big shed'. The 1968 ceremony was presided over by the Queen, and you can just imagine her internal triumph as she snipped through the ribbon: who's got the best coffered ceiling now, eh?

By the 1930s London had been the world's greatest city for over a hundred years, continually expanding and improving, getting ever bigger and ever better. Londoners and their administrators had become accustomed to the idea that it didn't matter what they knocked down, because whatever went up in its stead would be superior. London could do no wrong. Only in the sixties did it begin to dawn on residents that the city was actually in decline, that some of the old stuff might in fact be worth preserving – both as a reminder of past glories and because, in an aesthetic and perhaps even a practical sense, it was simply better than what would replace it.

The Euston Arch was the first faceful of cold water in this drawn-out wake-up call, but today we're all decadently resigned to our current hamfisted hopelessness. It's become rather too cosy, in fact, a bit of a cop-out: so entrenched is the mindset that blanket preservation has become the default option, that it's better to save even a rusty old gasholder rather than contemplate the expense and inconvenience of putting something better up in its place. Where once Londoners cremated their architectural legacy, today we embalm it.

Happy to have got this off my chest but wishing I could say the same about the hydrocarbons accumulating inside my visor, we throbbed and inched towards the notorious orange-bricked mass of Euston Road's most infamous public servant, the British Library. A soft target and an unmissably enormous one, the library took almost twenty years to complete, a phoenix yawning slowly out of hibernation from the ashes of what had been Somers Town goods depot, home to all those potato wholesalers.

It certainly isn't difficult to criticise the unmitigated shopping-mall brickwork on aesthetic grounds: unfairly counterpointed by the beguiling Hogwarts Castle that is St Pancras, the British Library eagerly welcomes most contemporary architectural insults – windowless superstore, overgrown electricity substation, secret-police interrogation centre. But, you know, it's rather more difficult to criticise it on library grounds. During my last visit, amongst all the school parties and academics, I'd been somehow infused by a sense of civic duty being enacted on an almost Victorian scale: shelves of new publications that grow by two miles every year, ten million important historical works extending back to Ancient Egypt and, of greater immediate concern to the schoolchildren and me, all sorts of intriguingly obscure little exhibits. Messing about with an archive CD jukebox I'd blundered across a 1968 recording of John Lennon acting the goat with Kenny Everett, which had sent me back out into the perpetually simmering traffic with a smile on my face.

Pall manipulated the bike through the ignoble shambles of Euston Road's conclusion at King's Cross, hung an illegal right and pulled over. I held a shaking left wrist up to the visor: nine minutes twenty-eight seconds end to end, a good 50 per cent quicker than my usual four-wheel run, but at the same time hardly faster than a brisk trot along a precise mile of pavement.

I was preparing myself for a kidney-bullying return leg that would slice no less than five minutes off this time when beside us a helmeted cyclist, his face already colouring up with blotches of rage, began screaming awful epithets at an adjacent van driver. A window was wound down and headgear removed, and an exchange took place which I'd love to have heard monotonically summated by the clerk of Bow Street magistrates' number one court: fuck off; fuck you; it's my fucking right of way; get off and I'll fucking do you; the fuck you will.

'Ah, the pleasantries of the world,' trilled a little Alan Bennett of a man passing us on the pavement once the debate had been cut short by a background volley of rabidly impatient horns. It was reassuring in a way that in general the blue set was still a bit lary, that gentrification hadn't smoothed off all its edges. But though the Islington effect would no doubt eventually seep down Pentonville Road, it was simply impossible to imagine Euston Road being any sort of community, being in fact anything other than just that: a road. We really have to do something about the traffic, you know.

CHAPTER 14

Electric Company

Think of a number between two and twelve. Ten, you say? Well, how remarkable – that's only four away from what the ticket clerk said when I asked him. I'd remembered to take my board up Euston Road but had somehow mislaid token and dice, and having procured a six from my human random generator mentally moved my car from The Angel, Islington, to Electric Company.

Even someone who's never been to London could probably tell you that Chelsea might not perhaps seem the optimum locale for the world's largest power station. But things were different a hundred years ago: the Thames was still a working river, and the area along its western Chelsea bank was lined with wharves, foundries, gasworks and even a manure merchants, all backed by tight streets of the near-slum dwellings inhabited by their workforces.

What's astonishing isn't that the 275-foot chimneys of Lots

Road generating station should have risen up above the west London skyline in 1905, but that they're still there now: no longer the largest but now the oldest thermal power station in the world, Lots Road's formidable, smutty engine-shed arched windows today look down on a street full of Porsches.

There are two chimneys now instead of the four that had contemporaries comparing it to an elephant on its back, and in place of the thick coal smoke that once belched out of them trail the wispy by-products of gas combustion. But at heart Lots Road is still doing what it's done throughout Monopoly's lifetime: burning decomposed prehistoric organisms to boil water to make steam to drive turbines to generate electricity. Smouldering poo-cakes to the Crossness Sludge-Powered Generator: here was my Electric Company.

Built to power the soon-to-be-electrified Underground, Lots Road did in fact excite much local outrage. Even by the blighting standards established amongst neighbouring industrial concerns this was, after all, an enormous project: sixty-four boilers, fed on the one hand by a 450-foot-deep artesian well and on the other by coal bunkers storing 15,000 tons of the black stuff; two 5-foot-diameter pipes drawing in millions of gallons of Thames water a day for cooling purposes; a jetty where huge barges were relieved of coal by gantry cranes or filled with ashes by a narrow-gauge railway. Even without its chimneys – each very nearly twice the height of Nelson's Column – the main building, 140 foot high and considerably longer than a football pitch, towered over the modest dwellings opposite.

Local artists, notably James Whistler, complained that the view of Chelsea Reach, as painted by Turner, had been lost for ever; children at Ashburnham School over the road said they couldn't hear themselves speak in the playground and Chelsea Borough Council sued Underground Electric Railways for 'removing the smoke from the tunnels but, by other means, discharging it over the citizens of Battersea and Chelsea'. No one listened to Whistler or the schoolkids, and when it came to court the council not only lost but had costs awarded against it. As if to taunt Turner's legacy, UER commissioned an impressionist to depict Lots Road looming dramatically out of a rouged dawn, and plastered this on huge posters that boasted 'This power house burns 500 tons of coal a day . . . for the USE and BENEFIT of the people of London.'

As the Tube system expanded so did Lots Road. More powerful turbines were installed, along with extra boilers and bunkers for an additional 28,000 tons of coal. Those pipes into the Thames were supplanted by one with a frankly petrifying 9-foot girth. A more protected control room was built in the thirties following a series of exhilarating mishaps: 'In the event of trouble the operator is exposed to flying fragments of broken machinery, and to the escape of steam,' revealed an earlier report, before drily concluding that 'these, in addition to the noise and commotion below him, are likely to distract the operator's mind from his work.'

Lots Road was still dropping coal smuts on King's Road swingers in 1967, but after a brief dalliance with heavy fuel oil in the seventies the plant switched to natural gas. Then, in the eighties, somebody calculated that the cost of generating each Lots Road kilowatt was rather dearer than the corporate rate charged by the National Grid. Coupled with the site's ratcheting appeal to speculators busily knocking up glitzy marina developments on the surrounding badlands, this effectively doomed the plant.

Inevitably placed under the aegis of some obscure privatised division named Seeboard Powerlink, Lots Road – already sold to Taylor-Woodrow for £34 million – is being gradually wound down; by the time you read this the builders will be in, digging up the boiler house floor for a swimming pool and dividing the enormous void above into flats for 1,000 wealthy professionals. If my kids went to Ashburnham School I'd no doubt be delighted to see them running happily home without blood trickling from their ears, but as it was I felt a terrible end-of-an-era pathos suffusing me as I walked up to the razor-wired entrance.

'Sorry about all that,' said station boss Richard Bettany, leading me up a grand but rather neglected Edwardian staircase. The security desk had grilled me without explanation for almost half an hour, thereby diminishing my pathos along with my patience. It had been the same when I'd phoned up Seeboard Powerlink's recalcitrant PR department: obtaining permission to visit Lots Road had proven inestimably more irksome than gaining access to Pentonville Prison. Aside from a vague mumble about 'the current climate', which in any case could just have been a feeble electricity-themed pun, I had no idea what the problem was.

Richard did, though. 'It's just that if something does, um, *go wrong* during your visit' – and I now understood this was a tactful means of describing my potential for perpetrating a terrorist outrage – 'we've only got battery back-up power for an hour, and even that's only enough for a quarter of the lights.' A covert nip with the wirecutters here, in other words, and the entire Tube network – tunnel-bound trains, deep-level stations and all – would be cast into silent darkness.

I followed Richard up deserted corridors and further echoing stairs, and at length into a panelled board room decorated with framed wiring diagrams. A lady came in with a tray of tea and biscuits, followed some time later by a bearded man in shorts, boots and a yellow hard hat, a man I was to know only as Martin. Looking at him I was fairly certain he would at some point refer to Lots Road's end product as 'juice'.

'Where, um, is everyone?' I asked with reference to the *Marie Celeste*-ean ambience, nibbling a custard cream.

'Well, everything's pretty automatic these days,' breezed Richard, whose creaseless, spotless boilersuit, particularly when teamed with Martin's ensemble, spoke less of the village black-smith and more of the Village People. Neither seemed certain how many people Lots Road had employed in its filthy, coal-fired prime, but we agreed it couldn't have been less than ten times more than the current skeleton staff of fifty.

'Monopoly?' said Richard, after I'd outlined the purpose of what I was aware as I described it seemed a fecklessly spurious visit. 'Oh, I *love* Monopoly.' Behind large lenses his eyes began to shine. ' "Move Directly to Jail" . . . "Bank Error in Your Favour" . . . *Monopoly*, Martin.'

Richard's prompting intonation failed to rouse the man in shorts. 'Yeah,' said Martin. If there was one thing I had learned, it was that although almost everyone loved Monopoly, those twisted few who didn't *hated* it. More so even than Marmite, Majorca or mutual masturbation, no noun in the dictionary's central pages cleaved society quite as neatly into two camps.

'It's funny, you know,' said Richard, maintaining his enhanced level of enthusiasm, 'but I always try to get Electric Company when I play.' He gave me a conspiratorial wink as he passed me over to Martin. 'A very nice little earner, as it goes.'

I didn't have the heart to tell him.

We forced open a reluctant door and entered the control room built in 1935 – another Frank Pick legacy – to replace the one so regularly peppered with turbine shrapnel. Rarely have I entered a realm of such eerie magnificence. Part-signal box, part-Frankenstein's laboratory, it was the sort of place Dr No would have held his final stand-off had James Bond been played by a young Cary Grant. 'No one's been in here since 1961,' said Martin, doodling on the dusty wood-block floor with a boot heel. Of the three desks I'd seen manned by sober, whitecoated baldies in a thirties photograph one remained, looking out from on high over the apparently unmanned and oddly silent turbine house. In 1905 that hall below had been tightly packed and stacked with bulbous, polished machines, each the size of a locomotive; now, a modest bank of blue drums, occupying a distant and lonely corner, effortlessly whirred out two million kilowatt hours a day.

As I was personally gratified to hear Martin explain, this represented a four-fold increase in his establishment's output of juice.

Beneath a fancy glass dome roofed over with concrete to keep the Luftwaffe out, I wandered about in the dark between gauges and panels, pinging a disconnected bell dome on the controller's desk and opening a drawer full of Bakelite identification plates and coils of fibre-sheathed cable. At this point a formidable and upsetting metallic slam echoed abruptly from behind one of the huge slate-insulated panels.

'That's a 600-volt open knife switch,' said a distant voice that suddenly didn't sound as much like Martin's as I'd have wished. In the unlit gloom I couldn't see him, and half-crouched as I was in the desk's knee-space I certainly hoped he couldn't see me. 'It was all live current here then – no other way.' There was a shuffle of footsteps, then a torch clicked on and shot a streak of pale yellow that panned slowly towards me across the church-like floor. 'Forty volts can kill, you know.'

'Martin!' I blurted, employing the upper end of my vocal register.

A little click and light filled the room. 'Sorry,' said Martin blandly, squinting over from the far end of the control room as I quickly straightened myself. 'Silly place for a light switch. Ten years here and I still get lost.'

Down we went, along further cold and empty corridors walled with Victorian-school-lavatory tiles, past vintage Underground maps and old mahogany plan chests with tarnished brass handles. In an establishment that once publicly trumpeted a rapacious lust for only the very filthiest fossil fuels it was peculiar to see a recycling bin neatly labelled 'Torch batteries only'. Finally, through a smeared window, I saw someone else: a man in hard hat and overalls, out on what had been the coaling dock, shovelling wet leaves from some sort of grating into a wheelbarrow.

'Is that a full-time job?' I said with a slight smirk.

Martin shot me a stern look. 'That's the water screen,' he said, importantly. 'We take 57 million gallons off the Thames every day to cool the machinery: we have to pay the water board to take the cold water out and pay them again to put the warm water back. If that screen gets blocked we've had it – one day we took 250 tons of leaves out.' If he'd been trying to impress me he'd succeeded. Looking at the leaf-lifter I now felt a calming, warm sense of continuity – here at last, here at least, was one Londoner whose job description had not changed for a century.

'So has it ever been blocked?'

Martin fixed the distant opposite bank with a look as flinty as a bearded man in shorts can realistically hope to muster. 'Boxing Day 1999,' he said, his voice thickening. 'Lost the juice for eleven seconds.'

Martin's lonely office, which we presently reached after a further disorienting blunder though industro-corporate history, was blessed with a harbourmaster's wonderview, its flaky-painted windows welcoming in a compass sweep of grand river prospects. At the edge of the coaling dock a cormorant stood as if crucified, drying its wings; in the background, a District line train sucked up the Lots Road juice as it rattled across a bridge towards Wimbledon.

'You'll miss that view,' I said, thinking of the prime penthouse this would shortly become. Martin nodded once and issued a lengthy, nasal sigh. Twenty-five years he'd worked for London Transport, starting out at the Chiswick bus works.

'That's an industrial park now and all,' he said, not as matter-of-factly as he might have intended.

He clapped a bare hand on a bare thigh and out we went. Wordlessly I followed Martin across rain-varnished cobbles and into the boiler house, past the meaty base of one of those chimneys, between the old narrow-gauge rail tracks, beneath enormous pieces of heritage hardware whose rusting name plates listed manufacturers that all ended in Bros and hailed from Wakefield, Newcastle-upon-Tyne or even London NW1:

Euston Road's postcode. As we tramped up the gantry stairs and walkways I detected the first ambient evidence – both thermal and sonic – of the production of those two million kilowatt hours a day. At last I could forgive Martin his shorts.

'This was the first steel-framed building in Britain,' he said as we climbed into a quieter hall, one relieved of so much redundant machinery that someone had found space to paint out a badminton court. I was about to put him right when I realised I'd been wrong: Lots Road 1905; the Ritz 1906. I shook my head in muted awe, contemplating an age when London built its power stations and luxury hotels to the same innovative and exacting standards, and was equally proud of both. 'And in fact the first of any sort built to metric specifications: it was a German design.' Oh.

Five minutes later I was doffing my hard hat by the security desk. 'It's a working museum here, really,' said Martin, shaking my hand with a prolonged intensity that suggested he was working himself up to something. 'The London County Council,' he announced suddenly; I'd seen their monogram all over Lots Road. 'Take a look at any 4-inch soil pipe in the world,' he continued, an invitation I could only be half sure was rhetorical, 'and you'll find LCC stamped on it.' He paused impressively and I grasped exactly what he was trying to say: this was just how I'd felt seeing those imperial measurements set in the wall at Trafalgar Square.

Realising his time was running out, with an eager blurt he tried to express a number of points at once. 'This place is riddled with asbestos, you know. It's all over the coal bunkers and mixed into most of the concrete. Riddled. And there's a refuse transfer station next door, and a sewage pumping house.' He stopped as abruptly as he'd started.

'Well, that's a few things for any future residents to bear in mind,' I said on cue, eliciting a disingenuous shrug. It was his last shot at saving Lots Road, to keep the working museum working.

Outside in the car, doing my board/token/dice thing, I ruminated upon Lots Road's inestimable ninety-six-year contribution to London. Just as Bazalgette's Water Works had kept us healthy, so this Electric Company had kept us wealthy: taking millions to work and home again, facilitating London's rapid suburban expansion.

Distractedly I concluded my business – a six to Marlborough Street: a small tut; a four to Chance: ah – a Get Out of Jail Free; a ten to Oxford Street. But as I drove away between the Porsche-paddocked pavements, I stole a final glance up at those chimneys and reluctantly concluded that, as proud as Lots Road's heritage undoubtedly was, it really wasn't terribly twenty-first century to contemplate Europe's most extensive mass-transit network droning to a halt because some pipe got blocked with leaves.

CHAPTER 15

The Greens

REGENT ST
CITY OF WESTMINSTER

OXFORD ST
CITY OF WESTMINSTER

BOND ST
CITY OF WESTMINSTER

Originally part of the Roman road from Hampshire to Suffolk, Oxford Street was thus titled only in the late eighteenth century when the relevantly named earl acquired the land along which it ran. Until then it had been generally known as Tyburn Way, after the infamous gallows – equipped to dispatch twenty-four felons simultaneously – near its western conclusion. Most Mondays for two hundred years an open cartload of malefactors rolled from Newgate Prison all the way down what is now Oxford Street, jeered and abused by drunk spectators. Anyone who missed the fun could always meet up with the hangman in a Fleet Street tavern and buy the rope off him at sixpence an inch.

Only when the gallows were removed in 1783 could Oxford Street begin to attract the right class of resident, and even then well away from the horrendous slums of St Giles around the eastern end, a place where things happened that made estate agents work that bit harder, things like the 1818 brewery explosion in which eight people were drowned in a flood of beer.

Perhaps as a result it never quite made the grade as a ponced-up residential street, and was soon known for theatres, music halls, ice rinks and – yes – shops. Because, let's face it, that's what the green set is all about: Vic had been given his fun with the oranges – all that cops and robbers business is blatantly boys' stuff – and Marge got her turn with streets Oxford, Bond and Regent, then as now London's premier retail thoroughfares. Around the turn of the century the street's drapers and dress makers were gradually supplanted by the first modern department stores. Waring & Gillow arrived in 1906 and Debenham soon after, but the Oxford Street we know today was effectively born in 1909 when American retailer Gordon Selfridge opened his vast store, which you won't be interested to hear sneaked the bronze in that steel-framed-building race.

Selfridge coined the catchphrase 'the customer is always right', though despite the determined efforts of his ruinous later life failed to interest quotation compilers in 'the boss is always in the casino with a couple of drunk sisters'. Just as the cinemas lured patrons in by posting their cosy interior temperatures out on the street, so Selfridge wooed women off the pavement with a promise of warmth, excitement and flushable porcelain fixtures, welcoming even those who had no intention of buying anything. Carpets and electric lighting – both then unheard of in retail establishments – and ranks of female lift attendants standing to attention . . . 'I was lonely,' read a desperately poignant early advert, 'so I went to the biggest and brightest place I could think of . . . I went to Selfridge's.' Almost thirty years later that towering colonnaded façade – deliberately suggesting a temple of shopping – remained a source of wonder. On Mass Observation day two Welshmen stood in awe before Selfridge's: 'It's as long as our main street,' breathed one to the other. So elaborate were the store's external decorations for the 1937 Coronation that the enormous gold lions and medals were promptly snapped up afterwards by an Indian rajah looking to tart up his palace.

If Gordon set the agenda, then his neighbours proved astonishingly adept at copying it. Department stores soon filled nearly the entire mile of Oxford Street, flanking a scene that in the thirties was almost indistinguishable from today's: a fearful ruck of taxis and double-deckers (forty of the latter in one memorable image); pavements of inadequate girth massed with shoppers; shops bedecked with familiarly phrased slogans – 'Gigantic shoe sale: stupendous bargains in fashion shoes at break-up prices'; 'Kodak: you press the button, we do the rest'. Only telltale advertised fixations with permanent waves and making-do-and-mending – one banner promised to repair any umbrella within twenty minutes – date the photos.

But at the same time the street had never quite been able to shake off the slightly rough-and-ready reputation of its Tyburn/beer-flood days. Mass Observation reports mention 'good-looking, partly drunken girls' wearing the hats of the sailors they've picked up. An observer working a night shift at Boots Oxford Street branch reported four customers in the hour after 2 a.m.: 'three to buy aspirins and one, a Cambridge undergraduate, to buy a draught for his friend outside who had just swallowed two bottles of sherry.'

Oxford Street has, in effect, proven ever-tolerant of question-able individual behaviour. Thomas De Quincey spent much time with the street's prostitutes and bought that first fateful dose of opium at a chemist's whose site is now appositely occupied by an establishment entitled New Look. The three-card tricksters were still at it until recently, as were the fake perfume scam artists.

Most famous of all, though it's a shame to bracket him with opium eaters and con merchants, was Stanley Green, a little man with round glasses, a crumpled raincoat and a slightly squashed peaked cap who one day in 1968 and almost every subsequent morning for the next twenty-five years caught the Central line to

Oxford Circus from his home in the distant suburb of Northolt. On his lap throughout the journey and above his head throughout the ensuing day-long tramp up and down Oxford Street was a placard, unforgettably headlined 'LESS PASSION FROM LESS PROTEIN'.

Beneath this arresting introduction were detailed the sources of nature's most dangerous nutritional aphrodisiac – 'MEAT FISH BIRD; EGG/CHEESE; PEAS incl. lentils BEANS; NUTS' – as well as notice of an additional threat that seemed to have occurred to Stanley at some later point in his crusade: 'SITTING'. This eclectic manifesto was described in more detail in leaflets as waywardly typeset as ransom demands, and after weaving warily around Stanley for the third time in a mid-teenage afternoon I bought one. Even the price was mad – by craftily electing to charge 12p Stanley involved me, as most of his customers, in the protracted mutual fumbling of coins of minor denomination.

The leaflet was entitled *Eight Passion Proteins*, and essentially summarised Stan's philosophy on the perils of the libido and how these could be magnified by dabbling with foodstuffs heavy in amino acids, particularly while adopting a sedentary posture. If Stanley had been the hectoring type you might have heard teenagers shouting uncouth invitations to a bring-an-omelette barbecue picnic, but in fact I never heard him say anything except 'Twelve pence, please,' and 'Guest of honour at your school sports day? I should be honoured.'

Stanley died in 1993, but lives on in the Museum of London, which holds copies of all his placards and booklets, and in our household, where 'Passion Proteins' is the derisive shorthand for any offbeat individual theory, most notably my insistence that bedroom slippers harbour contagion, which I don't mind because I know I'm right and to prove it I'm getting some leaflets printed up.

In the post-Stanley era, CCTV has rather put the mockers on Oxford Street's resident rogues and misfits. The perfume scammers, who spent most of their time sweeping their solvent-scented stock into a big plastic bread tray whenever the lookout spotted a silver-badged helmet, have now disappeared along with the fake-gold-chain boys and the sleight-of-hand artists. Peering over the heads and between the buses as I looked down from the Marble Arch end the only lofted placard in sight read GOLF SALE.

'He's a real little toad,' said the jovially forthright director of the Oxford Street Association with reference to the sporting-goods proprietor who hires the tone-lowering human billboards. 'Always pleads poverty, but every time I meet him he's wearing five grand's worth of gold.'

I'd met Sally Humphreys in her Selfridge's office, situated in what you might call the store's considerable back-stage area, and to prepare me for a day's trundle up and down Britain's busiest street was being treated to an overview of her kingdom. Stanley might have been barking mad but he wasn't stupid: when I asked Sally for statistics, the first of many she dutifully trotted out was the stupendous revelation that over two hundred million people shop in Oxford Street a year, an enormous and ever-changing audience for his passion play. It's also London's most popular tourist destination, patronised by over two-thirds of all foreign visitors spending £1 billion a year in its commercial establishments; and at the peak Christmas period its workforce swells to an improbable 60,000. 'A figure greater than the population of St Albans,' read Sally from her factsheet, wearing an expression that suggested this comparison could perhaps be improved upon.

Well acquainted with the footpads and knocking shops that once characterised Oxford Street, Sally seemed almost regretful that what she called 'the dodgy stuff' was now limited to the retail tackiness embodied by the Golf Sale blokes and a plethora of crap-mart souvenir shops bookending the department stores. 'Part of the joy of Oxford Street has always been that slightly seedy aspect,' she said, sparking up a fag as she consoled herself with residual memories of the street's last resident character: the evangelical nudist who regularly wanders about Oxford Circus. 'I watched him once on the CCTV. By the time the police turned up he was being asked by Japanese men to pose for snapshots with their wives.'

In the old days, even the bosses got in on the act. Sally revealed that Gordon Selfridge installed a secret lift to ferry young lady companions directly up to his office, and my research suggests Gordon's neighbouring proprietors were influenced by rather more than his commercial methods. In 1907, slightly further up the Roman road in Bayswater, the eponymous proprietor of Whiteley's was shot dead at his desk by a spurned illegitimate son, a crime arousing such sympathy that 200,000 Londoners signed a petition which successfully commuted the boy's death sentence to life imprisonment. Those who revere the stores of the John Lewis Partnership as a lone beacon of honour and principle on high streets scarred by cynical chicanery might be interested to hear how the chain's founder spent three weeks in Brixton Prison for continually flouting planning bye-laws; or how in 1906, hearing that his fellow department store proprietor Peter Jones was about to go tits up, old man Lewis ran all the way from Oxford Street to Sloane Square with £20,000 cash in his pocket: a brutal wad-on-the-table, take-it-or-leave-it offer Pete cravenly accepted.

After an enlightening résumé of the current commercial climate, Sally rounded off with a final volley of candour, railing against the 'sodding buses' that clog the street and bemoaning the 'disaster' that was Bird's Eye's recent sponsorship of Oxford Street's Christmas lights, a verdict I can't agree with as without them I'd never have heard my *Esquire* colleague Ivor encapsulate the event so memorably as 'peas on earth'.

Most entertaining of all was her account of the internecine feud between the three green-set associations. Each of the streets bills itself as offering the ultimate London shopping experience, a contest that extends to rival Christmas light displays. An alliance of sorts has been brokered with the Regent Street

Association (despite the latter's grievance at being relegated below Oxford Street on the Monopoly board), with both united by a special disesteem for the Bond Street Association and its double-barrelled director – someone I'd defend more stoutly had she deigned to grant me an interview.

'She wouldn't last five minutes here,' said Sally, the battle-hardened infantryman scornfully appraising a pen-pushing Oxbridge officer. 'They're always saying Bond Street shoppers wouldn't be seen dead in Oxford Street, and they won't even talk about buses or Tubes,' and here she adopted a grotesque parody of jiggly-headed, marble-mouthed elocution, 'because *our* customers simply don't travel on public transport'. I will allow you to imagine the grim triumphalism of Sally's smile when upon leaving I informed her that in order of current real-world commercial rents, Oxford Street not only topped the green set, and the London Monopoly board, but was nothing less than the fourth dearest address on the planet.

When a quarter of Londoners say that what they like best about the city is its shopping facilities, I begin to think I'm living in the wrong place. In common with many of my gender, the prospect of an extended retail quest for goods you can't plug in or uncork fills my limbs with gravel and my skull with some kind of viscous pâté. Walking back to start again at Oxford Street's west end I was already feeling the wayward tetchiness of a toddler in Tesco's; it didn't help to know I was being followed every step of the way on a screen in a CCTV room round the corner.

It was mid-November by now, but the most welcoming blasts of warm air issued from stores whose product ranges most stubbornly defied intelligent perusal: trainers, jeans, blouses for fat women, postcards of a pre-teenage Prince William. With weary inevitability, when I was lured in off the street – by an animatronic zombie constantly expressing green vomit into a bucket in the window of a novelty shop – the manager came up as I examined his pornographic mobile phone covers and angrily denounced me as a trading standards officer. Is it OK if I blame the raincoat again?

Sally had forewarned me of the street's polarisation, and it was indeed the case that the glitzier fashion chains and what Harold Clunn irresistibly dubbed 'the great dry-goods stores of Oxford Street' were topped and tailed by bureau de change cubbyholes and total liquidation sales. The middle market was clearly suffering: C&A, the most famous recent casualty, had three stores along Oxford Street in the thirties and the disembowelled hulks of the last two stand at either end of the upmarket stretch, plaster-dusted final-reduction starbursts still decorating doors chained against a threatened squatter invasion Sally had mentioned. It still astounds me to recall that the British Leyland of high-street retailing was actually owned by the Dutch.

Call it a coincidence, but it does seem odd that those department stores who failed to adapt to Oxford Street's evolving consumer trends – C&A, Waring & Gillow, Bourne & Hollingsworth, Swears & Wells, Marshall & Snelgrove – are united by the grammatical assassin known and feared by all high street retailers: the Ampersand of Death. Lilley & Skinner has popped its rubber-soled clogs, Marks & Spencer's problems are no secret, and if I worked at Hennes & Mauritz I'd be checking out the early retirement deals.

C&A was always a basket case, an establishment that hadn't so much boxed itself into a corner as sewn itself into a tank-top, but Selfridge's has been hauled back from the brink. In the seventies and eighties the store languished in *Are You Being Served?* torpor, its customers outnumbered by fussy little men scuttling about on frayed carpet tiles. 'They hadn't accepted that people didn't *need* to come to Selfridge's any more,' Sally had said, pre-empting my ruminations on the tourist shoppers. 'All the suburban malls and superstores had everything in the way of stock. What was needed was to recapture that sense of theatre, to make people *want* to come in.'

And so Selfridge's has gone back to its roots, these days no longer just a big shop but a place of entertainment. Walking past on the other side of the street, I noted that the lights I'd thought were flashing randomly in each window actually formed an animated ticker-tape scrolling festive messages along the entire frontage. It was the ooh-look factor, and coupled with extremely loud popular music, a daringly open-plan layout and tills manned by Miss Brahms rather than Captain Peacock it's proved an astounding success: more people now shop in Selfridge's every year than live in Australia.

Further along, Debenhams had resorted to more traditional inducements, filling plastic tumblers of generous capacity with complimentary wine and not bothering to stop me and a couple of blearily moon-faced grannies sidling back for seconds. Thus reinvigorated I very nearly started Christmas shopping, before remembering that Birna had assumed unilateral responsibility for this duty following the 1999 chisels-for-all debacle. Instead I breezed out into the street and shortly found myself interrogating, with the slurred pomposity of an intemperate trading standards officer, the youthful proprietor of a souvenir stall.

'This,' he said simply, responding to my inquiry as to his most popular product by tapping a forefinger on an 8-inch beefeater's felt hat.

'Moving eyes,' I noted, watching the plastic yeoman's pupils vibrate under his digital assault. Mantelpiece memory or target practice for Action Man: frankly, you could do a lot worse for a quid.

'It's all total rubbish,' he whispered disarmingly, watching a rare tourist finger his Big Bens. 'Everything's made in China. But you know – that's what they want.' Despite the current dearth of foreigners, earlier that week he'd sold over a hundred quid's worth of said rubbish to a single South American. And yes – sometimes he had to chase after a postcard-pocketing shoplifter.

Pressed further, he revealed that his family had run a stall on this site for forty years, adding that some of the other pitches – the ones I'd seen selling pound-a-roll foil wrap, cheap wallets, ambitiously priced fruit or 'Stop Looking At My Tits' T-shirts – had been passed down through four generations. Here, in effect, was the last bastion of the old Monopoly-era Happy Families economy: Master Crap the Costermonger's Son.

The buildings grew taller and pushed further outwards, crowding the pedestrians into a pavement bottleneck – Oxford Street's most blighting flaw – and suddenly I was having to weave and check my stride, showcasing a Londoner's talent for avoiding the jostling bodychecks so popular on foreign high streets. The Christmas shoppers were here, but, so soon after September 11, not many of the tourists for whom Oxford Street apparently exerts such an irresistible allure.

Why, in fact, is that? An enormous percentage of the goods on sale in Oxford Street are global ubiquities: if you want a U2 CD, a Gap hooded top and a pair of Nike Air Maxes you could have got them, almost certainly for less, in your country of origin. This leaves the luminous condom, vomiting zombie end of the market. All I'll say is that it does seem rather a long way to come. I'd only travelled thirteen stops up the Tube and reckoned that was slightly past the limit.

Further down the road makeover salesmen accosted women with barked inquiries into their hair-care regime; a pelican crossing beeped insistently; a wedged mass of buses and taxis juddered out diesel fumes. On I pressed through the bag-brandishing throng, its heads angled down, its legs striding purposefully. Oxford Street shoppers didn't stroll as once they had, or even look up: all the huge promotional flags and banners that once swung from fourth- and fifth-floor windows were gone, and craning my neck towards the abseiling window cleaners I noticed plenty of strident features whose existence had eluded me for a lifetime: a Barbara Hepworth sculpture stuck to the side of John Lewis; a great Scottish castle turret sprouting out above a steak house near Oxford Circus. That, though, was the thinnest of silver linings to the filthy storm cloud that hovers above the confluence of streets Regent and Oxford. Dominated by the unspeakable horror that is Nike Town – my own five-storey Room 101, a monolithic homage to lobotomised fashion and global marketing cynicism – Oxford Circus gets worse as you go down. Down as in under.

Oxford Street's four Tube stations are used by a hundred million passengers a year, and Oxford Circus, more or less the bull's-eye of Harry Beck's world-famous map, is the Underground's busiest. Interesting, then, that its concourse should have been conceived on a scale so Lilliputian that almost every day during the rush hour the modest stairways burrowing into it have to be temporarily barred off to allow the hulking logjam of commuting Gullivers below to disperse, wedging themselves laboriously through a tight isthmus of ticket barriers before stooping away down the low-ceilinged, circuitous network of compressed, excuse-me passages and escalators whose miserable breadth makes a mockery of those exhortations to stand on the right.

In 1928 Piccadilly Circus was blessed with a Charles Holden-designed, Frank Pick-commissioned overhaul that still warrants a visit in its own right: umpteen entrance subways leading into an airily grandiose booking-hall 'ambulatory' lavishly decorated with travertine marble panelling and bespoke bronze fittings; two great tunnels, each accommodating three escalators, sweeping passengers down to their trains. After Oxford Circus, here is the flip side of the Alice-in-Wonderland 'Eat Me' experience. The Moscow Metro is now universally held up as the majestic apogee of subterranean station architecture, but its designers were more than peripherally inspired by Piccadilly Circus. It's baldly inconceivable that the current authorities will even contemplate the expense and disruption necessary to sort out Oxford Circus Tube – Piccadilly Circus was a gaping crater for the three years its renovation entailed – let alone tackle the yet more chaotic free-for-all that is Tottenham Court Road Tube, down the other end of Oxford Street, a station whose booking hall calls to mind the kitchen at a party overrun by bored gatecrashers. Such a jerry-built, claustrophobic shambles is the subsequent descent to the TCR platforms that having brushed your scalp along increasingly obscure girder-roofed corridors lit by caged light bulbs you expect to be met at their conclusion not by a Northern line train but a hushed roomful of shingle-haired Wrens pushing squadron numbers around a map of southern England.

Beyond the Circus the street narrowed and the department stores were gradually superseded by narrow, gabled structures betraying this end's deeper, earthier roots. The 100 Club, where once the Sex Pistols and the Damned played; the site of De Quincey's chemist; young derelicts laying out cardboard in doorways. And in between them the purveyors of last year's jeans, offensive T-shirts and £10 watches: Oxford Street was ending as it had begun.

Having reached the round-the-clock disarray of the street's conclusion and being reluctant to leave it via Tottenham Court Road Tube's salt-mine underworld, I made for the nearest westbound bus. There can be no London pleasure more fulfilling than to step cavalierly aboard the rear platform of a Routemaster in motion, an act whose fluid choreography brings out the Gene Kelly in us all – at least at speeds below 7mph, beyond which it's a bit more of a Frank Spencer job.

Let me be the last to tell you what a great thing it is to travel through the West End on the top deck of a forty-year-old double-decker. The 710 Routemasters which still service Oxford Street have survived not through some romantic whim but for their peerless efficiency on busy downtown routes. Without that open platform and the presence of a ding-ding-any-more-fares conductor, Sally Humphreys would be wheeling out bus-berating epithets well past 'sodding' on the pungency scale.

In fact, London has only recently learned how to make bad and boring buses. Take the first double-decker, the open-topped, cart-wheeled Type B, launched in 1910. A frail and comic jalopy, looking at it you imagine drivers whose hands spent more time gripping starting handles than steering wheels – yet the extraordinary truth is that over 100,000 miles on the road, an average type B would break down just fourteen times.

Upstairs on my 94 to Acton Green, I smeared out a porthole in the window condensation. Receding behind me was the thirty-six-storey fuck-up that was and somehow still is Centre Point, a monument in cheap concrete and dirty glass to the vainglorious delusion of early sixties London, the other side of the Euston Arch coin. If Centre Point offered a suggestion of the bleak corporate wind-tunnel Oxford Street could so easily have become, I only had to look down at the pavements beneath me to be presented with a more heartening vision of its current reality.

As the first drops of rain coursed waywardly down my porthole, the Asian proprietors of a dozen novelty goods emporia instantly rushed out on to the street with boxes of umbrellas. What characterised Oxford Street's past, I was cheered to conclude, was still setting its agenda now: the no-nonsense, quick-witted capitalism that fired today's golf-sale sandwich men and beefeater barrow boys was the quintessence of Gordon Selfridge and John Lewis.

Thus reassured, I placed three plastic bags in my lap and settled back into a pleasantly vibrating seat to examine the purchases I'd contemplated not troubling you with. My £18 pair of Levi 501s were conspicuous by their bright red stitching and, as I would later discover, some painfully errant copper rivets; the face of that £10 watch was already starting to steam up in the top deck greenhouse. All I'll say about the beefeaters is that there were three of them. If Oxford Street's first law of retailing is to give the public what they want, then its second is that if it's cheap enough they'll buy it even if they don't.

*

I'm still not quite sure why Vic and Marge put Regent Street at the bottom of the green set: lower rents, perhaps, than Oxford, but higher certainly than Bond; less poncily prestigious than the latter but more so than the former. The kind of shops that survive along Regent Street wouldn't have lasted on Oxford Street: the silversmiths Mappin & Webb; purveyors of upmarket breakables Royal Doulton and Waterford Wedgwood; Austin Reed, Aquascutum and other gentlemen's outfitters of the type Harold Clunn chose to introduce with 'Messrs'. And, of course, it's all still owned by the Queen. 'Of all the streets named after famous men,' said the wit and critic Max Beerbohm, 'I know but one whose namesake is suggested by it.' Broad about the beam and born to shop, the Prince Regent was as his street now is. The brief he handed John Nash was to connect his Pall Mall residence to one planned in what became Regent's Park; completed in 1816, the new street represented the northern continuation of the architect's Strand/Trafalgar Square scheme, essentially forming a barrier between the noble squares of Mayfair and the mean streets of Soho, home in Nash's words to 'mechanics and the trading part of the community'.

Described by Peter Ackroyd as 'the most important exercise in city planning within the metropolis' – he might just as well have switched that superlative for 'only' – so perfectly designed was Regent Street that almost uniquely around the board it has suffered no demeaning change of use or drastic downturn in fortunes. The defining stretch of the street, that broad, graceful arc between Oxford and Piccadilly Circuses, was to be lined with 'shops appropriated to articles of fashion and taste'; 180 years on, give or take the Disney Store, Clans of Scotland and the English Teddy Bear Company, it still is. This isn't to imply that the original sinuous Regency grace has been dutifully preserved: worried that the charmingly Continental colonnade down near the Piccadilly end might attract 'doubtful characters' in search of shelter, shopkeepers had it torn down after just thirty-two years; flogged off for a tenner a throw, its 270 cast-iron columns now support railway platforms all over Britain and a church portico in Romford. And all but one of Nash's buildings, obviously, had been demolished by the end of the twenties – All Souls Church, up near the BBC radio HQ at the street's northern end, is the only survivor, and Harold Clunn even wanted that torn down for a theatre. Only Nash's sewers, some of the oldest in London, have made it through unscathed.

While maintaining a dignity appropriate to its royal landlords – those stucco-fronted buildings were repainted every year – Regent Street always knew which side its bread was buttered. In the 1850s its shopkeepers pioneered late closing, keeping their doors open until 7 p.m., and in 1882 it was the first London street to unveil Christmas illuminations. The human billboards have been around for a bit too: Edwardian photographs show sandwich men glumly advertising 'Bottesini Concerts' and 'The Pure Ice Company'. Established in 1925, the Regent Street Association is one of the oldest such organisations, and was soon producing its own promotional literature. 'A deliciously mad little hat to put you in the perfect holiday mood?' began one of its earliest – and surely most marvellous – brochures. 'Regent Street stores have them in abundance. Men's hats? Of course – from the bowler and the homburg to the ocean-going cap.'

Once more I am reminded of the downside of London life in the early Monopoly age. Yes, yes, I could have bought a house for tuppence and indulged my worrisome pyromaniac urges in every one of its many hearths, but at the same time, I'd have had to have worn a hat, and not just a hat but a bowler, a homburg or – deep, deep breath – an ocean-going cap. In the period photographs it's staggering how all the men carry their hats off with the panache of a Dick Tracy or the simple dignity of a Homepride flour man – or rather almost all, because in every one there's a chap in the background plainly ill at ease under a cock-eyed brim. I am that man. Putting any sort of hat on my head generates the same facile comedy as putting sunglasses on a dog. That's me in a bowler, a bouffant *Clockwork Orange* reject; there I am dwarfed under a fedora like one of the kids in *Bugsy Malone*, and – oh dear God no – here comes Little Timmy Osmond in a gorblimey flat cap.

I can only blame a subconscious urge to expose myself to slapstick situations by non-millinery means for the absolutely enormous laminated map of Europe I elected to acquire at a bookshop near the top of Regent Street that morning. Even rolled up it was as long as a scaffold pole, and by the time I stood pressing the Regent Street Association's bell I had already obstructed or injured more passers-by than Stan Laurel could have managed carrying a roofer's ladder around Tottenham Court Road Tube for a week.

'That's a big one,' said Annie Walker as I three-point-turned my cylinder into her fourth-floor headquarters overlooking Dickins & Jones.

'So they say,' I rejoined, building a free and easy camaraderie that was abruptly punctured when I heard myself telling her she looked exactly like my mother. Annie was busily preparing for the imminent turning-on-the-lights ceremony, coordinating a trio of Continental work-experience girls who flapped about us stuffing envelopes and rolling up posters. Noting from one of the latter that the self-styled 'Switch On' was to be effected by over-toothed popster Billie Piper, I wondered aloud whether Regent Street was deliberately moving downmarket – the last hands I remembered seeing on the lever belonged to a Prime Minister. 'Well, John Major,' said Annie, as if he didn't really count. 'And I certainly wouldn't say downmarket. Cosmopolitan, perhaps. More fashion chains.'

'Like Oxford Street?' I suggested mischievously.

'We are *300 per cent* superior to Oxford Street,' she said, rather shrilly. I'd been pushing my luck, and now gave it a final sharp prod with an enormous rolled-up map.

'Bond Street?' she repeated, as dismissively amused as the bloke in Jail being offered out by a lagered-up Uncle Pennybags. 'I was driving down Bond Street in a taxi the other day,' she recalled with a thin smile, 'and the driver turned to me and said "How does this place survive?" I don't know a single major Bond Street store which isn't in trouble.' She paused, giving me a brief moment to marvel once more at this rivalry's rancid gall. 'Have you been down Bond Street yet?' Not yet, I said, and she eased back in her chair. 'Regent Street,' she said, lowering her voice portentously, 'is the only boulevard in London.' I could see what she meant – the broad pavements and that elegant arc into Piccadilly Circus certainly make for a far classier stroll than is possible along Oxford Street – but walking up to her office I'd been aware of the overpowering Clunnish ambience imbued by those hefty structures run up along both sides in the twenties.

When Harold Clunn describes a street as 'one of the finest metropolitan thoroughfares in the world', you just know in his mind's eye he's being driven down it standing up in the back of an open-topped Mercedes staff car, and in the mid-thirties that slightly totalitarian atmosphere was unhappily bolstered by one of those flags with the funny bent cross fluttering on top of the German Railways Information Bureau at No. 19 (or Nos 19–21, as any bleak jokers at the next-door Czechoslovak Travel office might have had it). Not, of course, that anyone at the time would have found that particularly sinister: I'm still vividly haunted by a photo I'd seen of a cheery bus inspector at Trafalgar Square proudly displaying the swastika lapel badge that identified him to tourists as a German speaker.

The twenties overhaul that endowed Regent Street with these rather oppressive edifices in exchange for the elegance of Nash was, as ever, undertaken on economic grounds: setting the ground floors aside for retail use, the Crown Estate was able to welcome additional tenants in the four or five floors above. Annie's office, I'd noted from my directory, would in 1933 have been occupied either by the administrative headquarters of a brewers' chemist, a gown manufacturer, a travel agent, two wholesale milliners or a supplier of bus components.

There were loud protests. Once a gloriously stretched-out Royal Crescent, after its makeover a distraught *Country Life* columnist compared Regent Street to 'a nightmare of County Halls'. Most of the classy restaurants and cafés that had made the Regent Street experience a more rounded one were disappearing, he noted, and its ambience, once so suavely relaxed, was becoming unappealingly 'restless'. The article concluded with what its author clearly considered a grimly apocalyptic prophesy: that promenading pedestrians would be alienated and, in due course, the curtain would thus be lowered on a gilded epoch of 'casual shopping'.

Yeah, right. County Hall or no, nowhere else is casual shopping still practised more seriously. The average Regent Street department store has always seemed a little less, well, average than its Oxford Street counterpart. Liberty, of course, was made out of men-o'-war, and there was something aristocratically perverse about the spelling of that Dickins who teamed up with that Jones, but what really set Regent Street apart from any other in London – to my young eyes at least – was Hamleys.

In the days before we had Toys 'Я' Us, toys were them. My local toyshop catered for the sort of parents who didn't allow their children to watch telly, its dim shelves lined with diecast combine harvesters and nurse uniforms. But in Hamleys, all those state-of-the-art super-toys that had acquired near-mythical status in awestruck playground gossip were miraculously made flesh: the Airfix Boeing 747 with wings longer than your arms; radio-control cars that weren't actually connected to the handset by a telephone cable; the Subbuteo Stadium edition with a TV-camera rostrum and ballboys.

Squinting up at its many floors you somehow felt a historical connection with Edwardian children gawping at tinplate dreadnoughts – here was a shop that had been around a long time (though you wouldn't then have known it was established in 1760), a shop that had blazed trails in juvenile entertainment technology (though you wouldn't then have cared that 'ping pong' was coined there). There was something magical, something Willy Wonka about Hamleys: the bubble-blowing, plane-throwing clowns in the foyer; the model railway that circled the second-floor balcony . . . and ooh, look: there's my mother, seated behind a little baize table demonstrating to an amply-trousered audience the extensive creative possibilities contained within a Priscilla Lobley Flower Kit.

The Christmas she worked at Hamleys was one of almost incoherent excitement, for her children at least – show my mother a sheet of crepe paper now and she'll yawp like a poisoned crow. Almost every day after school my siblings and I went up and hung about the shop until closing time, embarking on protracted destruction derbies with the Scalextric demonstrators and running over to the board-game department for a covetous shufti in the Monopoly Deluxe box: gold tokens, a carousel for the title deeds and – eek! – hotels with chimneys. We also spent a lot of time with a neighbouring demonstrator flogging do-it-yourself balloon kits that essentially involved daubing a sticky globule of some powerful chemical compound on to the end of a stubby straw and blowing and blowing and blowing. At the time I wasn't quite able to explain the enduring thrill this activity seemed to generate, but because between all that blowing there was also some sucking I think I now understand: we were abusing solvents.

So Regent Street meant something special to those who accrued childish things and those who had put them away, and even back in the thirties Annie's Association was trying to explain what it was. 'Many a pleasant hour can be spent increasing one's poise and changing one's personality,' was the alarmingly ambitious definition of retail therapy described in another early brochure. But though Oxford Street, I could see, might reasonably be described as 'restless', Regent Street still manages to exude a sort of easy superiority befitting of its royal landlords, as if it doesn't actually *have* to work for a living but just finds it rather amusing to dabble with all this commercial malarkey, a bit like those Sloaney girls who get jobs in art galleries. The Queen was raised in Piccadilly and owns Regent Street, and the two streets are united by a certain sense of decorum, a shared antipathy towards in-your-face commercial excess.

But though they've banished the pound-a-slice pizza stalls and vomiting zombies, Regent Street does face certain blighting challenges to its image. One is another Day-Glo forest of Golf Sale placards: 'We pressured the shopkeeper into taking his sandwich men away once, and his turnover dropped by £35,000 a week. You do the sums: I can't imagine the chaps holding those boards get more than £40 a week.' Another was what Annie referred to with hauteur as 'the cloth shops', crusty old drapers whose windows are stacked with dusty rolls of pinstriped worsted and mohair.

I'd often wondered how these rather forsaken establishments survived in such a prestigious location, and now I found out. When the new buildings went up in the twenties, explained Annie, the Crown Estate doled out ninety-nine-year leases at little more than peppercorn rents: one can just imagine some retired colonel fondly welcoming in the chaps who had run up his grandfather's tropical dress uniform while splenetically skewering applications from any establishment considered unworthy of royal approval. Regent Street had just one Corner House, hidden away up its overlooked northern periphery; on Oxford Street, there were ten.

'Less than twenty years to go for most of the old drapers then,' I sighed, and Annie nodded, eagerly contemplating their more lucrative and image-consistent replacements. Personally I'll miss the cloth shops – I've no idea what 'barathea' is, but it's a great word to see in a shop window.

She rounded off with a dutiful résumé explaining how the Crown Estate was now marketing Regent Street as a 'branded entity'. Her parting words were delivered in a dreamy, Utopian sigh: 'If I could change one thing, it would be to rename Piccadilly Circus Tube station as Regent Street.'

I chortled at the hilarious improbability of this, but noisily bullying my laminated tube into the jockey-sized lift realised that the way things are going she might yet live to see her dream come true. It's not as if Tube station names are set in stone: Green Park was once Dover Street; passengers alighting at what is now Tower Hill were for sixty-two years met by signs reading Mark Lane, and they only settled on Lambeth North at the fourth attempt. And in an age of rampant corporate sponsorship there is no cow so sacred that you couldn't spray your slogan on its udders if the price was right. Opened in 1937, the historic Brockwell Park Lido in Brixton recently emerged from refurbishment with a huge pink and blue logo on its pool floor and a new name: the Evian Lido. We gaze down on our capital from a pod on the British Airways London Eye. It's just as well Post Office station changed its name to St Paul's in 1937, because otherwise people would now have to ask for day returns to Consignia, and I don't think they'd be able to do that without eating at least a small part of the ticket clerk's face.

A sudden and fearful rain began to beat down almost as soon as I stepped foot back on Regent Street, sending everyone scurrying into Dickins & Jones and Liberty. For a while I brazened it out, moistly inspecting the carnival of tat and fast food heaped together in Regent Street's forgotten northern appendix, like a funfair outside the palace walls. Here were Camilla Parker-Bowles masks and 'Small Pecker' condoms, as well as many examples of the phenomenon known as Big-Mouth Billy Bass, a voice-activated latex trout which bends in the middle and sings nine seconds of 'Don't Worry Be Happy' when you shout at it. I'm not sure what the royal landlady would have to say about Camilla and the condoms, but she'd certainly approve of the flexible fish. It's been said that the Queen has no sense of humour, yet she has no less than ten Big-Mouth Billy Basses installed in her palaces. Sorry – delete 'yet' and insert 'because'.

I could see the chaps out flogging umbrellas down Oxford Street, and with my new jeans beginning to shrink around me I splashed off towards the nearest vendor. I never made it. Fumbling for the requisite £3 – another special price, I'm sure you'll agree – I winded yet another approaching shopper with a gut-ful of Iberian peninsula, and belatedly grasped the hazardous impracticalities of an additional manual burden. What was worse – to shop till I drip-dropped, or arrive at Regent Street's southern conclusion with my brolly rib-tips festooned with toupees, spectacle arms and bloody earrings?

A close call, but one decided when I hit upon the obvious solution. A minute later I was striding past Liberty beneath an impressive acreage of unfurled laminate held in both upraised arms, like Atlas given a let-off. One of the drawbacks to this system, as I pondered watching a hapless Golf Saler receiving cider-scented grief from an obscurely furious pisshead, was that I appeared to be advertising a continent. Another was that it rendered actually going into any shops a logistical impossibility – though this wasn't an especially tearful tragedy, as the only one I might have wanted to go into was Hamleys, and the last time I'd been in there the boy who once quivered with incredulous glee had become the father mumbling truculently at the price tags as he homed in on a combine harvester.

The shops petered out as Regent Street swooped into its final parade. Here was the Café Royal, a regular House of Windsor lunch hangout in the Café de Paris era but now associated with an even more bizarrely feudal institution: gentlemen's evenings where dinner-suited patrons despatch many courses of fine food while two young men in big shorts batter each other to bloody oblivion in a central ring. Veeraswamy, London's oldest Indian restaurant; a Cheers bar done up in precise homage to the eponymous TV show, except that in this one nobody knows your name.

With lengthening strides I splashed eagerly towards Piccadilly Circus Tube; then stopped, lowered my head in weary recollection and in doing so emptied the Adriatic Sea down the neck of a passing child. 'What are you playing at, you great arse?' barked his mother at me, only in Scandinavian. It was all right for her. She only had to change a young boy's clothes under a brolly in the middle of the West End, whereas I had to turn around and walk up and down Bond Street in the pissing rain with a big map on my head.

Actually, I wouldn't be doing exactly that, because guess what – there is no Bond Street. Sort it out, Marge: you could have had New Bond Street or Old Bond Street, or just given up and gone for Mayfair, which – just to queer the pitch further – extends across both. (In the twenties the council proposed to cut the crap and call the whole thing Bond Street, but the local ratepayers voted overwhelmingly against it.) Still, just this once I'll let it lie, mainly because the street association's website – the closest I was allowed to get to a meeting – makes a particular point of referring to 'the Bond Streets', which you can call laudably precise or really fucking silly, depending on whether you're wrong or right.

Arriving at its proximate junction with Piccadilly, I realised I had no memory of walking or even driving down Bond Street. This seemed an exceptional omission – here was a pivotal thoroughfare of considerable length and global repute – but one that was eloquently explained as I peered into the window of Dolce & Gabbana to be met by a glare whose intimidating super-ciliousness even Alan Rickman could never hope to match. I hadn't been ignoring Bond Street – it had been ignoring me.

I don't expect my case was helped by the scene that

immediately preceded this encounter: as suddenly as it started the rain had stopped, and before stowing my rerolled map I'd elected to disperse its accumulated precipitation by means of a short but vigorous one-man light-sabre fight. But though that might have excused the D&G doorman's sneers, it could scarcely justify the pantomime loathing displayed by four further staff members who skulked close behind as I wandered around the store's sparse and otherwise uncustomered interior, poking my map into unpriced racks of fur-embroidered denim, lime-coloured leather and other season essentials from the emperor's new wardrobe. Literally shown the door, I felt like Cinderella being hounded back into the scullery by a surfeit of Ugly Sisters.

Well, *plus ça change*, I suppose. Old Bond Street was the work of Sir Thomas Bond, not a lordly landlord this time but a pioneering developer, who in 1686 bought up and pulled down Clarendon House – a mansion not yet twenty years old – and laid roads through its grounds. Its more extensive northward continuation New Bond Street has, in fact, enjoyed just fourteen summers fewer; the seamlessly connected pavements of both were swiftly lined with bijou upmarket homes.

But as Mayfair grew up to the east, Bond Street acquired a more commercial aspect, its narrow houses commandeered as shops for the burgeoning aristocratic neighbourhood. It got its big break in 1784, when the astonishingly influential Duchess of Devonshire orchestrated a boycott of the more fashionable shopping streets of Covent Garden, whose residents had voted against her mate Charles James Fox. By the end of the eighteenth century Bond Street 'abounded with shopkeepers of superior taste', and was patrolled by the Bond Street Loungers, definitive work-shy fops who inaugurated the street's long tradition of attracting ponced-up layabouts in dyed wigs.

Ridicule, it has been said, is nothing to be scared of, but for the Loungers it should have been. Their nemesis was the enemy within, the extremely mad Lord Camelford, who lived over what is now the Hermès shop and spent much of the early nineteenth century patrolling Bond Street with his footman – a black prizefighter – looking for Loungers to slap about.

Already court-martialled for mutiny after shooting one naval officer and challenging another to a duel, in his early twenties Camelford enjoyed a brief but glorious second career as London's lariest lord. When he couldn't find a Lounger to work over he'd take on the whole street: while the capital celebrated peace with France on the night of 7 October 1801, Camelford provocatively refused to join in, successfully luring an angry mob to his door. Eagerly rushing out alone with a bludgeon and a sword, the young lord was quickly beaten to the ground; having been hauled back inside by his servants he crawled out on to a balcony and opened up on the crowd below with a pistol. Three years later, having failed to get in deep enough shit even while touring Napoleonic France under a false name, Camelford challenged an officer known to be a crack shot to a duel in Holland Park, with predictably terminal consequences.

In the post-Camelford era, Bond Street gratefully returned to its business as a hoity-toity purveyor of flash stuff. As Regent Street moved towards the mass market, Bond Street continued to make its living by selling a small number of people a small number of very expensive things. For many decades a men's retail playground on the Pall Mall model – gun shops, dealers in awful sporting prints and the like – by the turn of the twentieth century the boot was on the other foot: a daintier one with painted toenails.

In 1937, when most of its customers were still local nobs, Bond Street's commercial establishments included 36 gown shops, 32 milliners, 5 motor dealers, 8 antique shops, 17 art galleries, 12 photographers, 10 tobacconists, 21 jewellers and – guh? – 58 cosmetic companies. Bin the garages, snappers, hatters and fag firms (even Benson & Hedges seems to have gone now) and nothing would appear to have changed, though in fact the street did also host sufficient vendors of more prosaic goods – there was a Lyons Tea Shop and even a Woolworth's – for one commentator to call it 'the High Street of some Utopian village'. At that time, Bond Street's retail establishments claimed to satisfy all human needs, but if you weren't allowed to shop anywhere else today you'd be seeing out your diminutively numbered days on an unadulterated diet of Charbonnel & Walker chocolates, effecting any DIY needs with a Dunhill shooting stick and getting tanked up every night on Chanel No. 5.

As in life, so, as ever, on the Monopoly board. Pretentiously overpriced as it has always been – '75 per cent off – all trousers on this rail now £400' – Bond Street remains the perfect embodiment of a set which promised prestige rather than profit. The greens offer a shocking rate of return: at £200, its houses cost the same as the dark blues, yet a hotel on Bond Street produces £600 less than one on Mayfair. Even overlooking its unexciting performance in Chris's probability program, Bond Street offers an abysmal price-to-earnings ratio: in terms of development cost to hotel rent, the king of no other set performs as badly. As Mike Grabsky had suggested, Bond Street is a rip-off.

But I don't think it was so much the shockingly exorbitant prices that upset me (to employ a literary device known as lying) as that wearisome, po-faced pretentiousness. It was terrible to think that what was now Dolce & Gabbana had in the Monopoly era been the raffish and sometimes raucous Embassy Club, the Café de Paris's main rival for the patronage of that Upper Three Thousand. Forcing my way map first into Prada through another five-man defensive wall I bumped into two women of late middle years, who I'm afraid I shall have to describe as painted crones.

'So of course I had to tell her she was making a complete fool of herself,' said the one who looked slightly less like Fanny Cradock, eliciting a nod of prim approval. To walk down Bond Street is to play a bit part in an episode of *Absolutely Fabulous* where everyone looks like Edina but acts like her dull daughter.

The street's AbFab credentials had been firmly cemented in my mind by an article I'd recently read about the phenomenon of kabbalah, described within as 'the hottest society pastime in London'. Madonna, Jerry Hall and almost anyone who has ever written 'socialite' in the box marked occupation are, I'd learned, among the 2,500 who have made the trek to the Kabbalah Centre above the Vidal Sassoon salon in New Bond Street. Based loosely – like, belt-off-and-dropped-round-the-ankles loosely – on Judaism, with a spicy dollop of the occult thrown in, to its adherents kabbalah is a 'pathway to truth', though to the rest of us it is a room above a hairdresser's where people pay £151 in exchange for a piece of red string. Worn round the wrist, this is both a spiritually recharging charm bracelet to help guide you along that truth pathway, and a handy way of identifying you to the shopkeepers of Bond Street as a valued customer: not only far too rich but childishly gullible to boot. 'Improving people's lives' is kabbalah's motto; precisely how the philosophy seeks to achieve this is predictably unclear, but frankly that isn't the point. In essence, the Kabbalah Centre seems to serve as a social club where people can say things like 'I found Buddhism was making me too morbid' and 'Is this spiritually recharging or what?' without immediately going down under a hail of angry blows.

Naturally enough, Bond Street can boast a proud heritage in this fertile field – right back to 1856, in fact, when Sarah Levenson, a former East End fortune teller, opened a shop at 50 New Bond Street selling exotic skin treatments under the bold legend 'Beautiful for Ever'. Beguilingly branded 'Dew of Sahara' and (splash it all over) 'The Royal Arabian Toilet of Beauty', these were eagerly acquired by proto-kabbalahan Bond Street ladies undeterred – indeed probably attracted – by prices of up to 1,000 guineas. Within two years Levenson was clearing £20,000 a year. Curiously unsatisfied with this income she began to forge love letters to her more grandiosely suggestive clients; purporting to be from prominent noblemen struck by the ladies' alluring Arabian-toilet complexion, these successfully procured purchases of ever more monstrously exorbitant cosmetics. One widow was fleeced for over five grand. Levenson was eventually charged with fraud, and at her trial contributed to many quotable exchanges, most notably in regard to a stock of twenty-guinea bottles of water 'brought by swift dromedaries from the River Jordan'. Having listened as she defiantly insisted that this fluid did indeed hail 'from the East', the prosecution lawyer paused dramatically before moving in for the kill. 'That might mean Wapping,' he said. She got five years, came out, did it again, got another five years and died halfway through her stretch.

On I happily wandered, prodding oncoming fashion victims with my map, past Cartier's topiarised Frenchiness, past gaudy caryatids guarding the Royal Arcade, past the marvellously eccentric Masonic castle of the Atkinson's Cosmetics building. Tiffany proved surprisingly awful, its windows decorated with what looked to my mercifully untrained eye like the sort of jewellery you'd try and grab in the jaws of one of those quid-a-go cranes at a funfair, but Asprey's – Bond Street shopkeepers since 1830 – exuded a regal timelessness beneath those Harrodsesque fairy bulbs. Almost everything it sold was ridiculous – straws, dice, miniature suitcases and other whimsical tributes to the silversmith's art – but, uniquely, the staff seemed not to have let this corrode their sense of human decency.

'The stones are at present in New York, sir,' intoned a low and plummy voice as I padded in beneath the chandeliers. Its source was a chap dressed like the father of the bride sitting behind a desk with a telephone held to his face, who when I caught his gaze raised an eyebrow and half a smile in endearing self-mockery. Idly perusing some of Jade Jagger's more capricious jewellery designs I was approached by a little bald man who inquired if I wanted any help: it was the first and only time a Bond Street retail operative essayed this stalwart gambit as if offering genuine assistance in a purchasing decision, rather than issuing a coded warning not to stuff displayed merchandise down my trousers. 'The contrast between the old and the new is less apparent here than anywhere in London.' Harold Clunn's overview of Bond Street in the thirties remains an apt one: it still effortlessly exudes an ostentatious exclusivity that is the antithesis of Selfridge's axiom about welcoming in all-comers regardless of whether they could afford to buy anything. 'Oh, what an entirely *wonderful* bag,' drawled a sweetie-darling voice behind; even the accents had barely changed.

In fact, as anyone who heard Posh Spice's address as she switched on the Bond Street Christmas lights in 2000, that isn't quite true. As the Upper Three Thousand dwindled towards post-war extinction, so the shopkeepers of Bond Street took a deep breath, and forcing out smiles bravely welcomed in a new aristocracy – rough of tongue and ill of breeding, perhaps, but it was either that or fall foul of the maxim connecting beggars and choosers.

The traditional lunching hour had long since come and gone, and having dismissed the option of despatching an £18 toasted sarnie in an overgrown toddler's highchair at the DKNY in-store café, I entered Fenwick's, Bond Street's resident department store and host to multiple dining opportunities, with only one thing in mind. Theft. Surveying myself unblinkingly and at length in the mirror above the sink in the Fenwick's Gents, I splashed cold water in my face as you were supposed to do in this sort of situation, then towelled off my big map of Europe as you weren't. I'd been treated as a potential petty larcenist in almost every shop – Bond Street had given me a bad name, and now I was going to live up to it. A bracing slap in the chops, a loud exhalation. Let's do it.

Rarely have I broached such a bastion of wealthily leisured womanhood: returning from my pre-blag comfort stop at the lonely beige urinal that had comprised the store's male facilities, I passed an airy gazebo-style hall ostentatiously decorated with mirrors and flowers – not even the Ladies *per se*, just a sort of antechamber thereof. The second-floor restaurant was correspondingly well stocked with London's ladies-who-lunched, many of them doing so with a tiny, boil-washed dog in their laps.

I patrolled the dining area's hushed periphery, but it was difficult to do so covertly bearing that 4-foot tube, and being followed about by several pairs of over-embellished eyes I accepted my criminal recce had for now been foiled: the joint was casing me. Momentarily thwarted, I downed a couple of escalators and found myself at the open-plan café. More people, more noise, more bustle – perfect.

'Waiting for a table?'

'No! No thanks. I'm, er, just looking.'

If I'd seen the waitress approaching I might have been better prepared, and the legacy of this unsatisfactory response was a dilatory five-minute tour of the nearest non-catering department. This might have put the store's undercover security operatives off the scent more effectively had it sold something other than girdles.

Sidling back to the café I took up a less exposed vantage point behind a display of single-estate olive oils. With every table occupied, I was focusing on the one nearest the escalator, where three middle-aged Mediterraneans in gaudily immaculate gold-buttoned trouser suits were preparing to leave. One pulled a fat purse out of a slim handbag and I watched as from it she withdrew a twenty-quid note with the seasoned insouciance of a dog-track punter. She laid it on a saucer beside the bill, then exchanging low-key Latin pleasantries with her associates strolled casually away.

Time had been freeze-framed but now jolted to fast forward. I moved out from behind the extra virgins and yes: there was my quarry on the tabletop, beckoning me over. A waitress emerged from the distant kitchen doors and I knew if she beat me there all would be lost. Chest vacuum-packed and mouth freeze-dried I quick-marched rigidly across and with a swift but hardly deft movement clattered a hand though the table's soiled crockery and grasped my prize in a blanched fist.

With all senses primed for fight or flight, but my brain already making clear which option it was backing, I buried the booty in a raincoat pocket and lengthened an already Fawltyesque stride towards the escalators. Scattering ironed slacks with my map I ploughed through the ground floor cosmetic concessions, barged the glass door open and hit the street. The hand on the shoulder came as Shanks's pony prepared to break into full gallop.

'Excuse me!'

Unburdened by the map I might have wrenched myself clear and run for it, but as it was I sagged in defeat and winced slowly around to face my captor. A slight young man in a very shiny black suit, he instantly withdrew his hand in embarrassment and with it pointed at the pavement behind us. 'Sorry, I think you just dropped something,' he said, as if it had all been his fault. And there, now slightly more in need of a wipe down than before, was my slightly used teaspoon.

Struggling to recapture the adolescent defiance which had inspired its liberation I continued to the end of New Bond Street, turned right and entered Tesco's Oxford Street branch. Here as intended I provisioned myself with twelve crumpets and a jar of piccalilli, before walking back down Bond Street perilously (and of course repellently) conveying the latter to the former by means of the spoon.

Bond Street boasts the oldest outdoor sculpture in London – an Ancient Egyptian bust over the door of Sotheby's – but it also has the most comically inept. Afterwards I would learn that those two bronze figures gurning at each other from either end of a park bench were supposed to be Roosevelt and Churchill, but sitting between them with jar in one hand, crumpet in the other and that big map unfurled across my lap to catch any errant yellow matter I thought: the ladies who lunch mightn't like what

I'm doing, but old Dick van Dyke and this fat Popeye here surely won't mind.

I was five crumpets into my protracted outrage against epicurean decorum when an angular woman swinging a glossy Louis Vuitton carrier slowed to a halt on the other side of the road. At first she seemed merely curious, but as I watched, her Botoxed expression slowly curdled until she was fixing me and my two metal companions with a look of incredulity mixed with hatred. I elbowed Dick manfully (and in fact painfully) in the ribs and leaned my head on Fat Popeye's shoulder; still she stared in appalled silence. I winked. Her eyes widened and she started to move away very slowly, as if evading a drunken Lord Camelford by stealth. 'It's OK,' I called out slightly manically, flicking a Day-Glo cauliflower floret off the Faroe Islands. 'Piccalilli first appeared in the eighteenth century.'

She clacked away down the street; I turned to Fat Popeye with a Marcel Marceau shrug and, with some difficulty, traded sauce-yellowed map for age-yellowed board. It was always going to get tougher towards the end of my tour, and only after a visit to Jail and a couple of full circuits did I land on a question mark past Free Parking to procure a card that baldly read 'Advance to Mayfair'. But Fat Popeye wasn't watching. Having taken the scene around us in with a sweep of his gimlet glare, he turned a cold eye towards me and in a voice purged of all nautical frivolity, began to speak. 'Never before in the field of human commerce,' he intoned, rousingly, 'has so much been paid for so little by so few.'

CHAPTER 16

The Dark Blues

PARK LANE
CITY OF WESTMINSTER

MAYFAIR
CITY OF WESTMINSTER

In fact I didn't actually advance to Mayfair. Most of the properties up until now had been sort of interchangeable within their sets: I bet you didn't remember that Trafalgar Square was King Red or Northumberland Avenue King Purple, but Mayfair was not just King Blue but King of Kings, an icon, a board-transcending legend. Succumbing to an inherent sense of Monopoly theatre, I decided it would be all wrong to go there before Park Lane. In making this decision I realised I'd cheated on almost every set – only the oranges and yellows had been covered in the correct order. But homing in on Monopoly's business end, where only GO separates the gutter from the stars, the pearls from the swine, it suddenly seemed important to play it by the board. Park Lane, the perennial support act, would have to warm the crowd up for Mayfair once more.

In the realm of urban appellations for hard-surfaced open ways, 'road' is fairly low rent – quite literally so in Monopoly, where it appears four times on the board's cheapo southern flank and not once thereafter. But 'lane', if anything, is humbler still, suggesting a narrow and dilatory earthen path, one thinly travelled by nursery-rhyme characters.

Such, for many centuries, was Park Lane's existence. Its still slightly skewed progress follows the boundaries of the Saxon strip farms it bordered; later it was menaced by highwaymen and other undesirables. When Hyde Park first opened to the public in the early seventeenth century, Park Lane was still a narrow path along its western edge, with a tall brick wall keeping the deer in and the poachers out. It was just that: a lane by a park. Only in the 1760s did the first houses appear opposite the wall, and it wasn't until the 1820s, when the bricks were replaced by view-affording iron railings, that Park Lane became an enviable address.

That constricted carriageway was now a problem: despite the poxiness of its miserable girth, Park Lane was the only north–south through route for the commercial traffic that is still today excluded from Hyde Park. Horse-drawn buses en route from Paddington to Victoria, elegant carriages attempting to manoeuvre their noble occupants into the calm of Hyde Park, costermongers' donkey carts, wagons and perhaps the odd flock of sheep: so hilariously bad-tempered were the ensuing jams at Park Lane's southern extremity that they became a fixture on many sightseeing trips.

Down at the Hyde Park Corner end on a mercifully benign November morning, the consequent overcompensations inflicted upon Park Lane were starkly apparent. Passing the first of the run of upmarket car showrooms that now define Park Lane at least as much as its hotels, I had recourse to consider just what an opportunity had been squandered here. One of the world's great city parks – 340 fetching acres of trees and water – lay alongside; yet somehow forgetting that this was what had originally attracted the wealthy to Park Lane, for decades the Clunnites had instead seen all those undeveloped acres as an opportunity to indulge their ugliest fantasies – a six-lane dual carriageway on top, London's largest underground car park beneath. Everyone, they seemed to believe, shared their ardour for the motor vehicle, an ardour so passionate that once you'd slapped your great big road down the last thing you wanted was to shield its traffic from sight. Quite the reverse: whether the resident of a humble thirties semi along the North Circular Road or a guest at the Dorchester, you would certainly want your windows arranged to give the fullest vista possible of the roaring, speeding majesty outside.

So Park Lane was reduced to a bypass, patrolled not by a leisurely procession of chauffeur-driven Hispano-Suizas but a furious, lunatic melee of cross-town chaos. And somehow, it's stubbornly refusing to admit it was wrong: you won't find many filling stations in central London, but there's one on Park Lane, and those showrooms – Aston Martin, Mercedes-Benz, Jaguar, BMW, Porsche – are still peddling a dream that has curdled right on their doorsteps.

It's hardly an auspicious introduction to a street fixed in the minds of the global millions who have played Monopoly on the London board as the second finest in the capital. The Duke of Wellington's home, Apsley House, nobly endeavours to cast dignity on the scene, but marooned in traffic it's shouted rudely down. Across those six lanes rises what is in effect the opposite gatehouse to Park Lane: the ten-storey Intercontinental Hotel, constructed in apparent homage to an irregular stack of fruit boxes behind a supermarket checkout. Apsley House has been famously endowed with the honorary address No. 1, London. The extrapolative contemplation that the Intercontinental might therefore be No. 2 set me off up Park Lane in what I suppose was an appropriately dark-blue state of mind.

At the turn of the last century, Park Lane was without question the wealthiest, stateliest thoroughfare in London. Regularly interrupting its grand terraces – once home to Disraeli – were huge and graciously appointed mansions, palaces in effect.

Modelled on an Italian palazzo, Dorchester House was completed in 1857 for R.S. Holford, who made a fortune supplying
London's tap water and blew £30,000 of it on a single staircase.
The foundations of Brook House groaned under the weight of
800 tons of marble; Dudley House incorporated no fewer than six
kitchens and employed one hundred staff. Grosvenor House
boasted a Corinthian colonnade based on Trajan's forum in
Rome; the ballroom of Londonderry House was graced by
unrivalled marble statuary.

Twenty-five years on only the owners had changed: anti-
surfactant tycoon Lord Leverhulme splashed out his soap dosh on
buying Grosvenor House from the Duke of Westminster and
Louis Mountbatten was lounging on the balconies of Brook
House. The smart but somehow jaunty Regency terraces between
them still imparted the air of an impossibly grand seafront, an
esplanade overlooking the rolling green ocean of Hyde Park.
Then, really very suddenly, it all changed. Grosvenor House was
eighty-five years old when it went under the sledgehammer in
1927; Brook House twenty years younger when it met its violent
end six years later. In between, a national outcry had failed to save
Dorchester House: the Italians tried to acquire what even Chopper
Clunn called 'a mansion second to none in the metropolis' as their
embassy, and there were other attempts to refit it as a museum or
even an opera house. Holford's heirs needed £400,000 to pay off
death duties, but campaigners could only raise £300,000 and in
1929 down it came. At the pre-demolition auction, that £30,000
staircase, still just seventy years old, was flogged off for 273 quid. If
there was room in my attic I'd have bid 274.

I don't suppose anyone needs telling what went up in their
place. Park Lane had been playing Cluedo for almost a hundred
years: in 1840 Lord Russell had his throat cut by his Swiss valet in
a house backing on to Park Lane, and thirty-two years later a
mistress of Lord Lucan (what was it with that lot?) was strangled
at No. 13 by her maid. With such a tradition of pre-empting

trends in the world of domestic amusements – and by this I mean board games rather than murder – it should have been no surprise that the street started playing Monopoly seven years before anyone else in Britain. Down came the houses, up went the hotels.

The Grosvenor House Hotel was opened in 1928, and the Dorchester three years later. In 1929, such was Park Lane's cachet that the Park Lane Hotel – the first in Britain with an en suite in every room – was thus called despite being on Piccadilly. The erection of these grand hotels marked the end of an era in the most starkly strident fashion. The great Park Lane mansions had already passed from toffs to tycoons, but with rate bills hitting £5,000 even they could barely afford to run a big London house on the *Upstairs, Downstairs* model.

Domestic service was by no means in decline: at the end of the thirties, over 5 per cent of the working population were servants, including no less than a quarter of all employed women. Most middle-class Londoners had a maid, and a modestly successful professional – a doctor, perhaps, or an accountant – would employ a cook, a housemaid, a parlourmaid and a nanny. The number of live-in staff had in fact been increasing for almost twenty years, mostly due to economic migration from the desperate north: the Unemployment Assistance Board damned 'the idleness and irresponsibility of young girls' not prepared to travel the country looking for domestic service, and one agency alone was sending 2,000 Durham teenagers to London to work as servants every year. The culture shock would have been a 10,000 volter: one commentator spoke of 'girls of eighteen who are unfamiliar with knives and forks'. From a how's-yer-mam mining village to the lonely, hostile metropolis; gazing at the blurred glowers on the top deck of a passing bus it occurred to me that throughout my extensive recent wanderings about the city in which I'd lived for all these years, I had yet to spot a single familiar face in the crowd. (Oh, except Anne Robinson.)

But a live-in cleaning lady was one thing; six kitchens and a hundred staff were another. Shaken by the sight of armoured cars patrolling Oxford Street during the 1926 General Strike, even those few magnates who still possessed the financial wherewithal to run that sort of household increasingly opted to do their *Gosford Park* stuff in the mobless sanctuary of the Home Counties. For the staff they left behind it could have been disastrous – domestic servants weren't allowed to claim dole – but as luck would have it there were plenty of just as miserably remunerated and drearily drudge-like jobs close at hand: as well as the 1,000 employed at the Lyons Corner House up at Marble Arch, many who had once trodden the servants' staircases at Grosvenor or Dorchester House were soon pushing trolleys out of the service elevators in the structures that replaced them.

Striding with relief past the awful Intercontinental, I briefly managed to ignore the enormous structure spearing the grey sky directly before me. Turning dutifully to the right, I inspected another Bond Streetian outburst of pretentious exclusivity: oh to be an autograph hunter at the Met Bar, where celebrities endeavour to leapfrog each other in the ladder-tournament of fame, or a cleaner at Nobu, where Boris Becker shags women in broom cupboards. Then, finally, I permitted myself to gaze up at the penultimate Park Lane hotel, one whose reputation flirts with infamy: the thirty-storey London Hilton. Erected in 1963, I'd been severally informed that in the manner of the Dorchester and the Grosvenor House the Hilton had replaced a great Park Lane mansion, in this instance Londonderry House. Photographs of the latter's interior in the days before its demolition in 1962 were terribly affecting – not the sort of crumbled-plastered, buckets-under-drips wreck you'd have imagined, but a proud and immaculate ancestral home, with portraits of many generations of eponymous marquesses and that famous ballroom, empty but for reclining marble nudes by your man Canova, of *Three Graces* fame. And the next photo in the archive box was an exterior shot of the half-finished Hilton, rising up through a cage of scaffolding before the newly laid dual carriageway.

What was interesting about this wasn't the Triumph Herald which had all six lanes to itself, or the great hoarding out the front trumpeting the emergence of 'London's finest hotel', but the unscathed neighbouring presence of a building that appeared to be Londonderry House. It had held out intact for thirty years longer than Dorchester House, only to be replaced not by 'London's finest hotel' but the modest and anonymous concrete stack that now hosts Nobu, the Met Bar and its accompanying hotel and a bevy of dull financial institutions with UK in brackets after their names.

Lucky old Londonderry, many may say. Now almost forty years old, the Hilton still manages to pip Centre Point in media straw polls of London's most vilified structures. In fact, in a kind of laugh-or-else-you'll-cry sort of way, I find it hilarious. With its three concave flanks demanding to be photographed at an oblique angle from the ground up, the Hilton is nothing more than a 328-foot model from a *Thunderbirds* diorama. Every time I looked up at it I imagined Virgil bouncing jerkily out of a smoke-filled reception area with an unconscious security guard on his back.

I followed Park Lane round its Saxon turn and there, rearing up before me in unfortunate emulation of Earls Court's exhibition centre, was the broad, sucked-in façade of the Dorchester Hotel. Opened in 1931, at £1¾ million this was at the time the most expensive non-public structure London had ever seen. It was clearly the sort of project where the accountants were bound, gagged and shoved under the table at site meetings: when someone fancifully suggested soundproofing the bedrooms with layers of cork and a particular variety of seaweed, not a voice was raised in protest and the next day off the trucks went to the beach.

Eisenhower requisitioned the Dorchester as his war HQ – not attracted by the lavish facilities, or indeed Les Girls, the hotel's multinational troupe of leggy cabaret starlets, but by the apparently unrivalled tensile strength of its reinforced concrete. As the Hilton was to in turn, however, the building dated with alarming swiftness; appropriately acquired in the seventies by the world's richest man, the 'Sultan of Brunei, it reopened in 1990 after a two-year, £100-million refit.

The first suggestions that this makeover may have erred into the realm of Arabesque gaud were the gold-painted traffic cones in front of each Bentley and Jaguar in the small car park in front, though I didn't quite get the chance to foster any supplementary impressions after being expertly wafted back out of the reception area by two doormen. All I heard was a tinkle of piano; all I saw were a couple of square-faced clocks and a carpet that together gave the impression of a pre-war West End cinema foyer rather than anything grander. Then it was off again up the narrow pavement, trying to blot out sirens and diesel.

In 1930, 2,500 hunger marchers from the north arrived in Hyde Park, where they fought pitched battles with police that must have made exhilarating but also rather worrisome viewing from up on your Grosvenor House balcony. Hunger marchers returned to the capital in 1934 and '35, and most memorably in 1936, the year of the Jarrow March. That year, more than one in nine of all births in Jarrow ended in the baby's death, an infant mortality rate that ranks with the poorest African countries today and a shocking reminder of what a split nation Britain remained. Your chambermaid on ten bob a week might be a Geordie migrant, and that might be her brother out there with his skull under a police horse's hoof; suddenly, Park Lane seemed a bit too near the class war's front line.

It might have lost some of its lustre, but it would be foolishly misleading to suggest – as I appear to be doing – that Park Lane's traffic hell and uninspired commercial structures align it with Monopoly streets of a different shade of blue. We are all snobs to some extent, after all, and in these terms the street remains a premium brand: Park Lane, remember, was preferred to Mayfair in the UK's set on that EU Monopoly board, and nose-up to a glitzy estate agent's window I saw flats in the street being advertised for £2,500 a week, which even accounting for such essential features as a 'luggage room' didn't seem an unmissable bargain. And because I did say we are *all* snobs, I might as well tell you that this estate agent's office was once the Grosvenor House, Park Lane branch of the National Westminster Bank, and that within its filing cabinets was a very thin folder marked Moore, T.S.P. (my word, how I'm regretting that prison confession). In fact, I'd actually opened the account there in my further education days on a friend's recommendation: with telephone number deposits in most of the branch's accounts, he accurately predicted they wouldn't bother with the odd telephone extension student overdraft. But I do have to say it was also quite fun to write out cheques with Park Lane printed on them – even though my incompatible personal presentation did result in much signature scrutinising and, on more than one occasion, a telephone call to the manager. It should have been a sad day when I received news of the branch's closure, but by the end of the letter I was strutting about the kitchen shrieking like a peacock: my account was being transferred to Curzon Street. It was the ultimate out-of-board Monopoly experience – I'd shifted my investments from Park Lane to Mayfair.

A couple of mothballed 'All Enquiries' blocks, then a surviving parade of breezy, bow-fronted Regency houses with a cobbled private road in front and ambassadorial flags above. And there, at No. 100, the solitary extant Park Lane mansion, Dudley House: once home to an earl and his six kitchens, but now the head-quarters of a company that identified itself, rather grimly, as Hammerson, wherein behind revolving doors two distant receptionists were perched self-consciously at the foot of a grand and echoing staircase. London, I mused sadly, was no longer defined by colourfully prominent individuals – Lord Camelford,

Gordon Selfridge, Stanley Green – but impersonal collective entities: corporations, tourists, street associations. Its story was now told not in the first but the third person plural.

Ultimately, Park Lane's malaise was not to do with the bricks and mortar you might call its permanent residents, but – once again – its passing trade. Euston Road had always been a bypass, but the fate of Park Lane – now a grim parody of itself, of the verdant tranquillity that had defined it – was the greater tragedy. It wasn't a lane, and unless you were looking out from the third floor or higher, there wasn't a park. Why, when those houses lined up along the North Circular Road were now unsaleably blighted, were people still queuing up to pay £2,500 a week to overlook an urban freeway barely less appalling?

Disorientated in the subway labyrinth under Marble Arch I emerged at the Hyde Park exit by mistake, and surprised that the gates were still open – none of this 'closed at dusk' idiocy here, apparently – I wandered in. After only a few paces the traffic roar was filtered by the trees to a muted hiss, and suddenly I was alone in dark, bucolic magnificence, the silhouetted trees and the contours of low, smooth eminences stretching endlessly away before me.

Looking behind at the hotel and apartment blocks winking their lights through the highest branches it was now clear that almost everyone who lived on Park Lane did so at altitude, comfortably above that third floor, at heights where the traffic would trouble the senses of only the suicidally curious. In the context of all this untrammelled acreage those six lanes seemed almost irrelevant, ants across the path of the world's largest and most splendid front garden. You can take the lane out of the park, but you can't take the park out of the lane. Or something.

Except as a packet of cheap fags and a defunct pornographic monthly, Mayfair doesn't exist. The only relevant address in the *A–Z* is Mayfair Place, a tiny stub of a road laid over part of

Devonshire House's back garden in 1924, and the name is shunned by Westminster Council and other official bodies. Swish and genteel as it was and is, I have no doubt that without the international influence of Vic and Marge's most eccentric choice, the quadrilateral area contained within Piccadilly, Park Lane, Oxford Street and Regent Street would not have accrued and retained such exceptional allure.

Monopoly made Mayfair just as, for many, Mayfair made Monopoly. Such was its magical, talismanic appeal, even seasoned players would do idiotic deals to procure it. Transgressing at least five of the deadly sins, possession of Mayfair seemed to offer absolute power, corrupting its owners and coveters accordingly – they could have made an Indiana Jones film about it. Mighty property empires were laid low by the Tolkienesque Mayfair curse: one street to rule them all. I once sold that transcendental title deed to a cousin for two grand plus the orange set. And he didn't even have Park Lane.

No one ever turned down the chance to buy Mayfair at face value, even if it meant entering the dark, tortuous maze where the mortgage monster roamed. No matter how many times you've played, when you're the first to land on Mayfair there's still a thrill; and when you aren't, you'll travel round the board with half an eye on how close your run-up is taking you to that hotel bill from hell. Two thousand quid – a £100 note was a handy sum in Monopoly, and that was, like, *twenty* of them. And you'd never even touched the sodding minibar.

The image of a bright red hotel, stark and oppressive in the centre of that strip of deep blue, is an iconic one. Though you might only land on Mayfair once in a deep-blue moon – in terms of 'hits' per game, Chris ranks it in the bottom half-dozen – when you did, you didn't forget it. The chicken-run up beyond Go To Jail was known in more than one family as Death Row, and once that big red 'un went up on Mayfair, a tense gladiatorial theatre ensued whenever a token clacked up to the board's eastern flank.

Even in our breakneck games, a respectful hush fell around the board. Some players would recklessly hurl down the dice with impulsive, Butch Cassidy bravado; for others, it was an agonisingly drawn-out, any-last-requests ordeal. Moist palms would be blown into, lips licked, hoped-for dice totals murmured mantra-like. This was the nearest we got to Russian roulette: even when the greens were also fully loaded there were empty chambers – Community Chest, Chance, GO – as well as the rubber bullets of Liverpool Street and Super Tax.

For the Mayfair hotelier himself, it was not a time for showmanship. The moment he'd switched his four greens for one red he had marked himself down as the man to beat, the man to hate, the pantomime villain. If, as so many Mayfair landlords tended to be, he was an honours graduate of the 'It's a pleasure doing business with you' school of rent collection, an advance down-payment on those Community Chest medical bills might be in order.

In the end, when you did wind up on Mayfair it would usually be via some farcical anticlimax: you'd land on Liverpool Street, only to hear those nose-thumbing whoops die in your throat as the next roll was a four, or you'd blithely plonk your Scottie on that Chance square next to The Angel, and, like a whistling, carefree milkman shot through the neck by a lunatic urban sniper, turn over ADVANCE TO MAYFAIR. Criminal psychologists and addiction counsellors could save a lot of time by scrapping all that blather about personality profiles and upbringing in place of a single yes or no question: have you ever landed on a Park Lane hotel then rolled a double one?

Occupying the first two weeks of a month I'm going to make you guess at, the annual fair held in the fields north of Piccadilly was about as classy as an event based around a seventeenth-century cattle market is ever likely to be. There were jugglers, puppet shows, tarts and the intriguing 'hasty-pudding eaters', who competed to ingest the greatest quantity of semolina in the shortest time. Bare-knuckle fighting was popular, as was 'women's foot racing'; for tuppence you could watch pinioned ducks being thrown into a pond full of spaniels.

It isn't difficult to imagine that such activities were felt to be incompatible with the posh new neighbourhood that had been gradually establishing itself west and north from Bond Street, attracting wealthy plague survivors keen to start a new life away from the City's half-timbered filth. In 1708, citing 'drunkenness, gaming and lewdness', the authorities suppressed what was then called St James's Fair, but thirty years later, now just the May Fair, it was started up again by the architect and developer Edward Shepherd, who built a market house behind Curzon Street, with butchers' stalls on the ground floor and an upstairs hall used as a theatre in fair fortnight.

Regrettably, though, the wrong 'uns returned, and after prohibiting the event again in 1750, it was soon accepted that the only way to stop semolina-chinned pissheads chucking pets in ponds was to stick houses over any remaining bits of field where such incidents tended to occur. Less than a hundred years after Thomas Bond laid out the first streets of what would become Mayfair, the entire area enclosed by the aforementioned thoroughfares – an area, it must be emphasised, very nearly the size of Hyde Park – had been completely developed with gracious homes.

Handy for the royal courts and parks, Mayfair has never seen its high-born reputation compromised: five years after Euston Station was opened, sedan chairs were still a common sight in its streets. At this time, the wit and author Sydney Smith claimed that 'the parallelogram between Oxford Street, Piccadilly, Regent Street and Park Lane enclosed more intelligence and ability, to say nothing of wealth and beauty, than the world has ever collected in so small a space'. He was Mayfair born and bred, of course. Gouge a Mayfair pavement with the funnel of your battleship and it will indeed bleed dark-blue Monopoly blood.

Until just before the Monopoly era, I could have taken the Piccadilly line to Mayfair. Opened in 1907, Down Street station was officially subtitled (Mayfair), but as if recognising that under-ground public transport wasn't quite the ticket for residents still mourning the death of the sedan chair, it closed in 1932. Walking up Piccadilly from Hyde Park Corner and hanging a left I walked right past Down Street station, those telltale ox-blood Edwardian tiles now framing a mini-mart. But there was an anonymous door in the wall which I knew was the entrance to an excitingly scary staircase down to the old platform level, and pressing my ear to its dusty keyhole I heard – and indeed felt – the pressurised hiss of air forced upwards by trains passing far beneath. 'Good OK?' said a voice, and righting myself I was presented by a concerned mini-martian. 'Trains,' I explained, pointing at the door, which I now noted was labelled IMR 'PB'. 'OK good,' he smiled back.

The defunct station was the first of many suggestions that Mayfair liked to keep itself to – and indeed up – itself. I'd done a few laps of Grosvenor Square in my time, and enjoyed a memorable victory over a traffic warden in Berkeley Street, but ambling back along Down Street and up to the twenties blocks built over Devonshire House and its grounds, I realised there were huge swathes of this considerable part of central London with which I was entirely unfamiliar. So huge were the swathes and so considerable the part, in fact, that to prepare myself I first repaired to a café and ingested a mind-altering overdose of caffeine.

If I'd imagined Mayfair was going to be an ordeal – and the toff-taunting foot-dragger inside me certainly had – then I was to be mistaken. I can go so far as to say that my day in Mayfair was both enlightening and really rather lovely. On almost every street so far I'd been met by a building or vista that had somehow snagged itself on a passing century and so resisted the tide of time, but in Mayfair it was as if the four thoroughfares that enclosed the area had formed a temporal dam. The only trace of the nobles who developed London in the seventeenth and eighteenth centuries were the names they left round the Monopoly board, but in Mayfair they'd somehow held out: the Duke of Westminster still owns a whopping 100 acres of the Grosvenor estate that made his family the richest in nineteenth-century Europe. I'd left my *A–Z* at home, but managed to navigate with wondrous accuracy from a photocopy of the relevant sheet of John Rocque's 1746 map in my dog-eared Mayfair factfile.

Liberated at last thanks to Vic and Marge's cavalier final choice from trooping dutifully up one particular pavement and back down the one opposite I roamed happily at will in a spirit of eager inquiry: here was a place where history had been made. Standing at the junction of Chesterfield Street and Charles Street I could see four blue plaques without moving: the Duke of Clarence, Lord Rosebery, Somerset Maugham and Beau Brummell – a future King, a Prime Minister, a literary notable and a big ponce.

Still insulating its inhabitants so effectively from the noise and filth of the city, Mayfair seems more like a bijou principality, a walled kingdom of immense wealth and privilege: Monaco, perhaps, without the Ray-Bans. And so it once was: this, I remembered, was where the Upper Three Thousand had worked, rested and played, or rather buggered about, rested, and buggered about again. The thirties were their last hurrah, and they made the most of it.

This was the golden age of the wizard wheeze: Bentleys chased each other through Mayfair at three in the morning, their Pimms-addled passengers struggling over the not especially cryptic clues of a West End treasure hunt; imbecilic Bertie Woosters pinched policemen's helmets or yodelled from the Berkeley Square lampposts. Parties were held with every guest dressed as a baby, and others where all-in wrestlers hired in East End pubs grappled on the Persian rugs – after one such gathering, the evening's sweating, pug-faced victor found himself betrothed to a high-born society lovely. They smoked, they gambled and – as anyone who's seen *Gosford Park* will tell you – said 'fuck' all the time. And check this out: 'As the period advanced, the "Mayfair accent" changed remarkably from an over-sweet rather French lisp to a rasping tone that had traces in it of Cockney, American and Midland provincial.'

The transatlantic element of the linguistic trinity suggested by Robert Graves had been heard with increasing volume across the capital for over three hundred years. Pocahontas was the first American to visit London (there's one for the next pub quiz), stretching that inaugural hand across the ocean with such graceful élan that it's probably best to gloss over her unfortunate demise at Gravesend on the way home in 1617. Obviously that whole war of independence business put a bit of a brake on the tourist trade, but in 1786 John Adams, later the second president of the United States, focused American attention on Mayfair by establishing the first US Embassy at Grosvenor Square.

As the comfort and reliability of transatlantic travel improved the area became very much the hang-out for future presidents: Theodore Roosevelt got married in Hanover Square, and in 1905 his fifth cousin Franklin honeymooned at Brown's Hotel in Dover Street, just down from Berkeley Square. But the American love affair with Mayfair was most fulsomely consummated during the Second World War, when huge numbers of US military and diplomatic staff set up camp around the Dorchester HQ of Dwight D. – another president-in-waiting, of course.

Throughout the war Grosvenor Square was known as Eisenhowerplatz, and the occupying army even managed to take some booty home. We might not have appreciated the stark idiocy of pulling all those grand residences down but the Americans certainly did: the drawing room of Lansdowne House, most splendid of the Berkeley Square mansions, has been reconstructed in Philadelphia's Museum of Arts and its dining room, rescued at the same time, now graces the Metropolitan Museum in New York.

As I trundled happily about, the evidence of the continuing American influence in the area was unavoidable – principally around that great Holiday Inn of an embassy in Grosvenor

Square. Here the effects of 'the current climate' were almost overpowering: roadblocks, twitchy coppers in flak jackets and posters in two almost adjacent shops in South Audley Street loudly announcing 'Yes: we have gas masks!'. There are memorials to both Franklin and Dwight in the huge Grosvenor Square garden, and great Stars and Stripes banners hung over porticos all around, most notably down Brook Street outside the Harrods-like block of Claridge's, chosen London residence of glitzy Yanks from F. Scott to Jackie O.

But it was in a slightly obscure and otherwise entirely unremarkable cake slice of park behind Mount Street that the full extent of America's romantic attachment to Mayfair was spelled out, in tiny plaques on perhaps two hundred benches crammed armrest-to-armrest on both sides of every path. Dedicated to the memories of Lytton Warwick Doolittle, Gustave Schimmer IV and additional names of incontrovertibly transatlantic origin, these told of a national attachment of long standing. Many were appended with touchingly personal postscripts, remembering 'two Philadelphians who loved London' or the 'American who made his home here'.

I can only suppose that by retaining its genteel eighteenth-century ambience, Mayfair somehow encapsulates the American ideal of England as a Regency theme park – a quarter whose gracious and immaculate streets might have been paved with gold, yet so ubiquitously privileged that even if they actually were you wouldn't catch anyone nipping out at 3 a.m. with a crowbar and a flat-bed truck. Mayfair sure knows how to ham it up for the Lytton Warwick Doolittles: all those rows of unadulterated and pristine brown-brick Georgian houses, all those cobbled mewses where the coachmen who once groomed their horses were now chauffeurs polishing Bentleys. And gee, Gustave – those plane trees dropping their leaves on to Berkeley Square were planted when George Washington was president.

Wearier than most of high-octane urban excitements, Americans must love Mayfair for its absence of traffic and bustle.

Dawdling up a steep and narrow path crowned unexpectedly by a quiet pub it was difficult to accept that six lanes of cars were steaming down Park Lane just to my left, or that a brisk and brief march ahead lay Oxford Street, flanked by Britain's busiest pavements. With so many of its stately residences now regally swish embassies or brass-plate company headquarters, Mayfair in office hours recalls the set of a costume drama during an actors' strike. So unusual are family homes in the area that they're obliged to deflect confused motorcycle couriers and Bahamian visa-seekers with little plaques warning 'This is a private residence'.

It only occurred to me later that these notices might equally have been posted to deter the least welcome of all mistaken punters. Mayfair has always had a connection with the ritzier ladies of the night: in the thirties, their pimps had them fitted for colour coordinated 'uniforms' that, when they began to fade, were passed on to those working less salubrious beats. Across all Europe, only Berlin could boast trendier trollops: there, apparently, a fashion for winter sportswear was followed so slavishly that girls stood on street corners carrying pairs of skis, an initiative regrettable in terms of both professional practicality and 'snow-job' jokes.

Mayfair's streets are still no strangers to urban courtesans – as Jeffrey Archer probably won't tell you, though there's no harm asking. (And asking and asking and asking until he goes all yellowy and dies.) Walking into Shepherd Market, a warmly fetching maze of mini-squares, I remembered its enduring connection with the sort of Monopoly player who, presented with that £2,000 hotel bill, might have squeaked, 'What – for an *hour*?'

The working girls who patronised the oddly proletarian takeaways and caffs of Shepherd Market were all still asleep, of course, but idling Tube-wards through its empty, flagstoned passages I could be thankful that I was at least heading in the right socio-economic direction for my imminent free fall back round the board. Because though this was, by tradition, the moment for my where-next roll of the dice, there was now no need, no point: seven sets down and just one to go.

CHAPTER 17

The Browns

OLD KENT RD	WHITECHAPEL RD
LONDON BOROUGH OF SOUTHWARK	LONDON BOROUGH OF TOWER HAMLETS

As a tearfully drunk Tony Blair might one day confess, I've grown to love the brown set. Something about them appeals to my innate sense of economy – for £500 you could roll out the red plastic across both their pavements – and they also seem to inspire a typically British sympathy for the underdog.

Like all players, in my early years I instinctively derided the browns and heaped jeering scorn upon their unfortunate landlords: thirty quid rent – what, with two houses on? Well, I'm rather afraid that makes you both ugly and stupid. To buy a single brown was to express footballing allegiance to Carlisle United; those who coveted the pair might just as well have paraded around the playground with a Golf Sale-style placard identifying their father as the openly gay owner of a Datsun Sunny estate. No, an affection for what must be the second most famous set on the board could only develop after many years' play, as a sort of post-modern perversion.

It was partly a tactical move: no competitor minded paying your puny hotel bills, because they did so in the happy knowledge of a narrow escape at Mayfair. They'd expansively peel off the notes as if about to ruffle your hair in the most patronising fashion possible, if only it wasn't so matted and nit-ridden. And just as no one ever wanted to do deals with the flash-arse proprietor of the dark blues, so as smut-nosed Master Brown you were nearly always indulged with extra leverage in the title-deed horse trading. The browns, no less, were imbued with a sort of stubborn grunge chic, a proto-punk pride in poverty.

It was nonetheless indicative of my shaming ignorance of London's right-hand side that I saddled myself with an epic trek from Bethnal Green Tube, which I'd imagined could only be a short lapel-clutching, knees-up jaunt away to the site of the modest place of worship whose pale stonework inspired fourteenth-century Londoners to christen both street and area with a disappointingly unintriguing statement of the bleeding obvious. The East End is a lot bigger than you'd imagine, particularly if you're me. For the first time, I was off home soil. Spherical shell-suited women were almost queuing up to elbow me off the pavement, and at my first junction I was faced by a whelk stall and a pub that aggressively identified itself as the Brit. It might have been worse if either had been open.

In truth, though, the East End has in historic terms become associated only recently with professionally violent connoisseurs of pickled seafood. So genteel and prosperous was the area in the early nineteenth century that strolling up Brick Lane during a visit to London, Tsar Nicholas I loudly blared, 'But where are your poor?'. The term 'East End' wasn't coined until the 1880s, and only acquired seriously downbeat connotations during the soul-searching inquiries into prostitution and poverty that followed in the bloody wake of Jack the Ripper, perpetrator of what are still known as the Whitechapel Murders.

It's been claimed that a greater proportion of London men visit prostitutes – one in eleven, apparently – than do the male residents of any other British city. Lord alone knows how they went about procuring this statistic, though my bet is that it didn't involve a show of hands in a crowded railway carriage. But my hands-on experience (yes, yes) in King's Cross had clearly demonstrated the tradition's endurance, one encapsulated in a thirties joke that neatly spans the board. Oh look: here it comes now.

Three impoverished sisters set out from the suburban flat they share for a one-night apprenticeship in the oldest profession; the eldest returns at midnight and the middle sister two hours later. 'What's six times two guineas?' asks the former, who'd been plying her trade in Mayfair. 'Well, what's seventeen times seven and six?' counters the latter with reference to her experience in Piccadilly Circus. At breakfast the youngest returns from Whitechapel with a breathless question of her own: 'What's 144 times ten pence ha'penny?'

Whitechapel's tarts were usually alcoholic and, as the above thigh-slapper suggests, always desperate. Blundering into a network of light-industrial alleys I quickly found myself in Ripperland: tight cobbled streets flanked by ghastly, soiled tenements. I peered into a basement stairwell full of half-burnt pieces of furniture and rat-nibbled binliners and to my horror saw a sheet of opaque polythene being drawn back to reveal a jagged hole in the wall; through this laboriously emerged a tiny man in a collarless overshirt. I had Hubert Gregg's funny feeling inside of me again, only this time it wasn't quite so funny.

A helicopter air-ambulance lowered itself noisily down on to the London Hospital, reminding me of a similarly unwholesome Whitechapel Road tradition of popular entertainment. Sauntering along the pavement opposite the hospital in 1884, and pausing to groom your vast handlebar moustache in the window between the pawnbrokers at No. 121 and the fruiterers at 125, you'd have found yourself being urged to come inside and behold 'The Great Freak of Nature'. Awaiting within, once you'd handed over your coppers, was of course Mr John Merrick, who as we now know was not an animal, squelch, suck, rasp, but a human being.

I hadn't realised that Merrick did rather well out of his notable deformity – he apparently cleared £200 during that Whitechapel run. And as well as being more lucrative, it must also have been inestimably less humiliating than his previous job: of all the rum facts I had recently acquired, there were none so very rum as the revelation that the Elephant Man once worked as a door-to-door salesman.

It was in the London Hospital that Merrick fatally cast aside that extra pillow, and his bones remain there to this day. Michael Jackson recently tried to buy them, perhaps unaware that the Elephant Man looked like that despite rather than because of a series of painful operations.

By the Merrick/Ripper era, the mercantile middle classes, initially attracted by the area's proximity to London's docks, had left their gracious homes in the elegant squares off Whitechapel Road and taken their liveried footmen with them. Driven away by the noisome fumes from sugar refineries and match factories, their former residences were split into cramped, unsanitary flats, and Whitechapel Road began to slip back round the notional Victorian Monopoly board. Dorset Street, scene of the Ripper's last murder, was the subject of a book entitled *The Worst Street in London* (renamed Duval Street, it later witnessed a horrible gangland killing and these days prefers to remain completely anonymous), and the Salvation Army and Dr Barnardo's both originated in Whitechapel. It even become *de rigueur* for Oxford graduates to take a year off after university to work with Whitechapel's poor and needy – much like the current trend for doing voluntary service in deprived and distant lands, and in conditions that would presumably have been no less alien or squalid.

Similarly attracted by the street-credible poverty were the exiled leaders of what was then the Russian Social Democratic Labour Party. Lenin was a regular visitor to the area, and it was on Whitechapel Road that Stalin met Trotsky for the first time, an encounter which may later have flashed through Leon's mind along with that ice pick. Stalin stayed at Tower House – a seven-floor tramps' hostel whose abandoned Gothic bulk still looms over the area like something out of Scooby-Doo – during the 1907 Fifth RSDLP congress in a hall on Whitechapel Road, a momentous meeting which consolidated the Bolsheviks' supremacy over rival party factions. The hall has gone, but check out what's gone up in its place, comrades: Whitechapel Road's only McDonald's.

Josef, Vlad and the boys wouldn't have had any trouble blending in: near the docks and offering plenty of unskilled employment, Whitechapel has always attracted immigrants and refugees. African slaves were a common sight on its streets, and in 1763 John Edenbergh, his profession listed as 'a black', was hanged for stealing horses in the parish. The Chinese, though concentrated slightly to the south, were also Whitechapel regulars: in 1805, the funeral of the first British-naturalised Chinese, 'John Anthony', was attended by 2,000 of his former countrymen. By the late nineteenth century, the pioneering social researcher Charles Booth described Whitechapel as 'the Eldorado of the East, a gathering together of poor fortune seekers; its streets full of buying and selling, the poor living on the poor'. And by then he was only really talking about one ethnic group.

Jews had for centuries regularly attempted to settle in East London, and just as regularly been murderously ejected. The first reported pogrom was in 1189, and less than a hundred years later a more rigorous onslaught completely wiped the Jewish presence off the London map. It was many centuries before they tentatively returned, though not tentatively enough to prevent 'Jew baiting' being considered 'a sport, like cock fighting' as late as the 1750s.

With that sort of reception lying in wait it would clearly take some especially brutal foreign persecution to drive you up the Thames, but when precisely this happened on a tragic scale in Eastern Europe in the late 1880s the numbers of Ashkenazi Jewish refugees on the streets of East London abruptly swelled.

The effect on Whitechapel Road was extraordinary. After cornering the market in second-hand clothes at Petticoat Lane market, Jewish entrepreneurs set up rag-trade factories and retail outlets all along Whitechapel Road and the streets behind. By the thirties, any gaps in between these had been filled with an eclectic range of Jewish-run enterprises: Sol Goldstein cycle dealer, Jacob Cohen trunk maker, Abraham Gold wholesale tobacconist. The Pavilion music hall became the Yiddish Theatre. The Houndsditch Warehouse was known, to Harold Clunn at least, as 'the Jewish Selfridge's'. Half of Britain's Jewish population, estimated at 165,000, lived in or around Whitechapel; with 4,300 pupils, the Jewish Free School near the top of Whitechapel Road wasn't just the biggest school in London or even Britain, but the largest educational establishment of any kind anywhere on earth.

Leafing through local history documents it had been touching to see how keenly Whitechapel's Jews endeavoured to honour their adopted homeland and its customs: there were 'Kosher coaches' to the Derby, and Jewish Scout troops (the 33rd Stepney); the 1935 Jubilee procession was routed along Whitechapel Road at local request and at Christmas the East End's two Jewish dailies were full of adverts placed by local businesses toasting the King. Barnett's on Middlesex Street had a royal warrant for providing the kosher meat to Buck House when one of the Rothschilds went to dinner there, and local rag traders fought over contracts for the honour of supplying the army with its uniforms. I saw a photograph of the Prince of Wales inspecting a bagpipe-toting Jewish Lad's Brigade at St James's Palace in the mid-thirties and almost blurted out: 'Watch that one – he'll be playing Monopoly with Adolf in a couple of years.' (Spare a thought for the Reich's beauty contest judges.)

It didn't work, of course: as early as 1886 the *Pall Mall Gazette* was claiming that 'Foreign Jews of no nationality whatever are becoming a pest and a menace to the poor native-born East Ender'. Few were interested in stories detailing the horrendous poverty endured by almost all of Whitechapel's Jews: the anecdotes I read featured tales of sleeping four to a sofa, of households that could only afford to cover their bare floorboards in lino if they sent at least three family members out to work. Suppers were cooked in the local baker's oven for tuppence, and eaten out in a communal yard as there wasn't enough space inside their tenement homes to seat the whole family. But for large sections of the British media the prosperous Jewish businesses that fronted Whitechapel Road told the whole story: introducing his overview of the thoroughfare, Harold Clunn could only restrain himself for two sentences before blurting out his stupendous rant about 'homes appropriated and businesses snowed under' by 'this invasion of Jews'.

I was beginning to understand just how contentious a choice for the board Whitechapel had been. Poverty, prostitution, abdomen-scouring serial killers – and, just months after Monopoly's debut on British shelves, an almost full-blown race riot.

Spurred on by the *Daily Mail* and his friends in high places, on 4 October 1936 Oswald Mosley organised a Blackshirt parade through the East End, passing the top of Whitechapel Road at Gardiner's department store. The climate had been heated for months: in deliberate emulation of events in Germany, Jewish shop windows were regularly smashed, and Jews spat at and beaten if they dared to stray from their Whitechapel heartland. Mosley's marchers never in fact made it to Gardiner's, repelled by 'the greatest East End crowd in living memory', but his British Union of Fascists still polled 19 per cent of the vote in the following year's elections and for Whitechapel's Jews enough was enough. Those who could afford to had already gone: the borough's population fell by 25,000 in the twenties as wealthier families moved out north or east, lured by ads such as those I'd seen in the *Jewish Chronicle* headed, 'Pleasant homes in Finchley: near synagogue, full-sized garage'.

The Yiddish Theatre closed in 1937, and soon only the poor and elderly were left behind: unemployed Jewish tailors, their careers ruined by mechanisation, touted glumly for work outside the clothing shops, and I saw a memorable photo of a Morris Traveller being unveiled in the livery of Stepney Borough's kosher meals-on-wheels service. Whitechapel's cowkeeper – caretaker of forty dairy cattle supplying kosher milk – held out until the fifties, and the Jewish Hospital for another couple of decades. The Jewish Free School was blitzed off the East End map, along with a fifth of all the area's buildings; last year, its nearest geographical successor, Swanley School on Brady Street, had eight hundred pupils in its registers. Two were Jewish.

As I turned into Whitechapel Road, I sensed it was right up my alley. I suppose it was Charles Booth's thing about the gathering together of poor fortune seekers that cheered me, even though I couldn't muster much enthusiasm for most of the displayed merchandise I came across. The rag trade remains the area's defining commercial concern, the street-front 'trade only' outlets now in Bengali hands. One shop specialised in big and very bad pants, another in holdalls the size of telephone boxes, another in 'a genuine English mesh classic', perhaps more familiar to you as the string vest.

It was silk-weaving French Huguenot refugees who inaugurated Whitechapel's association with the manufacture of clothing back in the early eighteenth century. Never a career for the idle or greedy, working in an East End sweatshop was especially tough in the thirties, when a Factory Inspector's report concluded drily that the 'weekly limit of working hours is often that set by human endurance'.

But despite all the poverty, Whitechapel Road in the thirties fancied itself as a genuine rival to Oxford Street. The East End, indeed, was never shy to take on the West: Gardiner's was happy to be styled 'the Harrods of the East End' just as Brick Lane, still more ambitiously, billed itself 'the East End Bond Street'. And yet looking at the photos and reading the local history the back-up is there: with five floors and a clock tower Gardiner's certainly looked the part, and the concerns in between were largely what you'd have found Up West: jewellers, umbrella re-coverers, a Lyons Corner House. Dolled-up mothers pushed gleaming prams down pavements crowded with well-dressed shoppers and promenaders, perhaps pausing to look at the watches or snap up a bale of straw at . . . Well, hang on there just a moment, Straw?

The West End Whitechapel had tried to emulate, I realised, was the West End of half a century before. The Haymarket just down Piccadilly closed in the nineteenth century, but Whitechapel's held out until 1928 – and only then not due to a decline in demand for horse fuel but because the LCC was worried about traffic congestion. There had once been breweries around Oxford Street, but those in Whitechapel comfortably outlasted them: three, all huge, were still going well into the seventies and the last didn't close until 1989.

If it's commercial anachronisms you want, nowhere is the area's passion for such things indulged more fulsomely than within the Whitechapel Bell Foundry, founded in 1420 and, I was astonished to learn, still knocking out them big ding-dongs today as the oldest manufacturing concern in the realm. Before I forget, let me urge you now to grant your patronage to this establishment, which almost uniquely in my experience achieves all of the positive aspects of the working museum without any of the blighting drawbacks – most particularly entrance fees and irritating souvenirs. (Scratch that last one: I've just remembered the handbell cookie cutters.)

But what a lot of history to squeeze into one place. Twenty-six monarchs have come and gone since the foundry's establishment, and at least one of them – George V – has paid a visit. All would have been familiar with the sonic output of their products: if it's famous and it goes bong, it was cast here. St Paul's and Westminster Abbey ring the hours out on Whitechapel bells; the Liberty Bell, an icon of Independence to all Americans, was carted down to the nearby docks, still warm, in 1752. And you walk into the foundry's Dickensian offices through a life-size outline of the most famous bell of all, the 13-ton job which, as every pedant knows, is itself known as Big Ben.

Better still than the informative display is the fact that the foundry is still doing exactly what it has always done. I peeked out of the tiny visitors' reception room: to the right a bald man in a pinstripe suit sat beneath a loudly ticking clock in a cosily panelled office, carefully skewering invoices on to one of those desk spikes; straight ahead, behind a stout clocking-on machine, men in blue overalls traversed a flagstone courtyard overhung with block-and-tackle yardarms and pulleys and arrestingly furnished with many large bells, some behind a sign reading 'HOT' (as I had just learnt, Big Ben took twenty days to cool).

Once they'd flogged the bell it replaced for scrap, Big Ben only cost £572 – there's one I should have kept in reserve for my price index. These days, such heritage craftsmanship doesn't come cheap: a 2-foot diameter bell is £3,450, and though that includes all your basic campanological accessories – clapper, clapper staple and a 40-foot rope ending, as you'd obviously expect, in a premium ding-dong, with a sally – it takes no account of p&p, which in the circumstances isn't likely to be settled with an s.a.e., unless maybe the 'e' was an elephant.

But if the bell foundry is the acceptable face of Whitechapel Road's sense of tradition, then its uglier, stubbled countenance is skulking about down the other end. Dorset Street might have been shamed by association with a notorious murder into changing its name, but the Blind Beggar – hardly a come-on-in sobriquet in the first place – seeks instead to reminisce fondly upon, one might even say cynically profit from, the tawdry homicide that made it famous.

Make that two. In the late nineteenth century, the Blind Beggar – then as now a substantial pub in a prominent location – was the headquarters of an eponymous gang of pickpockets and bullies, who one afternoon in 1891 taunted a passing Jewish couple with such persistence that having failed to goad the elderly husband into a fight, a gang member stabbed him fatally through the eye with an umbrella. Ready for a Blind Beggar baseball cap yet? No? Let's fast forward then, to 1968, and the brooding gang rivalry between the Richardsons and the Krays (in geographical terms, the Old Kent Road versus Whitechapel). There's a bit of a to-do about the division of Soho's pornographic retail opportunities, and – whoops – there goes the senior Richardson, George Cornell, calling Ronnie Kray a 'fat poofter'. And now here comes Ron, striding into the Blind Beggar where he's heard George is enjoying a bold off-his-manor pint, and George pipes up, 'Well, look who's here', and then Ronnie lowers his head into George's lap and with a contented smile on his lips falls happily asleep . . . sorry, shoots him straight between the eyes and runs away. The police turn up and all the bar staff and patrons say blimey, you're absolutely right, officer, there *is* a dead man by the pool table.

Drivers were pointing the Blind Beggar out to their saucer-eyed passengers as they queued at the lights out front, and walking into the pub's gloomy fug I was unable not to feel concerned. Fat I was not, but a typically lackadaisical approach to hair care might easily elicit the second half of George's fatal insult, and I wasn't sure how much retaliation I could get in first, even with the board's sharpest corner.

Beneath the display cases of Blind Beggar merchandise, groups of men wearing polo shirts designed to emphasise stomach bulk and tattoos slumped on vinyl Chesterfield sofas around low tables full of pints. Every face was jowled and white, every close-cropped hairline in full recession; unintelligibly mumbled conversations were punctuated with vindictive laughter delivered in club-style slow rumbles. A sign read: 'SMOKING POLICY: SMOKING ALLOWED THROUGHOUT'. Not a joyously welcoming establishment, perhaps, but I shouldn't have fretted. Studying the jackets thrown over the arms of most sofas, I gathered I was confronting the rather less worrisome *omertà* based on honour amongst postmen.

I had a half – it was 3.30, for heaven's sake – and sipped it slowly, there in Whitechapel Road's final bastion of love-your-old-mum, you-ain't-seen-me, whelk-stall bullshit Cockneyism. It all seemed woefully dour and rather bitter, sharing nothing with the raucous knees-ups I'd read about in the Mass Observation reports. 'Every pub roared with singing . . . all danced with tremendous gusto,' noted one observer, peeking into Whitechapel hostelries decorated with barrels and hanging joints of meat. I drained my small and, as I now saw, poofy glass and walked towards the door. In the thirties the Blind Beggar was run by a Jewish landlord, Leon Molen; Kray is an Austrian name and the twins had Irish, Romany and Jewish blood. And, come to think of it, wasn't 'oi', that catch-all Cockney call-sign, of Yiddish origin? None of these facts, of course, was congruent with the Blind Beggar's mythology, as was emphasised as I followed two waddling whelk eaters out into the street and a trio of jack-the-lad Asian boys with gelled hair swaggered past in front of us. 'Think they own the fucking place,' grunted one shiftless fatty to the other, and, I thought, that would be because they do.

The street market, amply accommodated by the broad pavements of yet another former Roman road, was pulling in its stock as drizzle began to fall: chilli bouquets and huge fronds of coriander alongside the usual stacks of watered-down washing-up liquid, sell-by-last-month biscuits and in-car phone chargers.

Wandering rather mindlessly along Whitechapel High Street into the oncoming rush of home-bound commuters streaming out of the City, I wondered if it would be the same for the Bengalis: all in and all out again in a couple of generations. Though they haven't quite made Whitechapel Road their own in such an all-encompassing way, what's known locally as Bangla Town is Britain's largest Bengali community and the parallels with the old Jewish population remain compelling. Synagogue to mosque, kosher to halal: the places of worship, clothes shops, takeaways and market stalls had changed hands almost as seamlessly and swiftly as a Monopoly set swap. And inevitably, the racists had switched targets just as smartly: that original 'white chapel' churchyard is now the Altab Ali Park, named in honour of a young rag trader murdered there in 1978.

So dedicated were my ruminations upon these matters that I walked straight past Aldgate East Tube station; a happy oversight, in fact, as looking about my unfamiliar surroundings I spotted a little stall whose jolly blue signboard rang a bell as loud as any knocked out by the foundry up the road. Tubby Isaacs. An East End legend. Seafood seller of long standing – established, in fact, as the signboard's small print revealed, in 1919. And listed amongst Tubby's marine offerings, handsomely trumping both whelk and winkle, was a preserved delicacy I had yet to experience, and I surely couldn't leave the brown set without doing so: the jellied eel.

Tubby, or at least the aged keeper of his flame, was a man of inappropriately modest build in a flat cap and glasses. Looking as if he'd just shuffled off the set of a nostalgic sitcom – one that I'm afraid might have to be called *Last of the Summer Brine* – here, clearly, was a fellow with a tale or two to tell about the old days. The surname suggested he might even be of Whitechapel's Monopoly-era faith, though of course unless he brought this up I'd never know. 'So – Jewish at all?' isn't a question that's ever going to be easy to slip matily into a brief discourse with a stranger.

Intending to cross that hurdle when we got there, I found

another rearing formidably up in front of it. That I had never previously sampled a jellied eel, I realised, was no simple accident of birth or demography; like ladies' fingers or a Brown Derby, jellied eels fall into that category of foodstuffs whose names alone pulled one's imagination and appetite in all sorts of incompatible directions. That I was hungry was not in doubt – never mind an eel, after a good seven miles of up-and-down Whitechapel action, I should have had room for a jellied owl – but even forming the request in my mind had my stomach yanking its drawstrings tightly in. Tubby didn't *fish* for eels, I thought, just heaved a shopping trolley into some stinkingly industrial canal and saw what was caught in the mesh when he hoisted it out a couple of months later. I blew hard, drew my tongue lightly across my upper lip and stepped up to the counter.

'A carton of jellied eels, please,' I said, with all the enthusiasm of a child forced to choose between raw tripe and a bearded great aunt.

Tubby didn't look up. He was old – actually, very old now that I looked at him closely, much too old in fact to be doing anything other than accidentally stealing things from Woolworth's. Poor soul. I raised my voice. 'Excuse me, I'd like a . . .'

'Glenn Millers!'

I can say this reply was not one I had anticipated. He'd said it far too loudly to ignore, but I tried anyway. 'Jel—'

'*Glenn Millers*, you nancy!'

I'd thought he'd been uttering some oath, perhaps the Gordon Bennett of the seafood-vending fraternity, but now realised it was something I'd said, or failed to say. Tubby was still staring at his trailer's floor, refusing even to look me in the eye until the terrible breach of East End etiquette I had so brazenly committed was put right. Glenn Millers? Glenn Millers . . . oh, please no, please say this wasn't some idiotically obscure rhyming-slang convention. No. What could it mean? I put the thought out of my mind and gave it another go. This time I almost made it.

'I'd like a punnet . . . or a portion, or a little jug of whatever, anyway something small with jellied . . .'

'Oh, you're having a bloody *laugh*!'

'No, I'm not,' I said. Then, because of the very low score this had achieved on the ripostograph, just to see what happened I quickly piped out 'Jellied eels!'.

He'd already lost his rag, and perhaps while looking for it found the handle he now flew off. 'Glenn flaming Millers! GLENN! MILLERS!'

It had been a long day, and I didn't need this. Whitechapel is no place for flouncing off, but I was unable to keep my elbows in as I ferried my rouged and burnished features off down the street. Stupid bloody Cockneys and their silly-arsed lingo. Pot of the old Glenn Millers, mate, you know, the old gut fillers, the old hunger killers, the old tastes-nothing-like-vanillas?

Still shaking my head, I slipped my one-day travelcard into the barrier at Aldgate East. But as I walked through and extracted it, I suddenly felt blood hosing into some sort of big hole in my brain, and I stopped, jammed the ticket back in the exit barrier and with lengthening strides marched furiously back down Whitechapel High Street. Damn it all to hell Isaacs, you're not getting away with this, I may easily have thought. I'm going back, and I'm going to get my eels.

Two minutes later I was standing back at Tubby's counter, nodding very rapidly as I noted a gaze still directed impertinently down at the floor of his smelly caravan.

'Hel-lo! Hel-lo up there!'

Tubby looked up, then glanced down at me with mild curiosity. 'Yes?' he said brightly, wiping his fingers lightly across his white coat. This sudden amiability was slightly disarming, but the emergency glass had already been smashed on my mental alarm box; there was no going back. 'Glenn Millers,' I said, enunciating with the gleefully haughty precision of Donald Sinden.

Tubby scratched an earlobe and looked a little uncomfortable. He seemed to be waiting for something, so I gave it to him. 'Oh, sorry. Glenn *flaming* Millers.' At this Tubby straightened himself, but there was more where that came from. 'Flaming Glenn flaming Glenn Millers,' I sort of sang, as if rounding off a limerick.

Tubby was already waving a rather shaky hand above his jars and bowls to help me refine my request, and when it trembled over a tub of halved slugs in aspic, the only visually credible candidate, I paired a curt bark with a brisk nod. Complying with slapdash alacrity Tubby slopped five into a small polystyrene beaker, thwocked it on the glass shelf between us and quavered, 'One ninety.'

One ninety? I thought. '*One ninety?*' I said.

I was still clacking coins on the counter when Tubby diverted his attention to the taxi pulling up behind us, and more particularly its unusually spritely driver, who presently arrived at my shoulder.

'Pint of whelks, Tubs,' he said, chummily. Tubby seemed inordinately happy to see him, looking instantly much less like that little bald man did just as Benny Hill was about to slap his head. Immediately he began shovelling marine gastropods into Styrofoam with a crowd-pleasing panache that Tom Cruise would do well to study should he ever be offered the lead in *Prawn Cocktail*.

He said whelks; he got whelks. What was wrong with these people? Suddenly possessed with the reckless defiance of a Russian toastmaster, after a quick glance at its modest but rather alien contents I upended the tub into my mouth.

The soured, fibrous flesh was pretty much as expected, as was the stubborn latex sheathing it, as was the gelatinous pork-pie padding embalming it. I hadn't, however, expected bones, not at least of such knuckled enormity. They say eating an oyster is like swimming in the sea with your mouth open, but taking all consistency issues into account this was more akin to biting the hand off a corpse dragged out after three weeks in the Thames. I was wondering what to do with the pickled vertebra painfully tenting my cheeks like a puffer fish when a muted round of tinny applause rose up from Tubby's feet.

'*Weakest Link*, innit?' said the cabbie, and following the tilt of his head I noted the tips of a rabbit's-ear aerial poking up above the counter.

'Spot on,' said Tubby. 'Dozy bunch tonight.' He tutted. 'Like: Who is Michael Schumacher's brother?' The cabbie rolled his eyes and snorted slightly: it wasn't even worth answering. Tubby continued. '*And*, right, whose big band had a hit with "Moonlight Serenade"?'

As he said this, something seemed to occur to Tubby; I was spitting out sheep's teeth into my polystyrene beaker when it also occurred to me. The cabbie issued a vague, wondering hum, one accompanied with a slow shaking of the head. 'Got me, Tubs mate. Sounds a bit before my time.' Tubby tutted theatrically. Or at least I imagine he did. By then I was downing the Tube stairs three at a go.

The Old Kent Road is in every literal fashion streets apart from its brethren on the board. All the other Monopoly addresses are contained either within the Circle line that girdles London's central area, or lie a single Tube stop beyond its perimeter, but if the Circle line is a bottle on its side – and in Harry Beck's map it kind of is – then the Old Kent Road is the straw that dropped out of its neck and got washed off right across the Thames and miles down some south London gutter. And it's so long: most of the Monopoly streets were contained in sheets V9 (West End) and V10 (City) on the 1914 Ordnance Survey maps of the capital I'd acquired in some outburst of academic enthusiasm – but sheet IX3 was just titled Old Kent Road, and even that chopped a bit off the southern end. Pottering up and down every individual street to date, I'd never once had to turn a page of my *A–Z*; standing at the southern end of OKR, as I'd already taken to calling it, ahead of me lay a two-mile north-easterly march across pages 39, 40, 54 and 55. I looked above the door of the mini-mart next to me. It was No. 915.

My aunt Helen lives in Greenwich, and it became a tradition for my father to drive us home from festive visits along the Old Kent Road. Because most of these excursions overlapped with our Monopoly period, the excitement generated was considerable. Regent Street, Trafalgar Square – by the age of ten I felt entitled to express a degree of worldly nonchalance about most of the streets on the board, but Old Kent Road was different.

In all honesty the very idea that Old Kent Road might actually enjoy any sort of extra-Monopoly existence seemed somehow implausible. That funereally joyless name and an absurd two-quid rent suggested a mythical, monochrome netherworld of barefoot urchins, rag-and-bone men and dead dogs. And yet there we were, bearing right past New Cross Gate station and approaching that first street sign labelled with those three short but evocative words. Pressing our faces to the near-side rear window in a fashion incompatible with today's more fastidious approach to passenger safety, my brother, sister and I eagerly scanned the passing pavements: was it, could it really be, *that bad*? Regrettably, because it was always dark by then we never really found out. My memory was of a long and very straight road lined with a great many chip shops, one of which we once persuaded my father to procure our supper from, as I recall a request he agreed to only with significant reluctance and effected with indecent speed.

Staring ahead at the endless, undeviating thoroughfare before me it seemed difficult to accept that in the intervening twenty or more years I could not remember once returning. The weather was trying very hard to make Old Kent Road alluring – the heavens solar and hugely blue, the air infused with a wintry crispness that seemed to emphasise how near I was to its bucolic terminus. I had to admit, however, that this initial stretch didn't seem entirely becoming: the guano-streaked shell of an abandoned pub opposite, a 'members only' club that looked more like a low-rent, high-security minicab office. Two ambulances were idling outside the mini-mart, implying imminent local excitement of the sort that at 10.20 a.m. I wasn't quite ready for.

I went into a café under the first railway bridge, one run by a silent oriental who if the sign outside was taken at face value wished to be known as Dave, and sat at the window with a big mug of tea, stoutly attempting to reminisce upon what had to be the Old Kent Road's happier times. This, I realised with a jolt, was the endgame. I'd brought the board along out of habit, but needn't have bothered: I'd already had my last roll of the dice. Instead of a dark-blue bang I was going out with a tired, brown whimper. It wouldn't do. The Old Kent Road, I decided, would surprise me.

It was Roman, of course, and not just any old *via* but Watling Street, the important road which connected Dover to London before heading on towards Leicester. The period artefacts that still regularly turn up during roadworks attest to the volume of ancient traffic, a volume that having been turned down a bit in the dark ages was cranked up to deafening levels in medieval times. Chaucer was one of the many pilgrims who strode past my café window; fifteen years after his death, the Old Kent Road was filled with crowds welcoming the conquering heroes as they marched triumphantly home from Agincourt. Lined with windmills, it made a jolly holiday route out of town towards the coast: the Kent Road that Dickens had David Copperfield flee from London along was still a rural affair down this end, its pastures and market gardens interrupted only by inns and taverns catering for the passing trade. In 1805, they were joined by another firm pitched at a more esoteric breed of Channel-bound traveller: John Edgington & Co. – marquee, tent, flag and canvas goods manufacturers and purveyors of exploring equipment. The splendid Edgington façade, decorated with an oil-painted mural of tents from the jousting age, concealed three floors of cannons, telescopes and ice axes: Livingstone's Stanley was just one of the notables who kitted himself up on the way past. And flanking Edgington's at the road's northern fundament – where, *à la* Bond Street, it rather pointlessly evolved into the New Kent Road – were grand Georgian residences erected by the landlords who owned most of the area around: the Rolls family, no less, one of whom was later to strike up that auspicious relationship with Mr Royce.

Holding on to these images, I swallowed the last of my tea, bundled all maps and directories under an arm for handy reference, bade Dave farewell and set off. Things looked up almost immediately: there, bravely decorated with appropriate murals, was the famous Gracelands Palace, a Chinese restaurant managed by the arrestingly eccentric Paul 'Elvis' Chan. Every night an amply rhinestoned Paul diverts his patrons with wholehearted renditions of The King's greatest numbers, wandering about what is hardly an expansive dining area, one hand on his mike and the other clamped to a highly active pelvis. Many of my friends have made the pilgrimage to the Gracelands Palace, universally describing an evening of peerless entertainment. Part of this, it seems, stems from the fact that Paul, though very loud, isn't actually very good – but that's OK, because he takes the consequent joshing in good heart, even when, as one friend reported, it extends to bellowed heckles of 'Elvis – leave the building!'.

But next along was an eighteen-storey tower block with a pub set into its basement, and opposite, lying in a considerable area of bleakly rubbled open space, was a Lidl: grocers to the underclass. The bad thoughts were coming back, and the history had already done almost all it could to help. Throughout the late eighteenth century the Rolls Estate prospered along with its genteel tenants, but in 1811 the Surrey Canal arrived, luring industries of a fetidity remarkable even by brown-set standards. Tanneries attracted outworkers who scoured the streets harvesting a natural astringent required in the production process: dog crap. There was a fat-rendering soap plant – and – all aboard for the factory tour – a 'hair and felt works'.

Merrily embracing the in-for-a-penny school of civil planning, a couple of prisons, a workhouse and a loony bin were stuck up the top, and an asylum for distressed publicans halfway down. And, would you believe it, off buggered the gentry, leaving their big old houses to be split into grubby bedsits. The farms and fields around were quickly crisscrossed with modest Victorian terraces, often occupied by City clerks who walked into work, and when the enormous Bricklayers Arms goods station opened in 1845 any spaces left in between were filled with back-to-back railway cottages, packed as tight as four green ones on that brown Monopoly strip.

Just as the foreign refugees settled in Whitechapel, so the areas around the Old Kent Road – Walworth, Peckham, South Bermondsey – were packed with economic migrants from the provinces and those whose old homes in the City were making way for new offices. So enthusiastic was the development that by the thirties this part of south London had not only the highest population density in the south of England but one of the highest in Europe: 280 residents an acre, each house home to an average 9½ Londoners. A modern footnote on my 1914 map expresses astonishment that within all its square mileage there was not 'a single acre of open space'.

Charlie Chaplin constructed his downtrodden street character from memories of a desperate early childhood on Barlow Street, just off the top of the Old Kent Road, and life was barely less harsh when Michael Caine was born down the other end half a century later. The porters at Bricklayers Arms were considered the aristocracy: a lot of the rest scraped a living at home, dyeing children's hats in portable boilers or peeling onions for the pickle factory up the road. A halved sheep's head was a treat, and healthcare was administered by a quack who drove about in a van emblazoned with an unmissable special offer: 'Buy one of my tins of foot ointment and I'll pull out one of your teeth!' The workhouse was still going in 1930, and eight years later a survey pronounced a quarter of the local housing stock unfit for human habitation.

The Old Kent Road's reputation by the early Monopoly era may be imagined from Harold Clunn's description of its former gentility during the Rolls Estate's heyday, or more particularly the way he prefaces this with the words 'Absurd though it may appear to our readers . . .'.

But hang on just a moment. Though even George Orwell might have called the streets around 'a huge, graceless wilderness' of 'smoke-dim slums', Old Kent Road itself remained a respectable and even exciting thoroughfare in the thirties. The Trocadero up at the top of New Kent Road was the largest cinema in the world, with 6,000 seats. And on the Old Kent Road proper the 1930 Astoria was joined in 1937 by the Regal; each had a capacity of over 2,000 and was full almost every night. The department stores at Elephant & Castle employed 1,000 staff and like their brethren up the Whitechapel Road were still keeping local shoppers away from the West End. And it was surely an indication of appropriate respect that in a city with more than three hundred bus services, the No. 1 should have been routed across the Old Kent Road. It still is.

And despite the emotional disincentives of their environment, the locals nurtured a community spirit that out-East-Ended the East End. They did everything together, even sharing holidays: day-trip piss-ups round the countryside in charabancs for those who could afford it, six weeks' summer hop picking for those who couldn't. When a local shopkeeper died, mourners lined the streets in their thousands; as they did, remember, to see off that final tram. The royalism was almost hysterical: when the Mayor of Bermondsey failed to turn out for the 1935 Jubilee, a baying crowd of 2,000 burnt his effigy outside the town hall. A popular local banner strung between houses on Coronation days read: 'Lousy but Loyal'. Even in the 1977 Jubilee they wrapped all the lampposts with foil.

The sun was shining almost straight into my eyes, somehow suggesting that hope lay on the horizon. But as is so often the way, that horizon never seemed to get any nearer. A drive-through KFC; a tool-hire depot; a self-storage warehouse; another sixties council block. Nearly every structure was large and at least relatively new, yet all seemed dwarfed by their own empty car parks and the wasteland between them, white space that I knew I wouldn't find on any of the old maps even as I battled them open on every junction. It wasn't until I got to No. 726 that I came up to a parade of original Old Kent Road Victorian shops, a marooned parade of seven on either side – ten of them were boarded up, including the third such pub. Two yawning fifteen-year-olds shambled past smoking dope. And then I looked up and there was the gasworks.

Actually I didn't need to look, having smelt it a mile off. 'It's closed, really,' said the security guard apparently in sole charge of its giant blue cylinders, 'we're just storing the gas here these days.'

'But you're not storing it very well,' I felt compelled to reply. 'The whole place stinks.'

He smiled flatly, a smile that said – well, call us old-fashioned, map boy, but down here we find it rather bracing.

At their peak, the capital's fearsomely poisonous gasworks consumed an annual equivalent of over 1½ tons of coal per Londoner, and the South Metropolitan was one of the largest. On the other hand, South Metropolitan gave employment to 2,000 locals, and its chairman, Sir George Livesey, was a noted philan-thropist who built a nice library over the road: it now houses a

Museum for Children which I'd eagerly have rushed into if it hadn't been closed.

The pre-Monopoly history of the brown set was full of contributions by genuinely saintly individuals, men and women who, fired by a sense of charity and justice, gave up their lives and/or wallets for the improvement of the many local unfortunates. Lord Rowton, Disraeli's private secretary, donated £30,000 to help build Tower House and five other London hostels; Lord Rothschild erected dozens of well-appointed apartment blocks to house Whitechapel's poorest. Salvation Army founder William Booth, Dr Barnardo, all those university volunteers . . . and what of Councillor Stanley Atkinson, whose bust I'd seen in the local history library: dead before he was my age, yet enough of decent merit still achieved to earn the legend 'Guardian of the Poor' below his marble shoulders? And today, we're converting tramps' hostels into yuppie flats and 'do-gooder' into an insult. Nothing is a more cynical inversion of charitable principles than 'care in the community', and it seemed that almost every time I passed someone else on the pavement – which in all honesty wasn't very often – they were being unusual. A man stood by his dog in a pile of leaves surrounded by holdalls and suitcases. Another was shouting at cars from under a bus shelter: 'And she forgot, and she's going down the motorway, and WHOMP!'

Number 620 was a barber's, and seeing two old men in grey shopcoats standing idly either side of a gas heater within I darted over the threshold, desperate now for some nostalgic sustenance.

'Oh, I've been in the trade – round here, round New Cross – for years and years,' said the elder.

'And years,' cracked his cheeky junior. 'Like, forty-five years.'

This was useful and heartening. After a little prompting, I was treated to gentle tales of queuing round the block at the Astoria, of 'the best furniture dealer in south-east London', of billard rooms, tailors, trams and pub after pub after pub. It wasn't quite pearly kings and singsongs, but it would do.

On the way out – I probably should have had a haircut, but didn't feel quite ready for the Roger Bannister look suggested by their establishment's ambience – I turned and asked whether anyone round here minded about the whole Monopoly business. They looked at me searchingly: it had clearly never occurred to them before. 'In Monopoly, you know, being the, um, the sort of . . .' I faltered, suddenly aware I might be about to offend. The old feller rescued me.

'Oh,' he said, '*that*.' For a moment we all looked out at the buses rumbling past. 'Well, it's always been *cheap* along here,' he concluded, 'but it was never *nasty*.'

I sighed understandingly, but his colleague seemed somehow dissatisfied by this response. 'It is now, though,' he said.

'What?'

'Nasty.' He nodded towards the world outside his window. 'Why d'you think everyone's packed up and gone? The Old Kent Road *is* pretty nasty these days.'

'*These days*, maybe,' conceded the elder immediately.

What had gone so terribly wrong? Where was the commercial vigour celebrated in 'Knocked 'Em in the Old Kent Road', a music-hall paean to costermonger culture that Shirley Temple had been moved to cover? In my visits to Southwark's local history library I'd been quite deeply affected by all the memories committed to paper by ageing borough residents, recalling an Old Kent Road that resounded with clanking trams and cries of 'Carbolic – you wannit!' or 'Racing tips – I gotta horse!'. It had sounded like a two-mile fairground, lined with glasseaters swallowing light bulbs and jars-in-the-window sweetshops; a huge black man unforgettably named Lord PooFun hawked patent medicines labelled 'African Herb Stuff'. Peek through a random threshold and you might have seen a coffin being hammered together or glowing horseshoes emerging from a forge. Even in the thirties there were butchers and bakers and candlestick makers. The Old Kent Road was a place where hot cross buns really were one a penny, where a muffin man really did parade up and down.

I suppose that was part of the problem. Like Whitechapel Road, OKR was always a couple of laps behind the rest of the board: the local council used horses until 1953, a year after that last tram was packed off down the road for its heartless cremation. But whereas Whitechapel was still pootling quite happily along at its own speed – now that I thought about it, almost no street had boasted such a tiny number of untenanted commercial premises – Old Kent Road had simply died on its arse. Whitechapel could draw on a long tradition of one group of poor fortune seekers arriving as the last lot moved out, but with no such tradition, OKR was left to starve. When the industries closed and the slum dwellers were relocated there were no longer 9½ shoppers in every house, and for those 915 modest commercial concerns that meant the end.

A new park created in the void left by the demolition of a great swathe of back-to-backs was sparsely populated by crushed cider cans, and beyond it the horizon opened up into a splendid turn-again-Whittington panorama of the capital, a winning skyline of towers and steeples and cranes. This, I suppose, was an update of the view that welcomed so many travellers into London, but surveying it I felt a guilty urge to rush forth through the urban wastelands and back to where things were being built and money being spent – away from the Poo, in other words, and towards the Fun.

At least there was a bit of activity at the park's edge: a busy crossroads, many active commercial premises and a generous scattering of pedestrians who even at this range seemed more approachably normal. And look! There, gazing at me from the crossroads' north-western corner, was a landmark that provoked an invigorating jolt of genuine excitement: the Thomas à Becket.

This was where Chaucer's lot had made their first stop en route to Canterbury, and where the Agincourt heroes had been feted; rather later on it evolved into the pub-cum-boxing-gym where Henry Cooper trained and sparred. And, standing outside in the mid-sixties, between those cries of pain or rage you might just have heard a very different sort of voice warbling ethereally down from the rehearsal room on the top floor: the sound, if only you knew it, of David Bowie inventing glam rock. 'Strange bedfellows!' you'd quip as 'Enery and Dave walked out into the street together, and then 'Enery would butt you extremely hard in the temple.

There didn't seem to be any sign of the gym, and the pub downstairs was now a half-hearted wine bar, but the building's darkly marbled Victorian flanks still radiated a residual sense of underworld infamy. For the Old Kent Road had indeed been a hard-bastard realm of full-blown Bob Hoskinsry: the area was, as we have seen, controlled by the Richardson gang, and local boy Frank Maloney – until recently Lennox Lewis's manager – recalls regular gangland assassinations. 'If you weren't into crime,' he says, referring to the early sixties, 'people thought you were a pansy.' Maloney was driving down the Old Kent Road with his dad one night near Christmas when a police van pulled them over: of the four cases of 'not entirely kosher' whisky found in the boot, three left the scene in the back of the Black Maria.

But then the Old Kent Road has always fancied itself as a bit tasty: they even used to have boxing tournaments in the primary schools. When the first batch of Belisha beacons appeared in the mid-thirties, three hundred of the glass globes were smashed along the Old Kent Road in a year; twenty years on, Britain's first Teddy Boys congregated on street corners around the Elephant & Castle. When they drained the Surrey Canal in 1971 a number of singed and doorless safes turned up in the sludge.

Criminal activity, at least, was one tradition that the locals seemed determined to maintain: careworn notices outside almost every surviving commercial concern variously ordered potential patrons to remove crash helmets or pay cab fares in advance; I've seen newsagents advertise their unwillingness to allow access to more than two schoolchildren at any one time, but never before a pet shop. Every other billboard heaped civic opprobrium upon those with a *laissez-faire* approach to road tax and TV licence renewal, and municipal poster sites of the sort that usually advertise evening classes or park concerts endeavoured instead to wean the borough's citizenry off less wholesome pastimes – principally claiming undue housing benefit and carrying concealed weapons. Continuity of a more generally acceptable sort, however, lay close at hand. It was the 'Est. 1928' that drew me into Ben Beber's tailor's shop at No. 288, under the endearingly hand-painted sign and into an uncompromisingly spartan interior.

With a now practised eye I quickly categorised the shop's three occupants. The two bald ones with tape measures round their necks: tailors. The one wearing an inside-out jacket covered in chalk and pins and stretching his arms apart: scarecrow.

'Have it ready by Christmas,' said one of the former as the latter removed his unfinished apparel; I was still noisily consulting my directories as he departed. The tailors inquired as to my business, and having told them it was soon established that the two were brothers, and that Ben Beber had been their uncle.

'We were originally over the road,' said the taller tailor, who, because I forgot to ask for names, we shall call Big Ben.

'At 340, I believe,' I replied, in a sort of smug drawl it's too late to apologise for now.

'That's right,' said Little Ben, circumspectly.

'All in here,' I said, patting my documents as authoritatively as their burgeoning resemblance to a papier-mâché Space Hopper permitted. I'd read in the local history library that the last Old Kent Road tailor – there had once been fifteen – shut up shop in the eighties; having just disproved this, as well as feeling rather scholarly I was also imbued with a renewed hope for the road ahead.

Well, what a capital chump am I. I'd hardly opened my mouth before the brothers blithely revealed their imminent departure: they'd be here to hand over the Christmas suits, and then it was off to a brighter commercial future elsewhere. By the time you read this No. 288 will be under new management, or more likely no management, that wayward sign torn down, the hardboard-lined interior hidden behind whitewash. 'People round here like a bargain,' explained Big Ben, 'and a tailored suit is not a bargain.'

'Down to the council, too,' added Little Ben. 'They keep hoicking the rates up to drive us out.' I was still too taken aback to speak, but neither Ben seemed unduly affected. 'See it from their point of view. If it was you in the rates office, what would you prefer – faffing about with fifty little blokes like us or just firing off a couple of letters to B&Q and Toybus?'

'Toys " Я " Us,' corrected Big Ben, softly.

Little Ben dug out an old photo of their uncle's original shop over the road – along with many neighbouring premises now replaced by a huge Tesco's – and together we looked at it with a sort of matter-of-fact poignancy. They seemed as resigned to their fate as the barbers, and having recovered my composure I didn't think they'd be upset by a few direct questions.

'Embarrassed? I don't think anyone cares that much. Having a business on the Old Kent Road isn't *embarrassing*. Just . . . not very profitable.'

I imagine they'd spent too many years on the Old Kent Road to appreciate the extent of its unfortunate reputation amongst the Monopoly-playing millions. But I somehow wished they'd taken it more personally, stoutly defending the OKR when I'd insulted it. Part of me wanted to goad them into a response, to rail loudly against the Old Kent Road's risible futility in game as in life, its international infamy as a yardstick of shabby destitution, perhaps even its shitty brownness.

'Only two quid rent, weren't it?'

I nodded. In fact, I even delved into my backpack and ferreted out the title deed, still hoping to stir up an emotional denouement. 'Ooh, your heart always sank when you got that one,' smiled Big Ben, with a disloyal shudder.

'Well, you didn't *have* to buy it.'

'Eh?'

'You didn't have to buy it. You could have left it for someone else.'

'Oh, I got it: you played the slow way. We used to deal out a load of cards at the start.'

'The shorter game,' I said, unable to stop it coming out in a shocked whisper. It was always there at the end of the rules, but I'd never come across anyone who'd played it, or at least admitted to having done so. *The shorter game*. How could these fine, bald tailors have even considered such a diluted and childish parody? The Shorter Game deserved to be ranked along with other lamely derivative pastimes not worthy of association with the original, like French cricket or Junior Scrabble. Why not forty questions? Or paper, scissors, bomb? Honestly. After a perfunctory farewell I left.

I was beginning to understand why no one wanted to stick up for the Old Kent Road these days, why the only business I'd found happy to associate itself with this benighted thoroughfare in the phone book was Old Kent Dismantlers. I'm not sure what the opposite of the Midas touch might be – perhaps I should ask some retired local authority architects – but the road seemed thus cursed. And every time you tried to cheer it up or talk it round it skulked bitterly away.

There was a greasy spoon next to the dusty mausoleum of South London Pistons and I went in: egg, chips and beans and two fat slices of crusty bread delivered to my table in less time than it takes to uncrumple three old maps and a 1933 Post Office directory. All, I realised, was not quite lost. My residual hopes were now distilled into the tale of George Carter and Sons: partly because the name so clearly inspired Dennis Waterman's *Sweeney* character, but mainly because of a quiet little man who in – let me see, seventeen minutes' time – would put on a street performance that had been running for over a century. Outside George Carter's gaff, Old Kent Road's show was still going on.

Hats were always important on the OKR: the headwear class-code that was already breaking down north of the river lingered on here well after the war. But millinery was also a major local industry: the bowler had been invented just up the road, and firms in the area were still taking on apprentices. One company was successfully exporting fezzes to Egypt, as close to that sand-to-the-Arabs trading achievement as you're ever likely to hear.

George Carter had started selling hats from his shop at 215 Old Kent Road in 1851, and by prudent diversification into tailoring soon expanded into premises on either side. But despite this success, old man Carter remained a quiet and modest chap who unlike most of his commercial neighbours disapproved of vocal commotion; so much so, in fact, that near the end of the nineteenth century – dates differ – he devised a rather round-about method for reminding his staff it was lunch time without having to open his mouth. A specially commissioned clock installed above the shop's main entrance was topped with a bust of a bowler-hatted and fulsomely moustachioed gentleman – said to have been modelled on George himself – who at 1 p.m. every afternoon, in a great, clinking whir of cogs and springs and things, dramatically doffed his headgear.

George died but his son took over the burgeoning business – by the twenties there were thirty-three branches around the capital – and all the while the little chap raised his bowler at 1 on the dot above the Old Kent Road flagship store now spanning Nos 211–217. The son died, and his son picked up the reins – in the fifties, British men were still buying five million hats a year.

Only with the old man's great-grandson at the helm did retrenchment set in. The Carter empire was in retreat through-out the sixties – somehow you couldn't imagine David Bowie pressing his face covetously up to the window – until in 1976 the inevitable presented itself, and Mr Carter dutifully bowed to it. Wonderfully, though, the proprietors of what was now Carter's Tyres appreciated the clock's status as a pet landmark, and in the mid-eighties even had it restored: an especially zealous scribe on the local paper was delighted to report that the man with the hat also did his stuff at 1 in the morning.

If I tell you I had especially timed my visit to be outside 211 at 1 p.m. you will have some idea of the weight I had attached to this rare – in fact, in the post-Beber world, unique – connection with the Old Kent Road's lively pomp. I'd got to the café, No. 192, at 12.30, and began hurriedly despatching the rather wonderful food before me.

'What you got there, then?'

It was the waitress. I vaguely explained while she smoothed out the relevant documents with gratifying fascination. ''Ere!' she called back to the kitchen, after extensive perusal. 'Guess what this place was in . . .'

'1914.'

'. . . in 1914?'

Steam and sizzling came out of the hatch but nothing else. She shrugged, then shouted 'Coal merchant's!'

This was good, and it was about to get better: just three minutes to go until doff-time. I paid up, fumbled together my reference library and made for the door. 'Not far to Carter's, is it?' I said, thumbing up the road.

'Not at all,' she said, airily. 'Right over the road.'

I looked across. 'Isn't that a pub?' This was a question that in the interests of accuracy should have kicked off in the past tense.

'Not that. *There*.'

She indicated the adjacent terrace of shops – newish but still obviously unoccupied, with two floors of flats above. 'But . . . 211 should be further up there,' I said, weakly. 'Well, there it is all the same,' she said. 'Old place burnt down couple of years ago. Awful lot of smoke. Shame, really – used to be this lovely old clock out front.'

Blankly I walked out, and adopting a rather robotic gait set off for the Old Kent Road's proximate conclusion. Automatically I noted the survivors and casualties. The last Rolls Estate house, a compact Regency villa set back from the road, was occupied by the Dynamic Gospel Church. The World Turned Upside Down, a crazy-name, crazy-place Victorian pub constructed in a style I can only describe as Taj Mahal Gothic, had been replaced by a dull cube squeezed between the Peabody tenements. And then there it was, squashed over a huge area like the Monty Python foot: the Bricklayers Arms interchange, a large and lonely roundabout leapfrogged by a four-lane flyover.

When I'd asked the local history librarian what characterised the Old Kent Road, he'd confidently replied, 'Shopping.' Only then he'd cupped his chin thoughtfully, and added, 'In the old days, that is.' I requested an update, and he didn't hesitate: 'The flyover.' Harold Clunn had seethed about the traffic flow in this part of London, and given the excuse of Blitz damage around the top of the New Kent Road, in 1961 his vision finally bore fruit of the very sourest variety. By 1966 the Elephant & Castle had ceased to exist in any human sense, replaced by what the London County Council called 'the Piccadilly of the South'; or, as everyone else saw it, two huge roundabouts and the world's worst shopping centre.

Fresh from this triumph, what was now the Greater London Council set its sights slightly further south, at the confluence of Tower Bridge Road and the New and Old Kents. No bombs had dropped here – in fact, the Old Kent Road survived the war almost completely unscathed – but . . . well, crossroads are just so . . . *angular*, guys, and, you know, this is the *Old Kent Road* we're talking about. Haven't you ever played Monopoly? Whatever we do can hardly make it *worse*.

The Bricklayers Arms goods depot, a lovely Gothic library, the splendid Edgington edifice with its murals and flagpoles – more than a hundred Georgian and Victorian buildings went down on the Old Kent Road, and many hundreds more in the streets around. Most of the Monopoly addresses have a national route number – Park Lane is the A4202, Pentonville Road the A501 and New Bond Street the B406 – but unless you were particularly interested in making a taxi driver weep like a child you'd never refer to any of them in that way. Yet so effectively has the Old Kent Road's identity been stripped away you could drive all the way to 915 and not realise the thoroughfare you'd just motored down was anything other than the A2.

The flyover was opened in 1968, slicing literally seconds off journeys that in any case became quickly bogged down in the old Old Kent Road, the one from No. 122 upwards. Looking at that lofted arc of stained concrete I felt like Charlton Heston on the beach at the end of *Planet of the Apes*. It's a pity Harold Clunn wasn't around: I could have told him he'd finally really done it, the maniac, then repeatedly god-damned him to hell.

The traffic scheme's drastic precedent set the breaker's ball rolling. As well as almost every shop along the Old Kent Road, whole streets disappeared behind it. Tragically, they thought they were doing the right thing: getting rid of the slums and clearing some open space in an area so claustrophobically overcrowded it had hardly been able to breathe for a hundred years. So up went those Trotter-family high-rise estates, many so poorly constructed that within ten years they were crumbling. Most notorious was the North Peckham Estate, where Damilola Taylor was killed in November 2000, and where 3,000 condemned flats are currently being demolished after just thirty years in existence.

Why had Vic chosen Old Kent Road? Throughout his Brixton

childhood, it was in its colourful costermonger heyday, and even at the dawn of the Monopoly era remained vigorously, brashly commercial. The board had to kick off with a pair of low-rent addresses, but there was no point humiliating anyone: the street markets of Whitechapel and Old Kent Road were cheap and cheerful, and equally proud of both. They wouldn't mind.

Whitechapel still wouldn't, but there was no one left on the Old Kent Road to care one way or the other. Its post-war history was a void: when the anti-globalisation anarchists had drawn up their usual suspects list for their May Day 2000 Monopoly protests they'd found over a dozen corporate targets even on Whitechapel Road, but along OKR they could only manage one McDonald's and that Tesco. The few commercial premises that seemed to thrive along the Old Kent Road, I reflected, were those selling a form of escape: minicab firms, long-distance call centres, off-licences.

For a while I shuffled about in the subways underneath the flyover and its associated gyratory system, breathing in piss and solvents and generating meditations to match. I realised I'd found no trace of the establishments that might have lightened the mood, the transvestite nail bar at No. 169, or the Family Fish Restaurant, where Paul McCartney used to stop off on the way home from Linda's chemotherapy sessions to buy her a bag of chips and a pickled onion. When he'd first driven down it to his Sussex farmhouse the Old Kent Road was still a *Penny Lane* kind of a street. Now it was more of an *Eleanor Rigby*.

*

So this was it, not just the end of one road but the lot, the terminus of my final Monopoly street. And though in the horribly downbeat circumstances that should have sent me eagerly off and away it didn't, because it wasn't supposed to finish like this. It had started as an intention to overnight at a hotel on every set, an intention that foundered both on grounds of logistics (there weren't any in the oranges) and budgetary prudence (remember that £305 minimum tariff at the Ritz?). Plodding round the board I'd gradually distilled this extravagant proposal into one that granted appropriate homage to Monopoly's defining preoccupation with hotels, yet wouldn't require me to keep the bailiffs at bay with a wardrobe full of purloined toiletry sachets wedged against my front door. I'd top and tail the Monopoly spectrum, staying at a hotel on the flattest of the flat-cap browns and the toppermost of the top-hat blues. From the Old Kent Road to Mayfair.

Once I'd settled on this scheme, it had been the plan to throw logic and reason out of the window and epilogue my journey with the Mayfair part of the bargain – a reward for all my yomping about in the midnight rain, though more accurately a reward for Birna, effectively stuck in babysitting jail for twenty-eight turns while I occasionally traipsed through, Just Visiting. As soon as that last roll had taken me to the brown set she'd been straight on the phone to Claridge's, booking us in for a night at what a thirties social commentator had winningly described as 'the most aristocratic of the great Mayfair hotels'.

And tonight was that night, because the depressing truth that had gradually emerged over many days of subsequent exhaustive inquiry was this: there were no hotels on the Old Kent Road. I'd asked the local historians and the local paper and trawled through page upon yellow page of the relevant directories, all to no avail. Just for the hell of it, I'd carried on asking all the way up the road: the barbers, the Bebers, the waitress and perhaps half a dozen retail operatives in between. Used to be, they all said, yes, used to be a load: as the bloke in the local library had told me, the Old Kent Road was London's overland connection to the rest of Europe from the Roman era until the railway age. For almost 2,000 years I'd have been able to appraise Old Kent Road's accommodation options at my leisure; now, though, it couldn't even offer me a room above a pub.

Birna couldn't appreciate why this discovery should have

proven anything other than joyously, air-punchingly liberating. Our budgetary outlooks might be separated by a single square on the Monopoly board, but that square, regrettably, was the one with the big red arrow on it. My sole regret regarding this whole Claridge's business was that Birna had given them her real credit card number. Hers was that she'd been born 140 years too late to arrive by sedan chair.

When I phoned her up on my mobile from the roundabout she was packed, ready to go out of the door, and certainly in no mood to tolerate disconsolate mumbling about the Old Kent Road's room/inn situation, about needing to take some rough with my smooth.

'Cobblers to that,' she retorted. 'You've *taken* the rough already.'

'Have I?'

'Come on, you just walked up the whole length of the Old Kent Road.'

'I'm supposed to walk down it again now. I always do that.' The Mayfair hotel suddenly seemed a vacuous indulgence, a mockery of the original plan. What was the point of doing one without the other?

'No time for that,' said Birna. 'I've booked us in for afternoon tea at 5.45. If you get the Bakerloo from Elephant & Castle it'll only take half an hour. Where do you fancy going for dinner?'

'The Driscoll House Hotel.'

'Where? Tim? *Tim?*'

Well, now. Well, well, well. There before me, oddly marooned at the gateway of the New Kent Road, was a large and enigmatic structure of briskly institutional design, a six-floor, four-square Edwardian block that announced itself as the Driscoll House Hotel. Rooms £30 a night, £150 a week, breakfast and evening meal included. The slightly off-limits address didn't concern me – it had always seemed monstrously snobbish of Vic and Marge to besmirch the Kent Road with an Old when they'd diplomatically united the Bond Streets. Here it was: my Old Kent Road hotel. 'Listen,' I muttered urgently, 'I'll call you back.'

The Driscoll House reception, entered up a small flight of stairs round the side, was a dim office haphazardly stacked with confectionery and newspapers – part St Trinian's tuck shop, part doctor's waiting room, a combination powerfully reinforced by the scent of school dinners and Benylin. I pushed the door open with my map-ball and found myself on one side of a huge, stationery-strewn desk addressing a woman on the distant other. 'Tomorrow night? Ooh, don't think so. Big party of Russian schoolchildren coming in. Just one night you want?' It was clearly an unusual request. I nodded. 'Just a sec.'

She rose and disappeared through a side door and I began idly inspecting my arrestingly peculiar surroundings. What *was* this place? It looked like an old girls' school and smelt like an old people's home. Kurdish refugees maybe, or distressed publicans but *Russian schoolkids?* There was a sort of information factsheet Sellotaped obliquely to the wall and I read it: 'Situated on one of the main South London Roads,' it began, 'Driscoll House warmly welcomes men and women guests from all over the world of every race, colour or creed.' Well, that was nice. Slightly mad, perhaps, but certainly well meaning. I read on. 'The main Building has 200 single rooms . . . priority is given to the long-term guest . . . there are 8 Pianos for the use of residents . . . during the past 80 years, 50,000 guests have stayed from 210 different countries . . . in the interest of others, no one with an infectious or contagious disease may stay in the hotel . . . visits are made to the Galleries of Parliament to listen to debates.'

With a sort of comic foreboding, I read it all over again. I'd got to the contagious diseases bit when the receptionist returned. 'Sorry,' she said, 'Mr Driscoll says there's three rooms left tonight, then we're full of Russians until Christmas.'

Mr Driscoll? A barking-mad family-run hotel that spanned the Monopoly era and beyond. It was perfect; I felt as if I'd been led here by some divine Uncle Pennybags brandishing his enchanted cane in the clouds above. Tonight it must be. 'I've just got to make a phone call,' I said, and dashed outside. Then I dashed back in, blurted that I'd be very interested in having a chat with Mr Driscoll, and dashed out once more.

'*I'm not cancelling Claridge's,*' retorted Birna, who wasn't about to let the surrounding presence of what sounded like a well-populated pavement impinge on her shrillness: I could just picture her swinging her overnight bag through the pedestrians in furious accompaniment to her words. She waited until I'd detailed the scenario, majoring on the looming unavailability of accommodation, before playing her joker: 'I can't, anyway. Why do you think they ask for your credit card in advance?'

The strident alacrity with which Birna agreed that I should stay on the New Kent Road while she stayed in Mayfair should probably have depressed me more than it seemed to. But though my unalloyed excitement at discovering Driscoll House was now slightly alloyed, the itinerary I sketched out walking back up the hotel steps presented a satisfactory compromise: wake up at the crack here, then nip on to a Bakerloo train and meet Birna for breakfast at Claridge's. Checkout wasn't until noon – I could still fit in five hours there. Not at this stage realising that Monopoly was doing to me what it had done to Mike Grabsky when he packed his wife off to Malaysia alone, I marched happily back into the reception.

'Mister . . .?'

'Moore,' I replied, to the large-spectacled, elderly gentleman who was now standing by the desk. There was hardly a wrinkle on his face but that slight quaver in the voice suggested he couldn't have been under eighty.

'Terence Driscoll,' he said, holding out a large hand. 'I hear you wanted a word.'

I think it was my overeagerness that did it. Peeling off the map-ball's crumpled epidermis I began to lay out a messy timeline across that huge desk, nattering helplessly as I did so about Charlie Chaplin, homburg hats, Henry Cooper, the Family Fish Restaurant and tanning factories. My interview had become a lecture, and there was a new steadiness in Terence Driscoll's voice when at length he next employed it.

'I think there's been a misunderstanding,' he said, peering in wary disbelief at the desk as if I'd just halved a sheep's head on it.

'Sorry?'

'This is a student residence. For students. Foreign students.'

'But . . . but you warmly welcome men and women of every creed,' I said in mounting distress, paraphrasing clumsily from the factsheet.

'*Students* of every creed. Now I bid you good day and must ask you to leave.'

'No!' I yelped impulsively, which as a polemical gambit perhaps left something to be desired.

'We don't have a bar,' piped a voice through the side door. It was the woman who'd greeted me initially.

'I can live without a bar for one night,' I said, in a pleading whine that was too little, too late.

'Can you?' returned Mr Driscoll, rather unnecessarily. One of the smaller tragedies of the unfolding situation was that I would never now get to call him Terry.

'We have to think about security,' said the woman, adopting a sort of strident bleat. 'There are . . . *young girls* staying with us.'

Good God. Not sure whether to blush or blanch I wanly crumpled up my documents and walked slowly towards the door.

'I'm ninety years old!' cried Mr Driscoll as I pushed it open with an armful of Ordnance Survey.

'Happy birthday,' I mumbled without turning.

Birna was on the Piccadilly line when I phoned her back. 'We're about to go underground,' she shouted above the usual terminal-velocity Tube-train rattle. 'What is it?' In a numb and unpunctuated monotone I explained. 'He actually bid you good day?' There was a pause, then Birna said: 'I'm losing reception. Just go to Claridge's.' I was walking down Bond Street, past that silly bench statue in fact, when Birna next phoned.

'Where is this place?'

'Well, you know: here. Mayfair.'

'*No.* This hostel place. I'm at Elephant & Castle.'

I stopped dead. Sheet IX3 detached itself and I distractedly pinned it to the pavement with a foot. *'What?'*

To put her sacrifice into context, it might help to explain at this point that Birna not only owns, but regularly wears, a velvet Coronation gown weightily accessorised with ermine-effect trimming. And there she was, walking under a south London gyratory system after dark in her Claridge's finery while I battled my shambolic mobile library across Mayfair. 'It's, um, New Kent Road,' I said blankly. 'Number 172. But you don't . . . this is . . .'

'You want to know what it's like, don't you?'

I did, and said so. At the same time, however, I felt it only fair to brief her. 'If you're really sure you want to do this,' I said quickly, 'you're going to have to look like a student. Slouch or something. Take your make-up off. And no questions – they don't like questions.'

'Fine,' she said, stoutly. 'I think this is it now. "Established 1913"?'

'That's it. Just wait there a minute.'

Though still tremblingly moved by this act of heroic martyrdom, I knew it would come to naught if Birna didn't learn from my mistakes. I took a deep breath. 'You might need to do a voice.' Clicking footsteps but no reply. 'Foreign students only. Do your Icelandic accent.'

A pause, a sigh. 'Anything else I should know?'

I thought back to the most heinously memorable clause in that eclectic factsheet, and placed it in mental context beside Birna's habit of leaping out of bed at 4 a.m. to disinfect the cooker hood filter. 'Actually, yes there is,' I said. 'They've got eight pianos.'

And so it ludicrously came to pass that as I rustled awkwardly through the revolving mahogany doors of Claridge's, Birna was squeaking along crevassed lino up an endless, dark corridor two storeys above the New Kent Road. And that was before I checked in and found that I didn't have just room 105 at my disposal, but 106 as well. We'd – I'd – been upgraded to a suite. Bundling maps-first through one of its entrance doors, I found myself in Poirot land, two huge rooms of hexagonal chrome fittings, angular walnut inlay and illuminated globes held up by arched-back nudes.

The bath was an imperial sarcophagus of Dr Foster depth, and if our bed at home was a king size, here was God's own divan. There were buttons everywhere marked 'WAITER', 'VALET' and 'MAID'; I couldn't begin to imagine under what circumstances each might be required, but there was another knob marked 'PRIVACY' which I hoped you didn't need to keep permanently depressed in order to prevent all three of them bursting in at once. I flicked through the information leaflet and discovered that if at any point I found myself with any syringes I needed to dispose of, I merely had to dial 0. Before I padded out and down to tea I flicked on one of my two tellies: it was tuned to Al-Jazeera.

I phoned Birna again as I sat before a pageant of starched linen in the foyer tea room. 'Are the waiters still wearing knee breeches?' said the lost and tiny voice that answered, still retaining a vestigial Scandinavian lisp. She'd been to Claridge's for tea once many years previously, an experience inevitably accorded generous space in her memory bank.

'Don't think so,' I said, looking in mirrors and between the silver columns for any periwigged footmen. 'It's all twenties now. What's your place like?'

Birna might be putting on a brave face, but she still had some work to do on the voice. 'It's not as bad as prison,' she whispered reedily after an interval which suggested this had been a close call. 'I think it might be a halfway house.'

A halfway house, I thought but didn't say, would be one on Vine Street or Strand. There was nothing halfway about the Old Kent Road. Whereas I, of course, had gone all the way. 'What about the foreign students?'

'There aren't any. No one under forty. Actually, hardly anyone over forty. I've seen a man with a backpack full of the *Big Issue* and an old lady with . . . with a hump.'

A lunatic guffaw very nearly burst free from my throat at this point, but I swallowed it down with a gulp of Darjeeling and talked on. 'So you're in your room?'

'Mm.'

'What's it like?'

'I don't think I want to talk about it.' There was a small noise which I hoped wasn't a sniff. 'How about yours?'

'I don't think you want to hear about it.' I should have said 'them'. 'Listen, I'd better go. My tea's here.'

'Yes, I understand. The little éclairs are good.'

'Oh, I'm not having any of that stuff. Just a cup of tea.'

'I don't think you should do that. Look at the menu.'

And indeed there was only the one option, and that involved not just tea but access to a broad selection of pastries and sandwiches. With or without a pianist tinkling out 'Let's Call the Whole Thing Off', and preferably without the over-tanned blazer-wearer loudly giving some poor girl the full Leslie Philips at a table behind me, that £26 bill seemed not just a bit steep but a genuine threat to the new world order. Advancing straight from the Old Kent Road to Mayfair in half an hour was a huge mistake: I'd gone down with the financial equivalent of the bends. *Twenty-six pounds* – that was only four quid less than bed and board at the Driscoll House. On the other hand, by cramming every last cake, sarnie and – what the heck – asteroidally misshapen sugar lump into my gaping maw, I rendered the subsequent ingestion of still more extravagant evening victuals not just unnecessary but medically impossible.

Slumped bloatedly behind the fantastically overbearing chairman-of-the-board desk in my double-sofa sitting room, I wearily embarked upon the arduous task of re-collating my abused maps and photocopies into some semblance of order. There was the lunatic façade of Edgington's the year before it went down; here – flatten, tauten, rip, blaspheme – was sheet V5 of my Ordnance Survey collection, cluttered with the potato markets, 'coal shoots' and milk sheds of King's Cross in 1914. It all took some time, and when it was done I tugged out my old board and centred it in the gilt-embossed acreage before me. If I wasn't sick of the sight of it now, I thought, I never will be, and I can't have been because laid out across leather and burnished wood, that palette of glorious colours warmed by the soft spotlighting of a standard lamp, it had never looked better. It was the perfect Monopoly desk, indeed the perfect room; perhaps, I speculated, not so very different in design and ambience from the setting in which Vic's son Norman had played that first game in Britain sixty-six years before. And so I laid it all out, cards in their relevant on-board zones, title deeds fanned out in order, motor on GO, wad in hand.

But I didn't actually roll the dice; been there, I thought, done that. And then I thought: been where and done what? What had I found out about London? It was almost impossible to generalise, inevitably, because though London might have shrunk since the thirties, it remained far too large to encapsulate meaningfully, not so much a city but a nation: I don't think I shall ever now forget that more people shop in Selfridge's than live in Australia. But today it was more of a multination, a city that was home to more Cypriots than all but one in Cyprus and more Jews than any other in Europe. London told its stories in two hundred languages.

And what a lot of stories it had to tell: I'd only covered twenty-two streets out of the city's total of almost 50,000, yet those alone had yielded so much history that fitting even half of it into my head had necessitated the mental equivalent of sitting on the suitcase. The one certain legacy was that henceforth I would only ever be able to walk about London with associates who were either stone deaf or tirelessly scintillated by the words 'And on your left . . .'

I had learned many things about my city that I probably should have known already, but more than a few I probably shouldn't, and with particular reference to Crossness Southern Outfall Works, now wished I hadn't. I had seen the runic legend DRY RISER on the outside of a great many buildings, but never decoded its meaning. I had travelled back through time, from the medieval alleys behind Fleet Street to the imperial pomp of Trafalgar Square, and sometimes through national borders, to Parisian Piccadilly or Reichstag Regent Street. I've never been to the outskirts of Bucharest, and now that I'd walked up the Old Kent Road I don't need to.

Looking around the board before me I pondered the constants: that those who now worked in Whitehall or shopped along the green streets or lay flat on their bare backs in Leicester Square requesting in song to be shown the way home were still doing the same things in the same places as their urban predecessors a century before. Fleet Street looked the same but wasn't, most of Oxford Street didn't but was.

A lot might have changed, but a lot more hadn't, and that went for the whole of London. The City is now the wealthiest region in Europe, yet 43 per cent of London's children live in households with incomes less than half the UK average, the highest proportion in the country. London's skyline is about to be radically redrawn with half a dozen Canary Wharf sized towers going up in the decade ahead, but in general bickering and prevarication remain the planners' watchwords: no sooner had the fate of that perennially vacant Trafalgar Square plinth apparently been decided than a campaign starts up to replace the rolling art show with a statue of the Queen Mother. London was

like a game of Monopoly: dominated by ruthless but unpre-
dictable speculators with both eyes on a quick buck, haphazardly
developed and redeveloped, and unlikely ever to be finished.
After fifty years of decline the city's population is growing again,
but no one seems to have even started thinking about where all
these new Londoners will sleep and work and how they'll travel
between the two.

And I could only conclude that the reason no one had bothered
is that London has always muddled through in the end, and it had
done that because its inhabitants had learned to concentrate not
on long-term grand plans but on the day-to-day practicalities of
city life – we looked after the hours, in other words, and somehow
the years seemed to look after themselves. Because ours was the
original modern metropolis, so Londoners have evolved into the
ultimate urban beings, and if that means being grumpily taciturn
on occasion it also means treating your fellow citizen with almost
beatific tolerance, whether he looks or sounds very different from
you, whether he's utterly lost or utterly plastered, whether he's
toting a ball of crumpled cartography or a stout placard
proscribing the sedentary consumption of fish and lentils.
Londoners wrote the rule book for considerate metropolitan
living: we are world leaders in queuing etiquette, the only capital
urbanites to have learned that it is possible to hurry through a
crowded street without the use of force. And it occurred to me
that to do what I'd done in any other city would have involved the
extra-cutaneous excretion of a lot more distress-related body
brine: I'd not once been in any way concerned for my own safety,
or rather when I had it was down to my own whimpering
inadequacies.

Only the traffic consistently flusters London, and suddenly
enthused into direct action I whisked the racing car off GO,
swallowed hard and put the top hat in its place. Free Parking,
obviously, was the one square you'd have to bin if the board was
to be meaningfully updated; but how, I pondered, would you

update the rest? London was certainly slipping ever westwards, and an estate agent I'd talked to said if he was asked to design the game from scratch he'd include Notting Hill, Knightsbridge and Chelsea. Mercifully, though, he hasn't been, because thinking about it the only streets that didn't deserve a place on the board now were generally the same ones who should never have been there in the first place: the oranges, Northumberland Avenue, the light blues. All such postulations, of course, overlook the uncomfortable truth that if Monopoly hadn't existed, it would no longer have been necessary to invent it. The great shared history that is Monopoly could only have been written in the twentieth century; board games have had their day. The likes of Trivial Pursuit and Pictionary were the last hurrahs of a generation reared on dice and tokens, and even these were really just parlour games: stripped down to the bare bones, with no arcane rules or covert deals or great wads of cash. Looking again around the board it suddenly seemed a great pity. Hardly anyone actually lived in the Monopoly zone any more, and it was looking as if we'd even lost the desire to recapture the freewheeling, high-rolling city-centre thrills left behind when we all moved out to the dull suburbs.

Recklessly incited – here I was, for heaven's sake, *in a hotel on Mayfair* – I leapt up and did something unusual: I threw open the minibar and yanked out a half bottle of champagne. If I'd managed to find the tariff chart it probably would have gone straight back in again, but I didn't, and standing on my balcony sent its cork spiralling high over the Bentleys beneath. The festive pop echoed back off the Georgian brickwork opposite, quickly followed by another sound as I lapped the overflow from the foiled neck, the sound of my conscience coughing. Prompted, I took a big hit of fizz and dialled Birna's mobile.

Two squares round the board, her spirits seemed to have bottomed out. Supper had finished before she'd found the basement kitchen, but a very friendly Armenian-looking factotum had creaked open a 'big school-dinner warming oven thing' and presented her with a huge and rather tasty plate of curry, eye-catchingly topped with a dollop of mashed potato. He'd also refilled her orange juice twice and quietly informed her that although her room was small, she was to think of the whole hotel as her home: a statement which interestingly didn't seem to have struck her as one steeped in sinister foreboding. As I talked to her she'd just watched the end of *Robot Wars* in a dark room with a number of silent and expressionless men in late middle age – again a scenario which clearly wasn't half as bad as it sounded – and was currently patrolling a long corridor lined with a multi-denominational selection of dusty religious statuettes. 'It's actually very interesting here,' she said, and though I listened carefully it didn't sound as if she was reading from a script with a chisel pressed to her throat.

Succumbing to those Old Kent Road miles, I'd actually dropped off on Sofa A when she rang next. 'There's a letter Sellotaped to the wall here from the King of Benin,' she muttered eagerly. 'It looks like he stayed here once and they tried to get him to pull strings with some planning application.'

These were not the sort of words to foist upon a still-waking man. 'Guh?' I said, but there was worse to come. 'And remember that nice man I told you about?' 'Whu?' 'That Armenian bloke. He told me the President of Togo was a guest here when he was a kid, only he ended up getting shot in his room.' 'What? There?' 'No, no. Back in Togo. Some sort of coup. Oh, and this place was originally a Catholic girls' school.'

Birna was beginning to sound like Thelma in *Scooby-Doo*. What was Driscoll House doing to her? I might never know, but it was still doing it well past midnight.

'A *ghost*?' I repeated, now tucked up in that huge bed watching the news in German.

'It was first seen here in 1952,' she breathed with a sort of ethereal glee. 'A silver lady . . . some say an angel.'

338

'Listen,' I said, 'this is above and beyond the call of . . . of everything. I'm going to send a cab over.'

'Don't be silly,' Birna replied dismissively. 'I'm *fine*.'

So fine, in fact, that she didn't show up until it was gone 11 the next morning, by which time I'd begun nibbling her share of the trolley-load of fried comestibles that a jolly but unbreeched waiter had wheeled dramatically in through the door of 106 as I peered uncertainly out of 105.

'I've eaten breakfast already,' she said lightly, taking her ease on Sofa B.

'You had it . . . *there?*'

'It would have been rude not to. Anyway, I'd paid for it.'

These last four words might have defined large parts of my adult life, but I never thought to hear them from Birna's lips. The management of the Driscoll House were clearly one house short of a hotel and now they'd been at my wife's little green ones.

'It was just very interesting, all that stuff about ghosts and the King of Benin. And, you know, the room was clean and had hot water and everything. Everyone was friendly. Odd, but friendly.'

Birna had eaten sausages next to a *Big Issue* salesman; I'd lost my minibar virginity and – dramatic brass fanfare – pressed a pound coin into the room-service waiter's hand, albeit rather too tightly. The Old Kent Road and Mayfair had taught us both a lesson; Monopoly had made us better people.

'Though having said all that,' she announced, pressing the sleeve of her coat to her nose, 'I do smell like I've been on remand. I'm going to try that enormous bath out.'

I looked at my watch doubtfully. 'Better make it quick. We've got to check out in half an hour.'

'Half an hour plus another twenty-four.'

We exchanged even gazes, then Birna waved a hand lightly over the board I'd set up the night before. 'Come on,' she said mischievously, 'we've all played Monopoly. No one swaps Old Kent Road for Mayfair.'

'Not without a sweetener,' I mumblingly conceded. Not only had she upgraded us to a suite before heading off to Driscoll House, she'd also checked it was free for another night.

'It's interesting, isn't it,' she continued blithely, plucking the relevant title deeds from the desk and consulting them closely, 'that our bills last night exactly matched the respective rent with two houses.' And with a big smile she held the cards up towards me.

You know what that brown bill was, but I'm afraid its dark-blue equivalent appears to be stuck in my craw. Go look in the cupboard under the stairs and check for yourself.